FASHION

Fashion Sketchbook

FIGURE TEMPLATE

_____

_____

_____

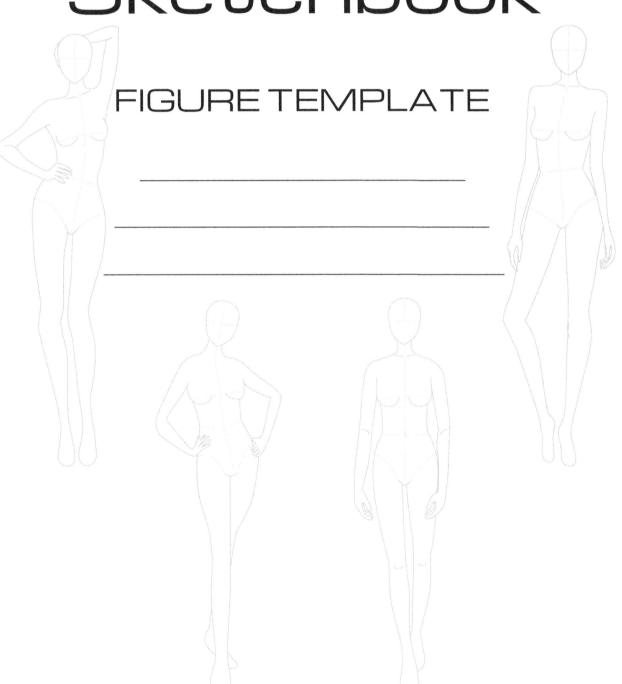

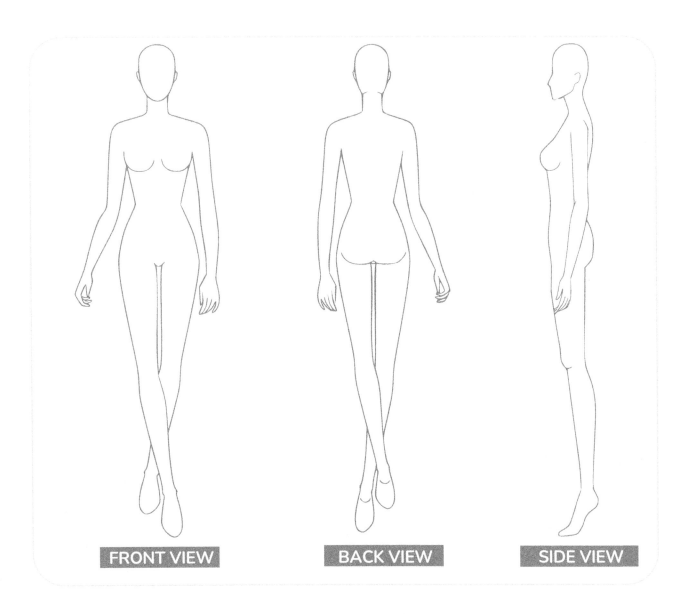

FRONT VIEW   BACK VIEW   SIDE VIEW

COLORS ◯ ◯ ◯ ◯ ◯ ◯ ◯ ◯ ◯ ◯ ◯ ◯ ◯ ◯

MATERIALS   PATTERNS

ACCESSORIES

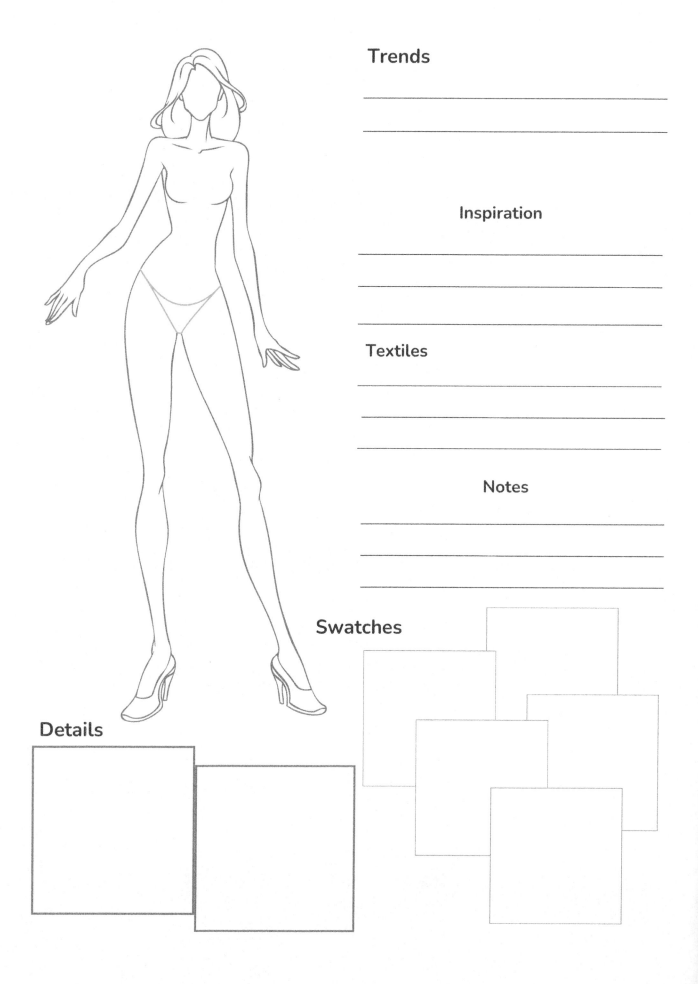

Trends

Inspiration

Textiles

Notes

Swatches

Details

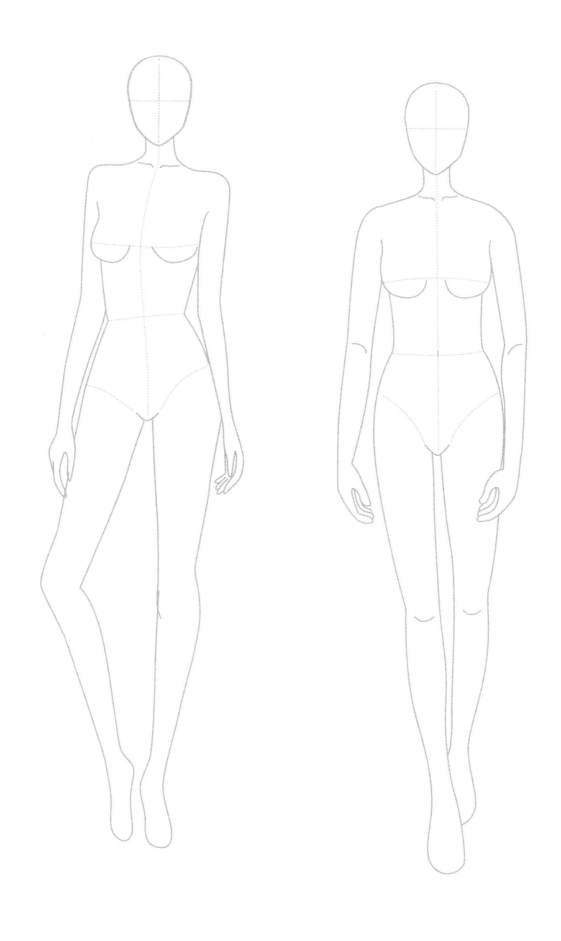

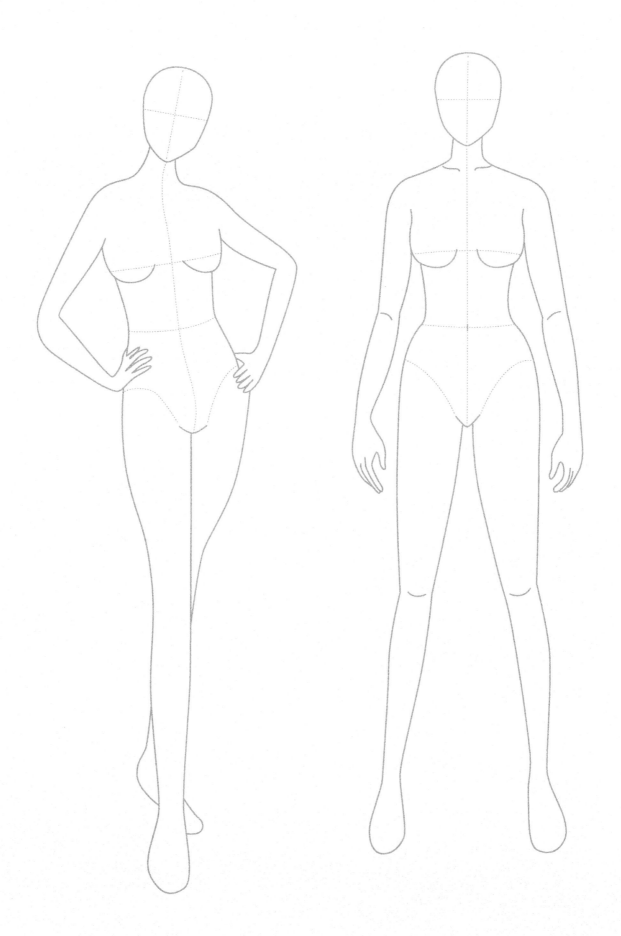

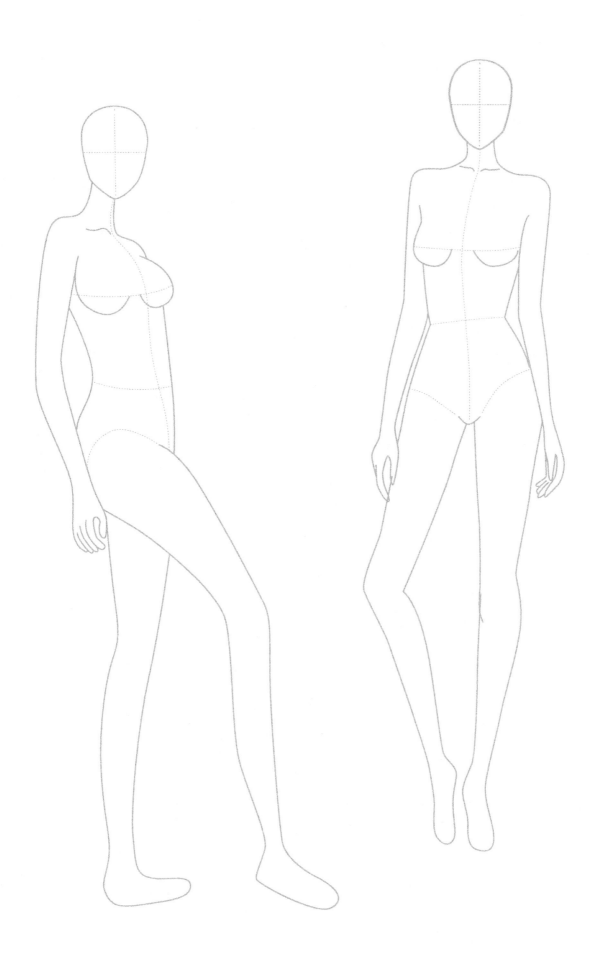

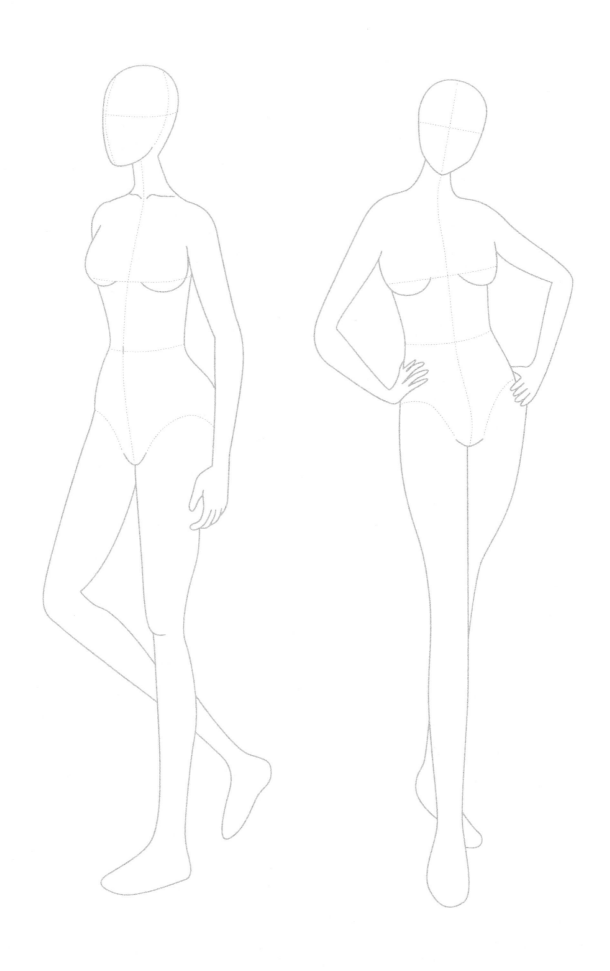

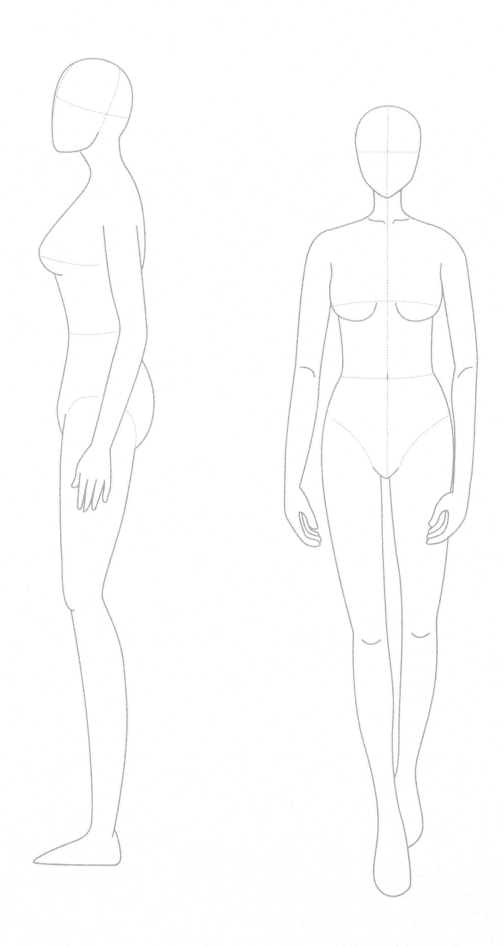

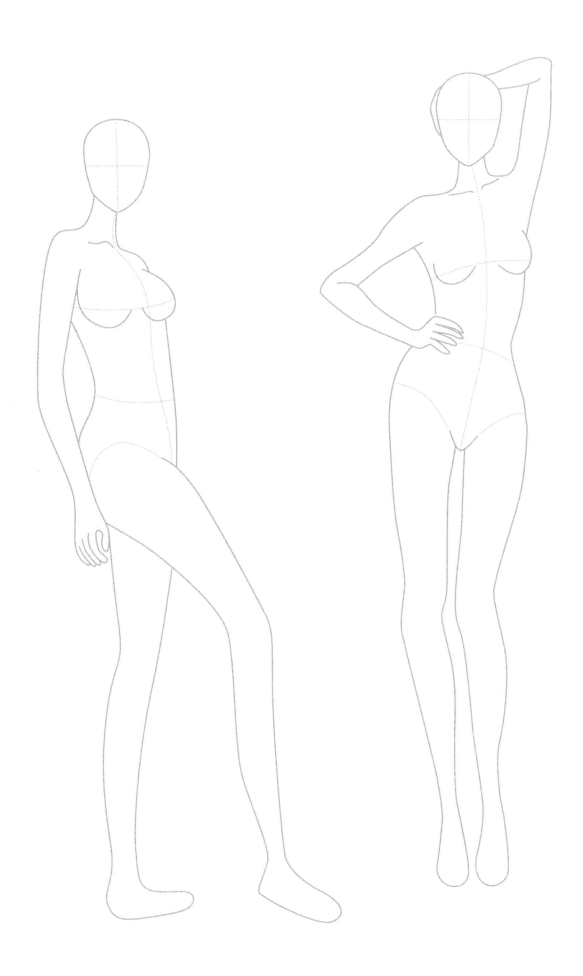

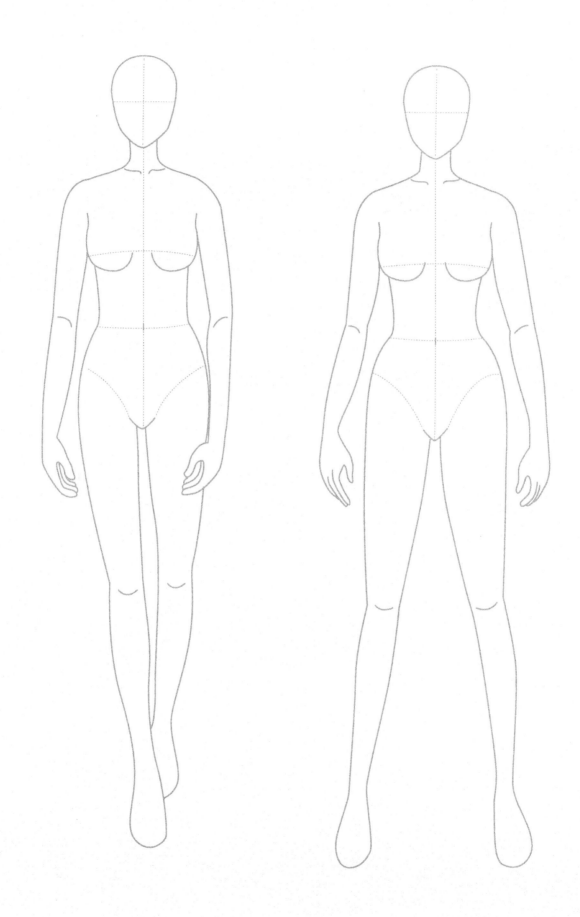

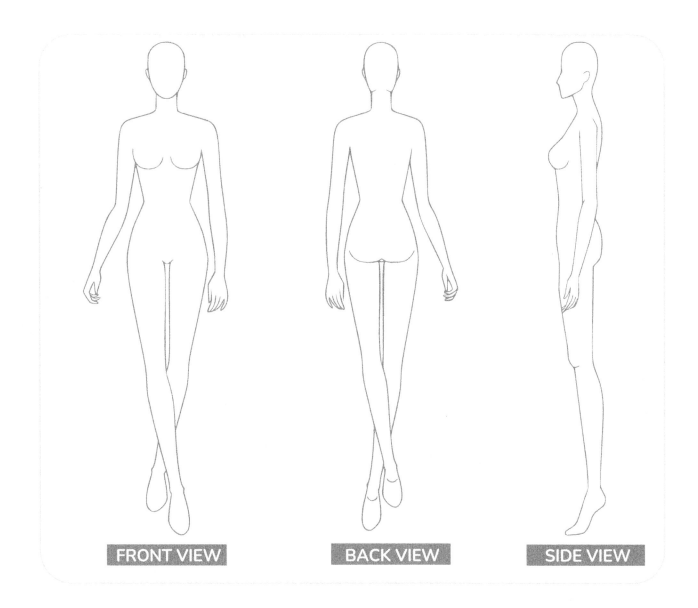

FRONT VIEW   BACK VIEW   SIDE VIEW

COLORS ◯ ◯ ◯ ◯ ◯ ◯ ◯ ◯ ◯ ◯ ◯ ◯ ◯ ◯

MATERIALS   PATTERNS

ACCESSORIES

Trends

_____

_____

Inspiration

_____

_____

_____

Textiles

_____

_____

_____

Notes

_____

_____

_____

Swatches

Details

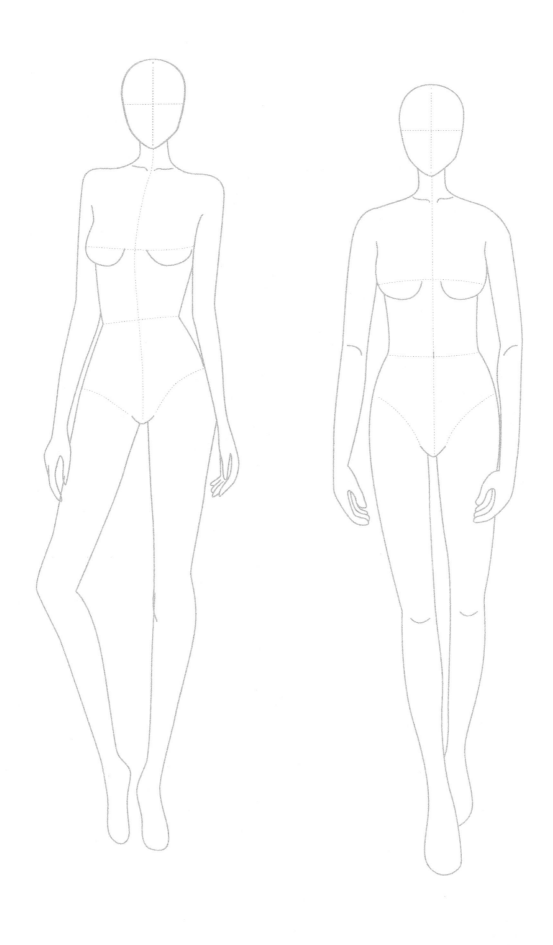

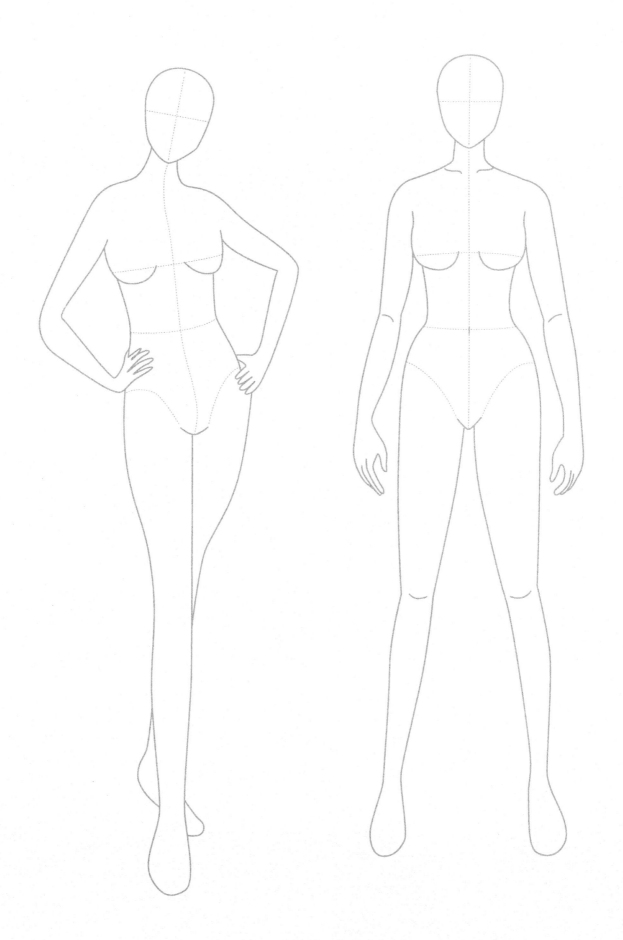

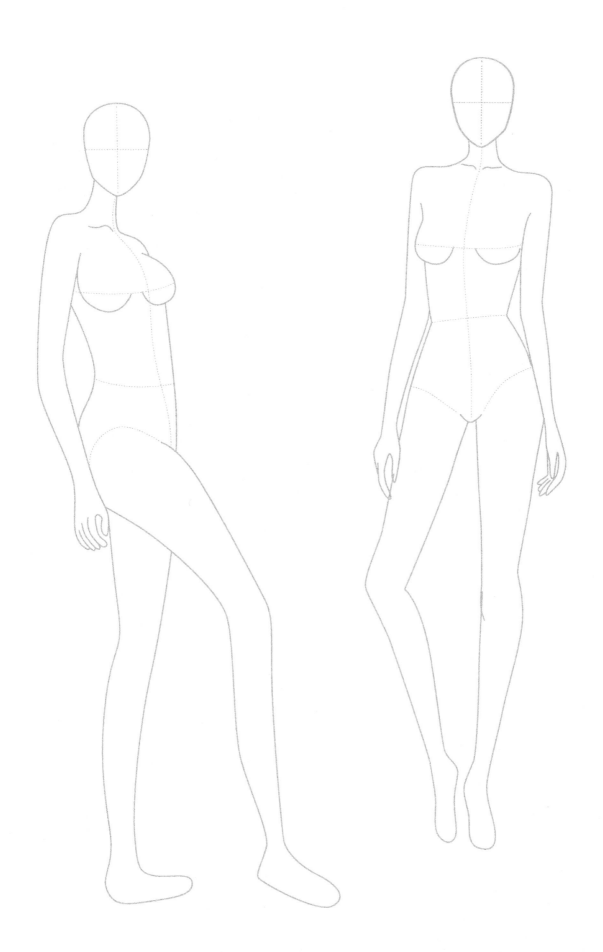

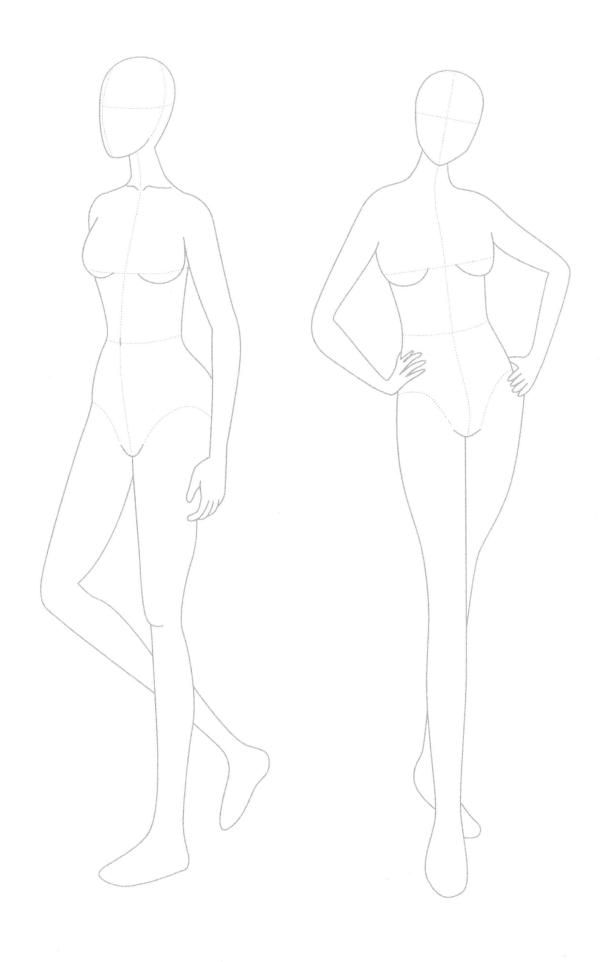

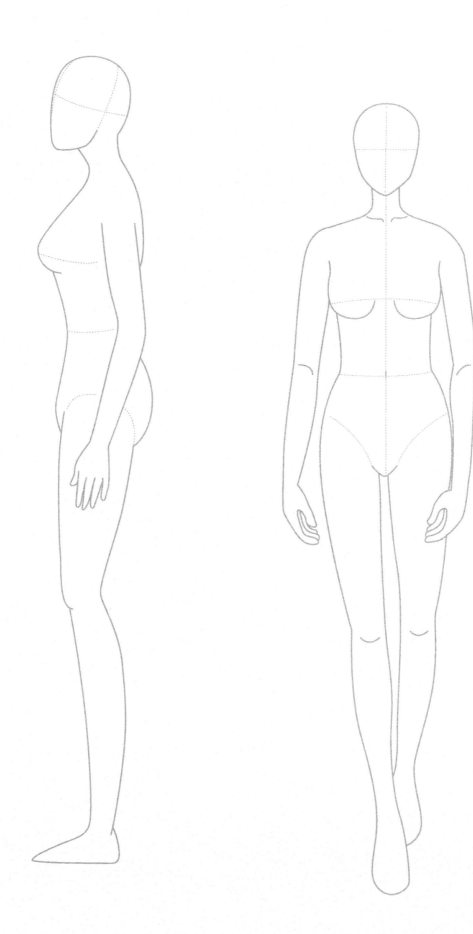

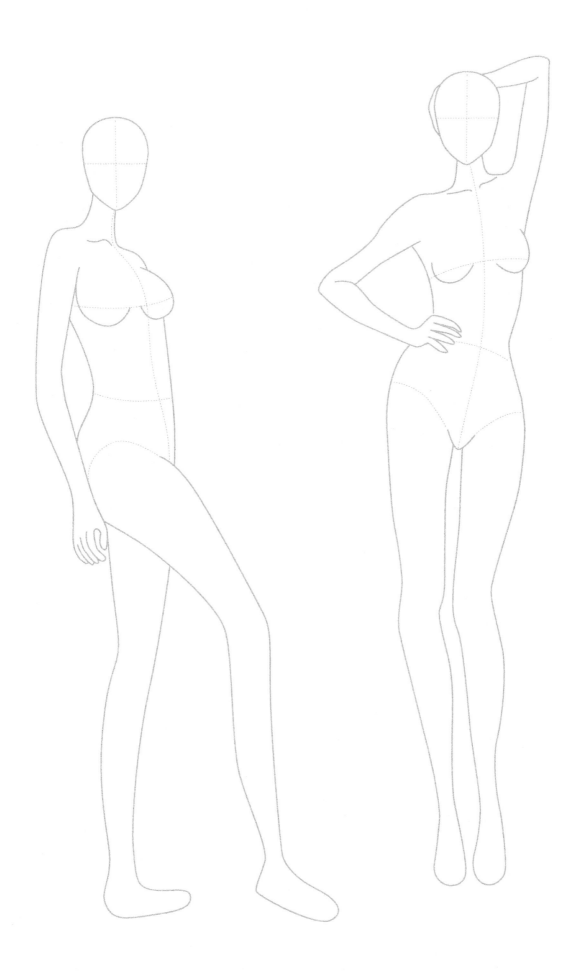

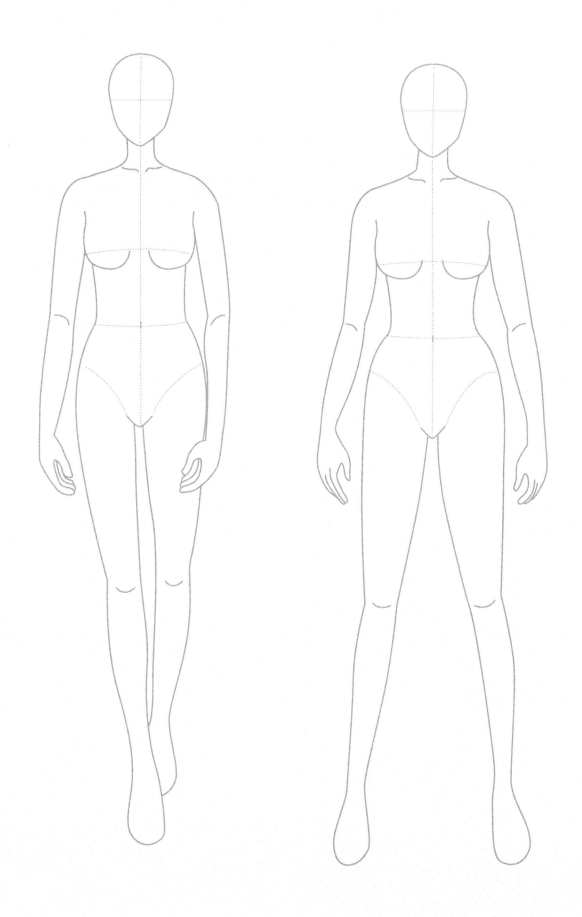

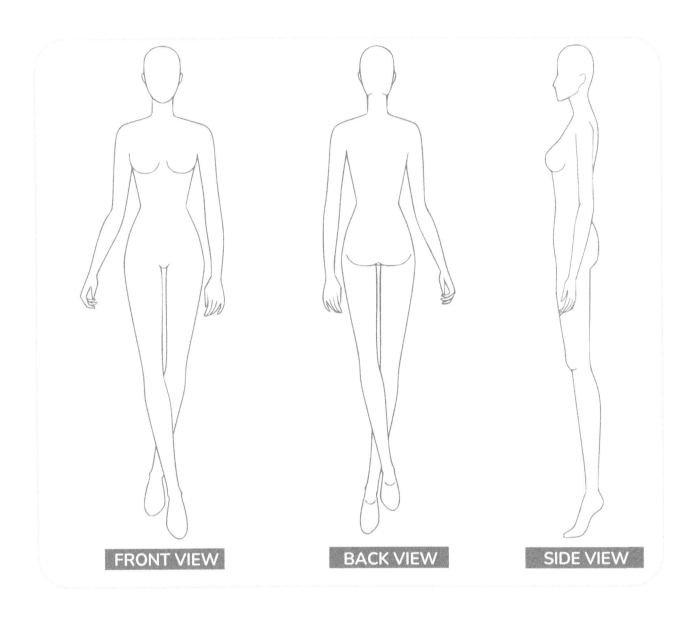

FRONT VIEW

BACK VIEW

SIDE VIEW

COLORS ○ ○ ○ ○ ○ ○ ○ ○ ○ ○ ○ ○ ○ ○ ○

MATERIALS

PATTERNS

ACCESSORIES

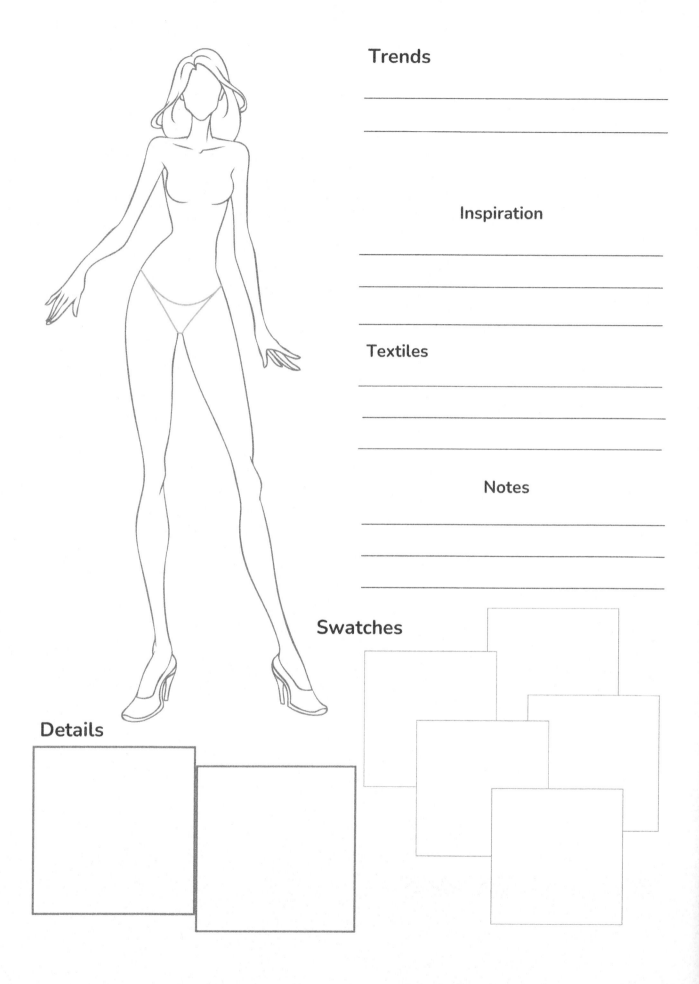

Trends

Inspiration

Textiles

Notes

Swatches

Details

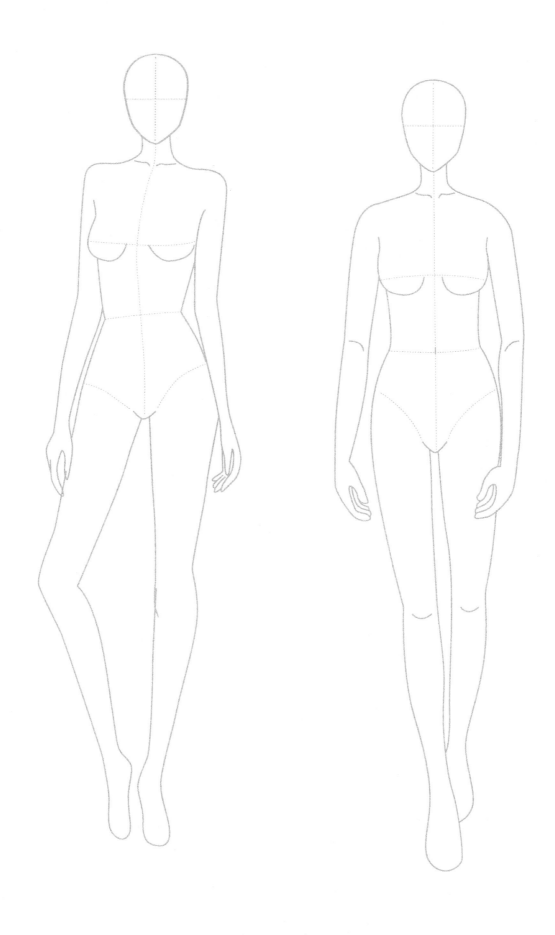

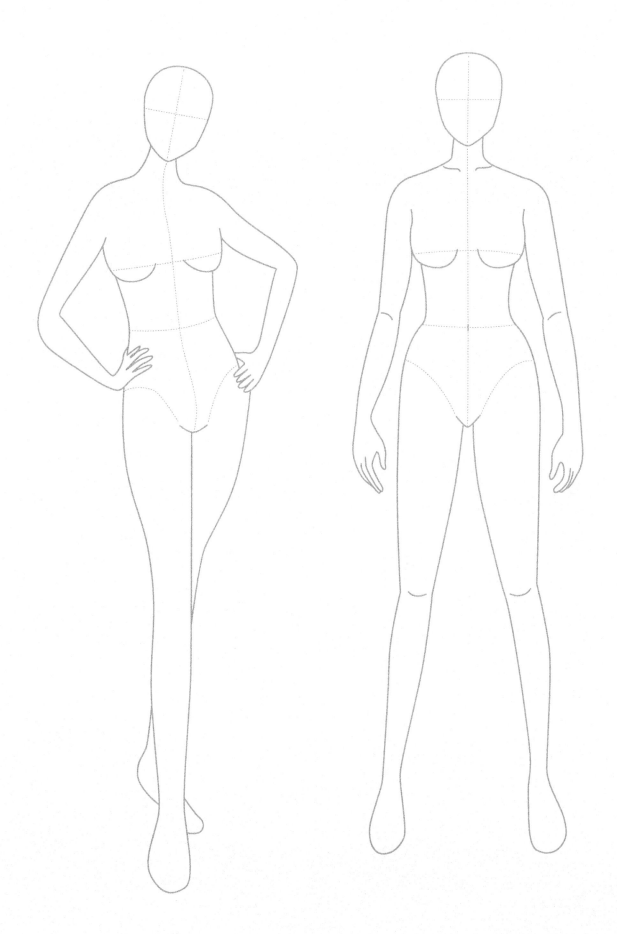

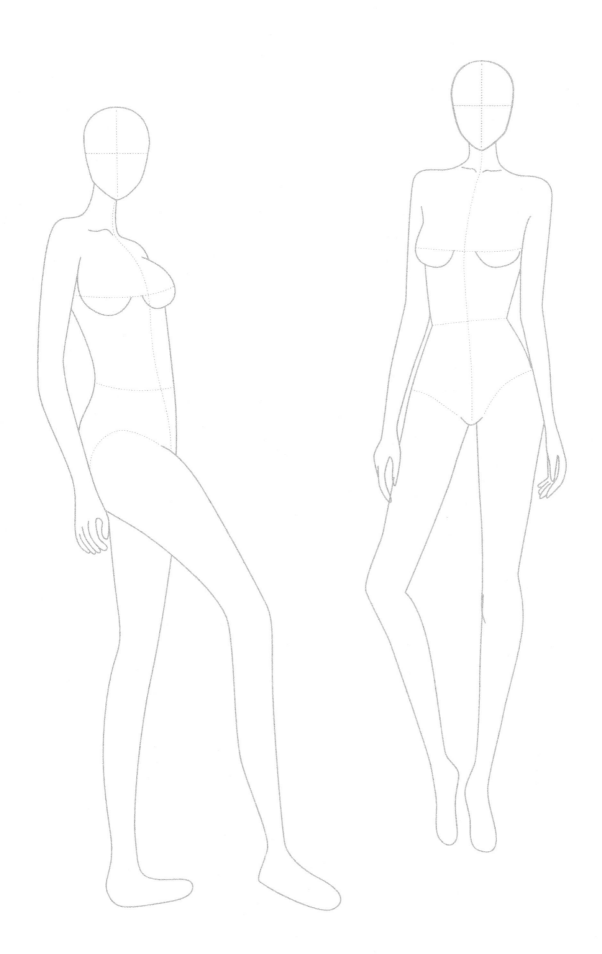

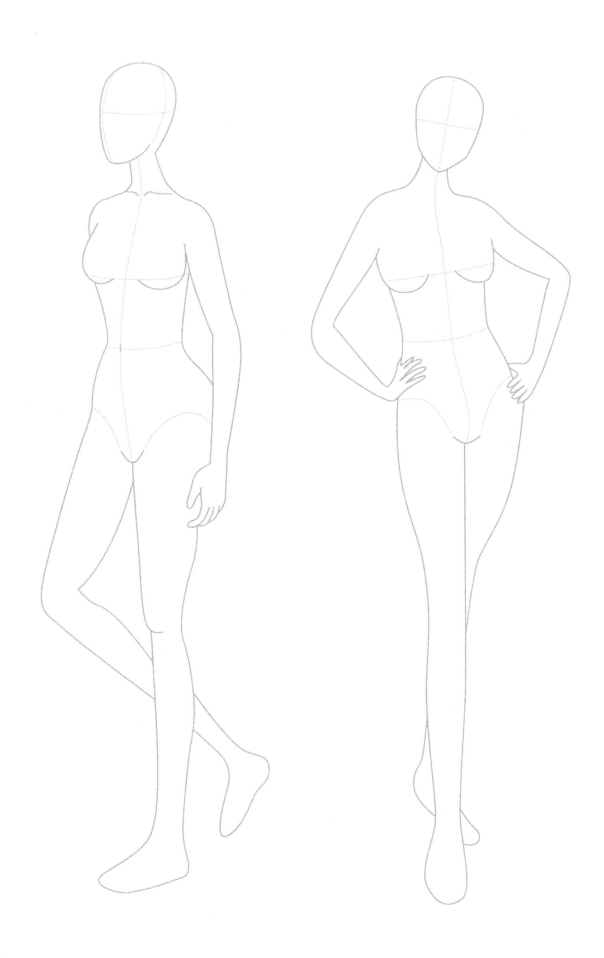

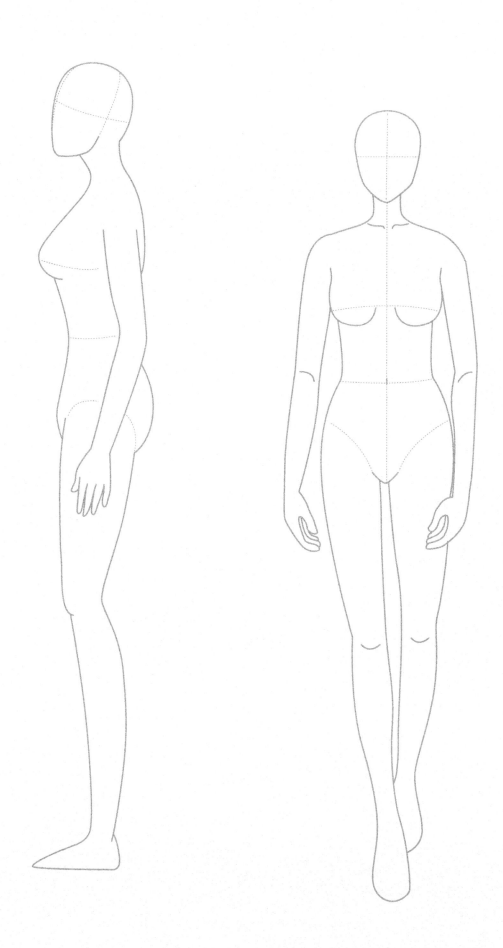

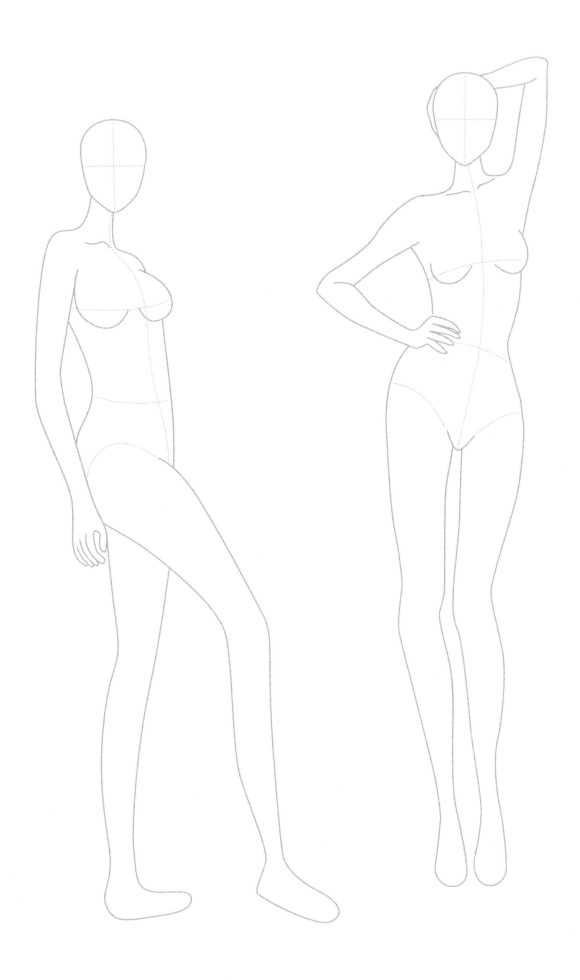

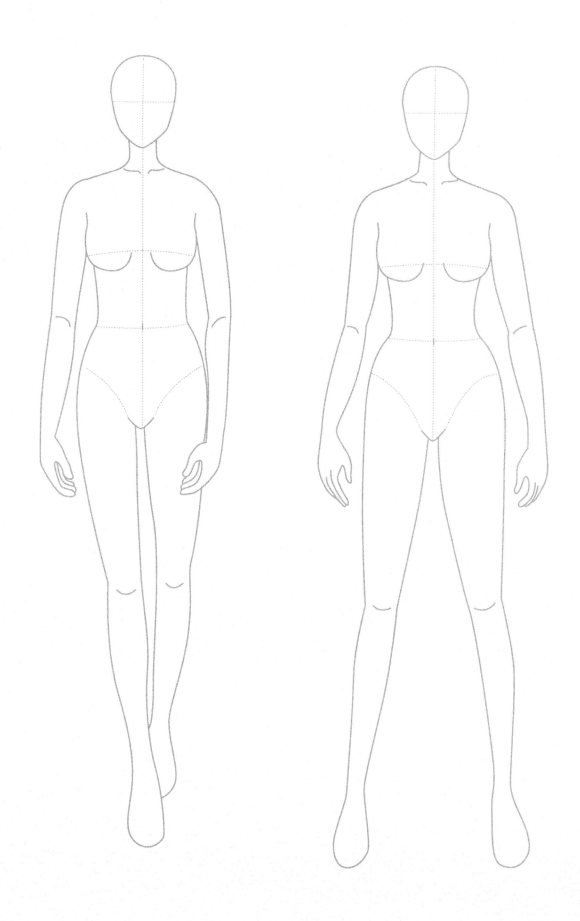

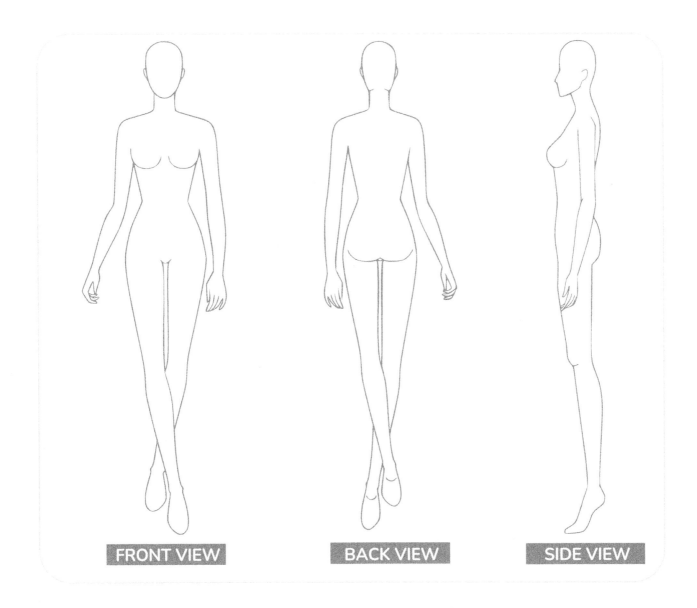

FRONT VIEW   BACK VIEW   SIDE VIEW

COLORS ◯◯◯◯◯◯◯◯◯◯◯◯◯◯

MATERIALS

PATTERNS

ACCESSORIES

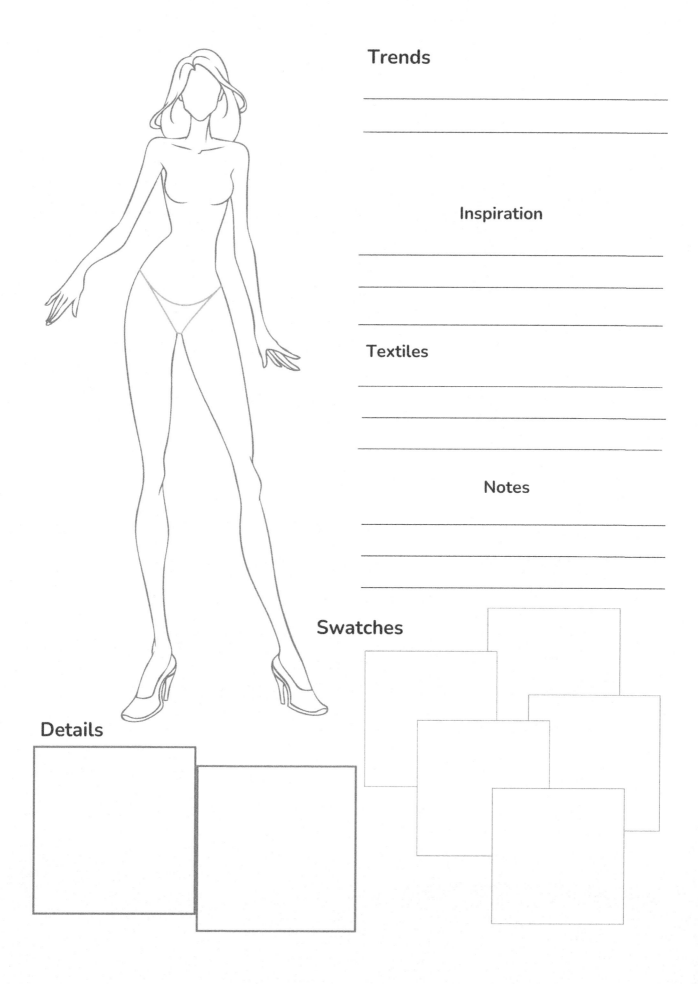

Trends

Inspiration

Textiles

Notes

Swatches

Details

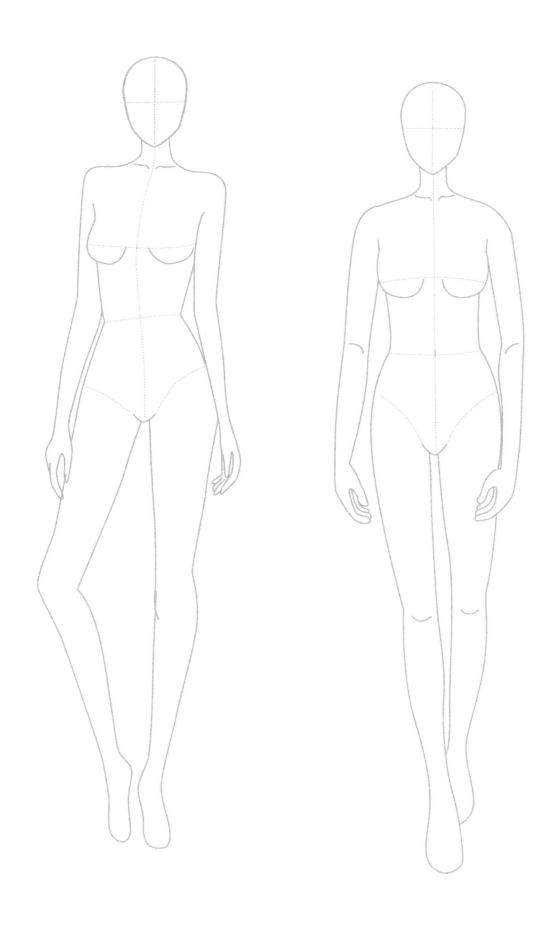

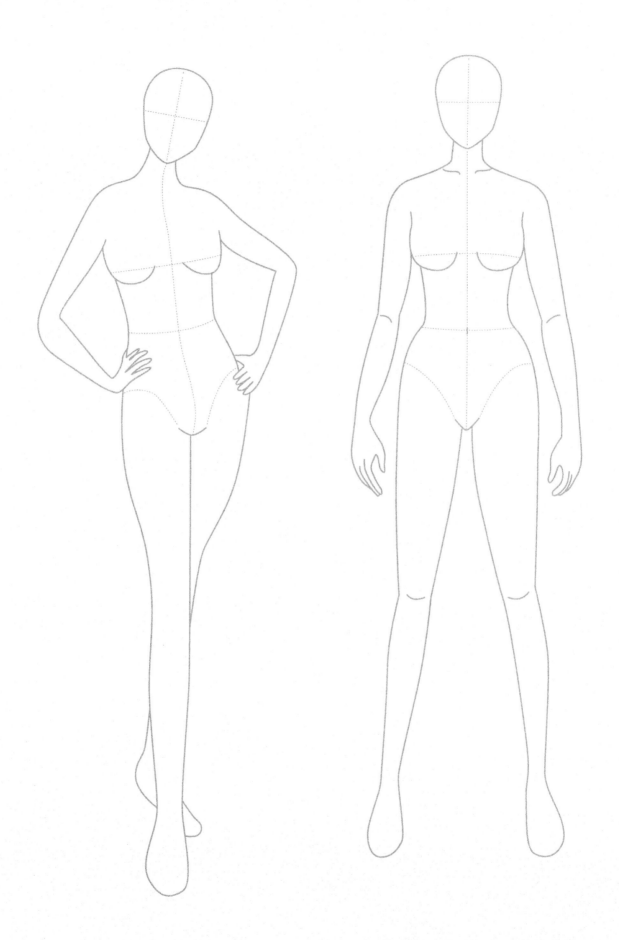

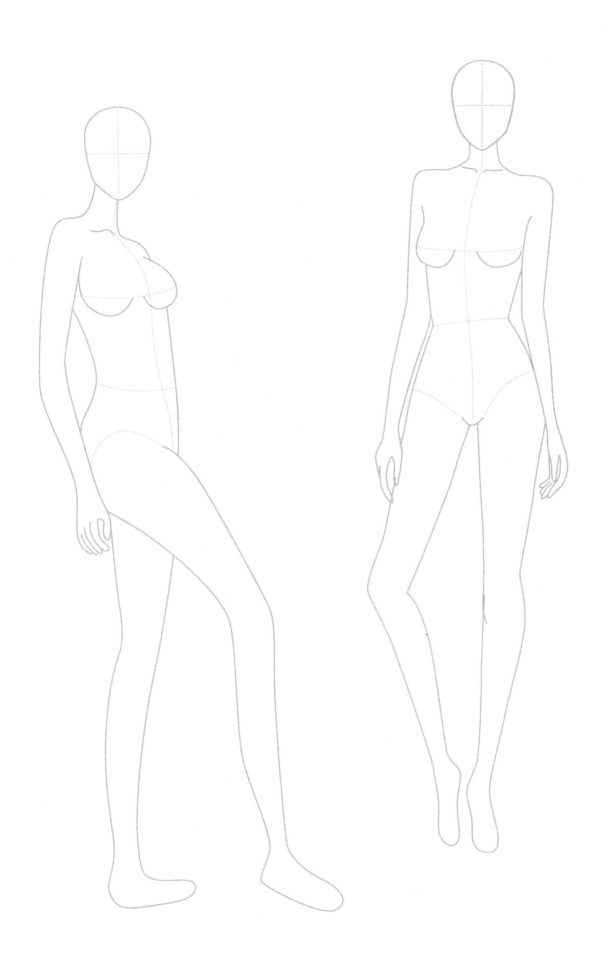

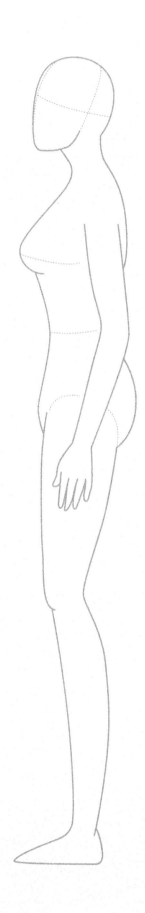

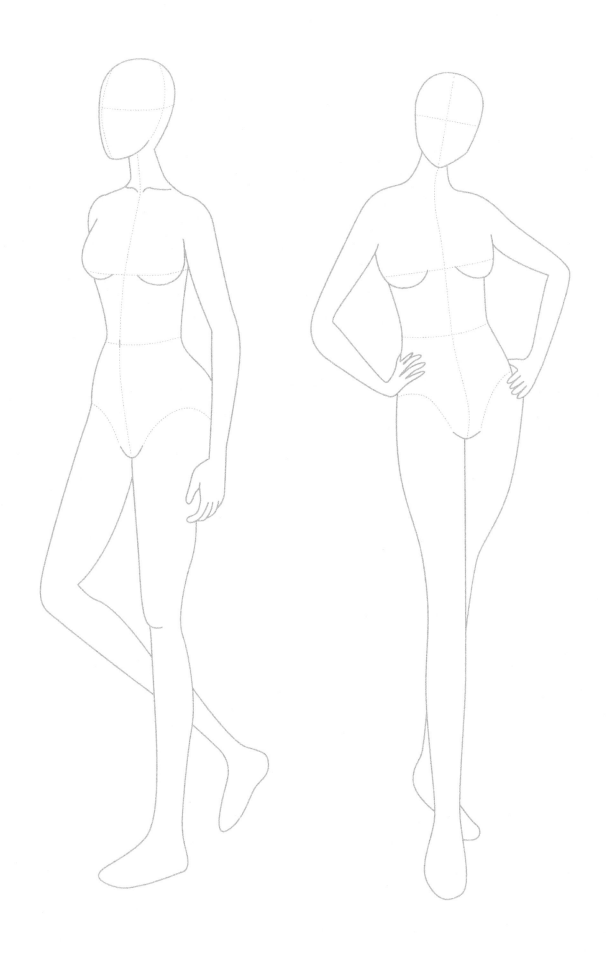

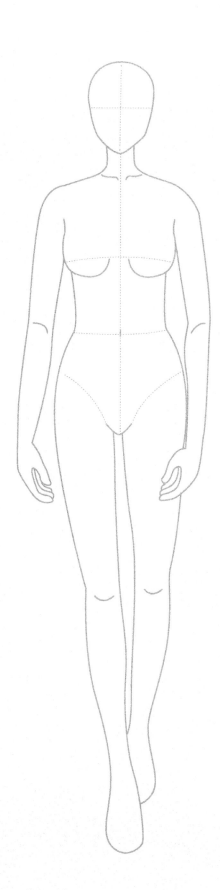

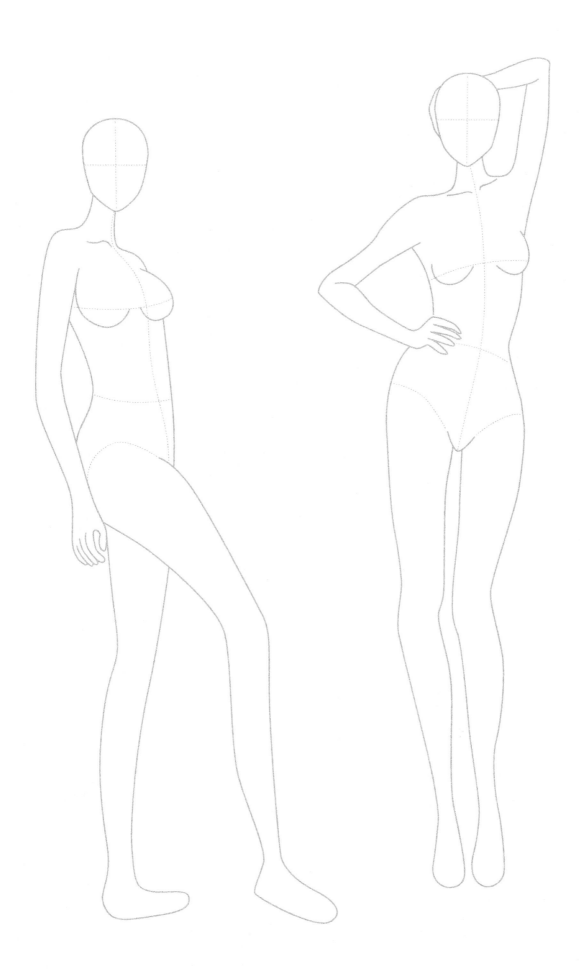

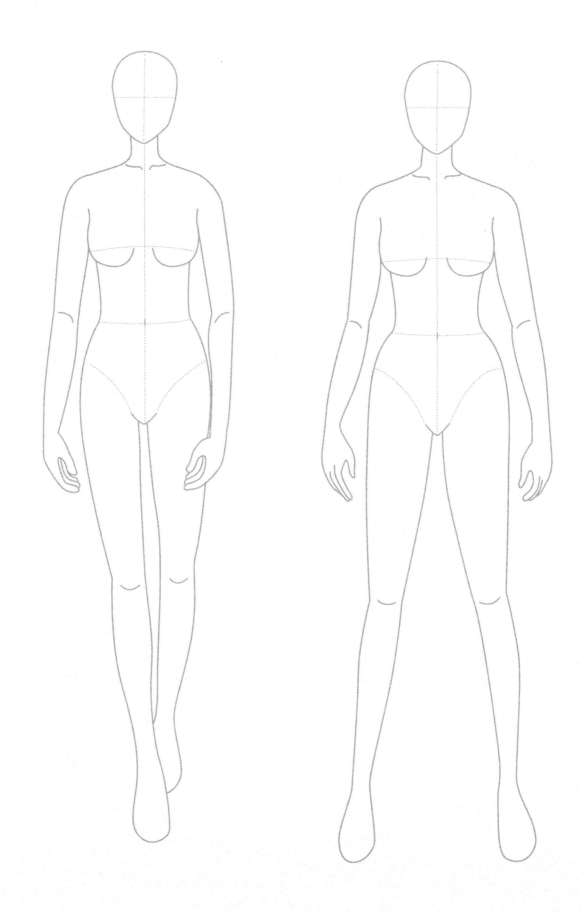

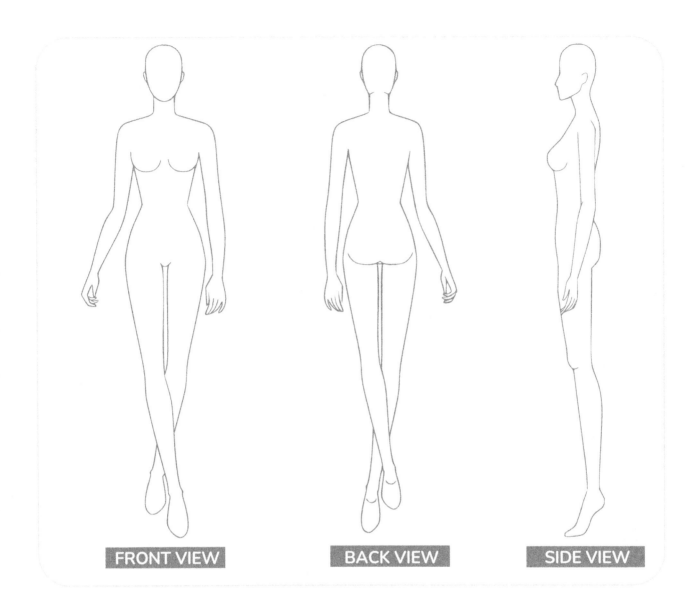

FRONT VIEW   BACK VIEW   SIDE VIEW

COLORS ○○○○○○○○○○○○○○○○○

MATERIALS

PATTERNS

ACCESSORIES

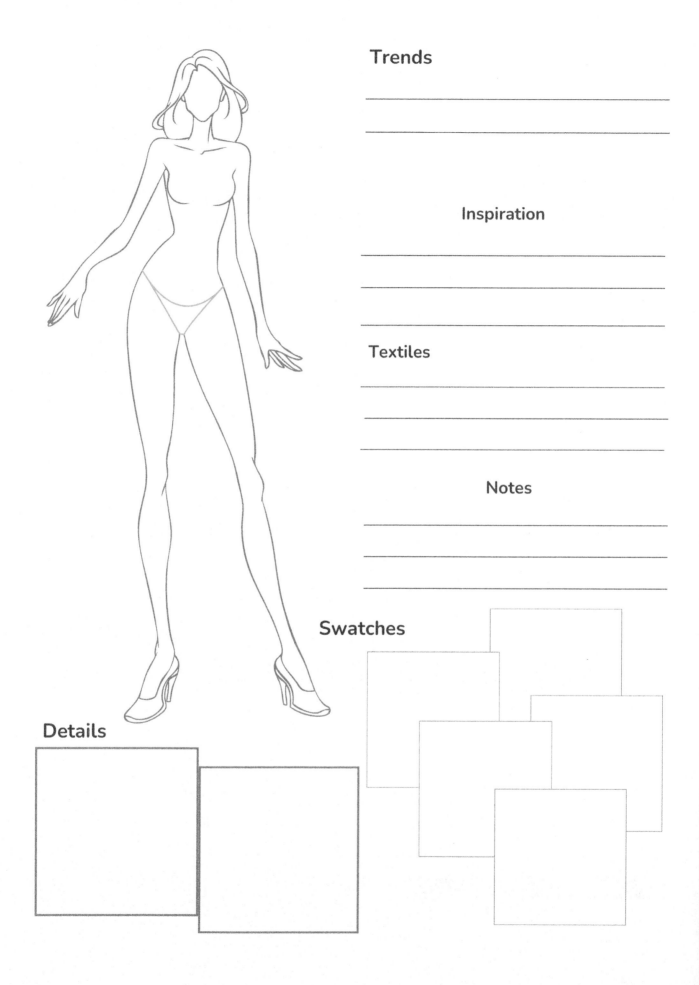

Trends

Inspiration

Textiles

Notes

Swatches

Details

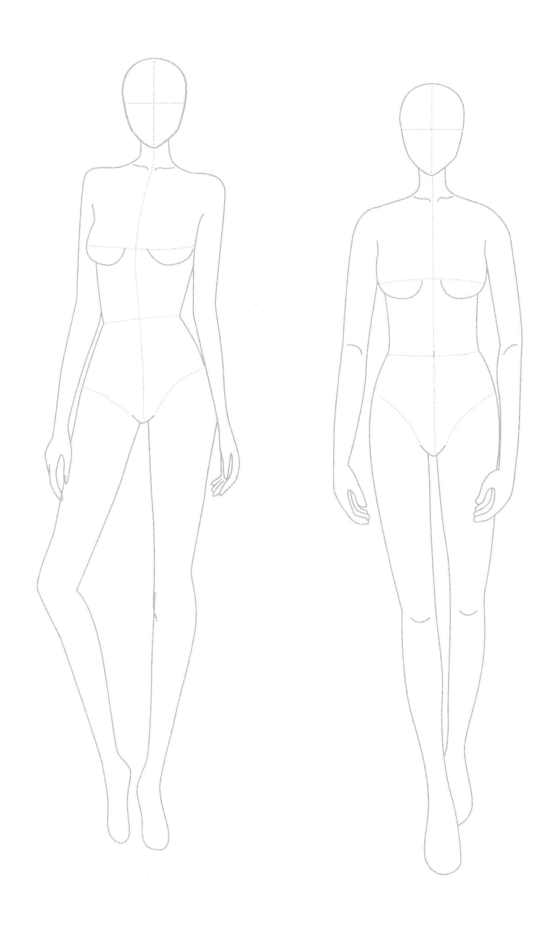

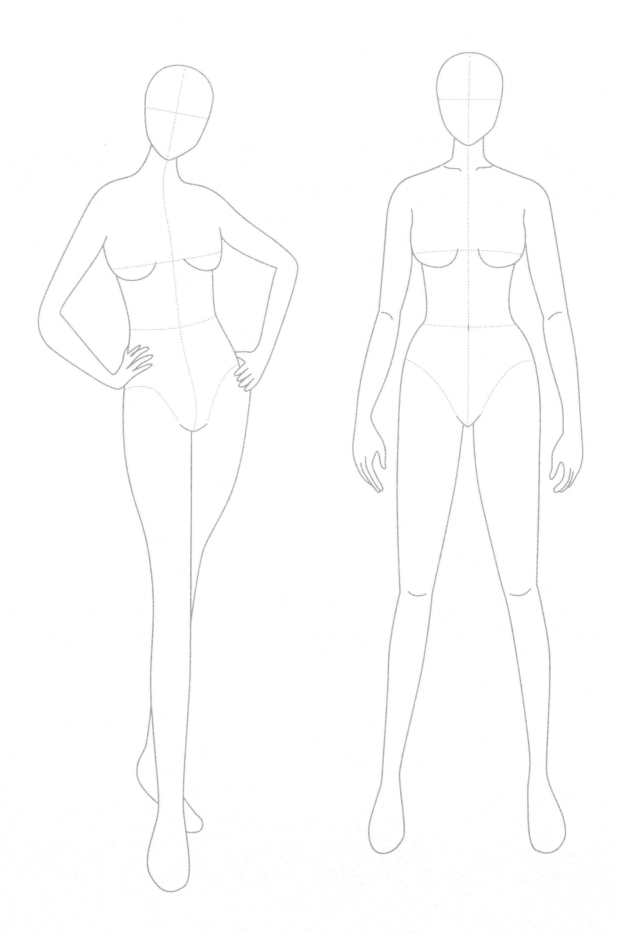

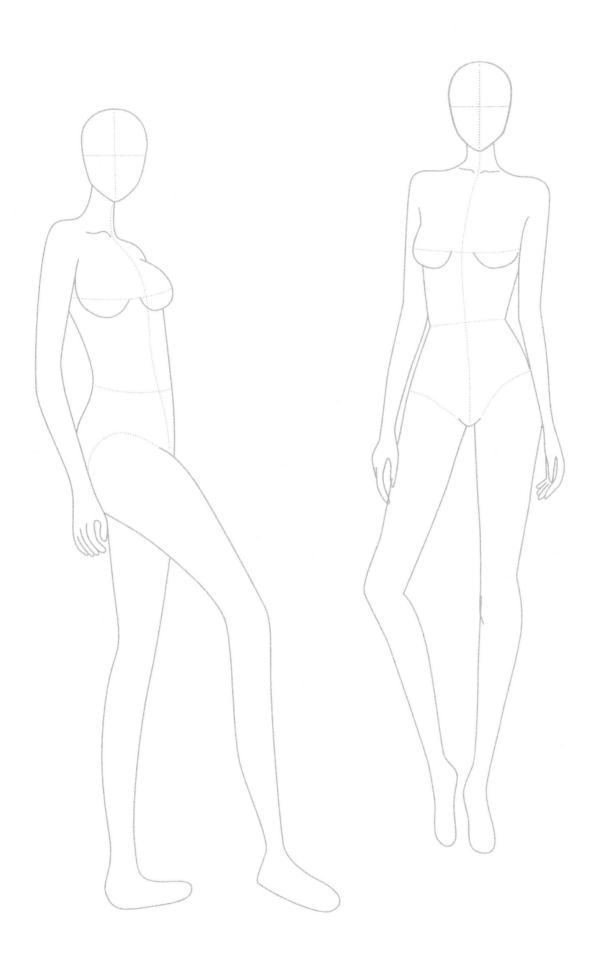

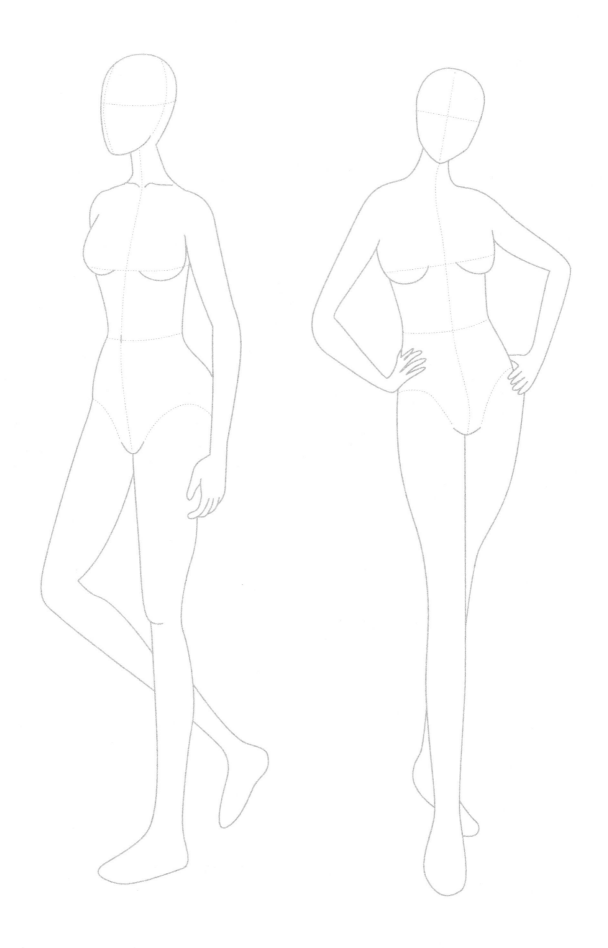

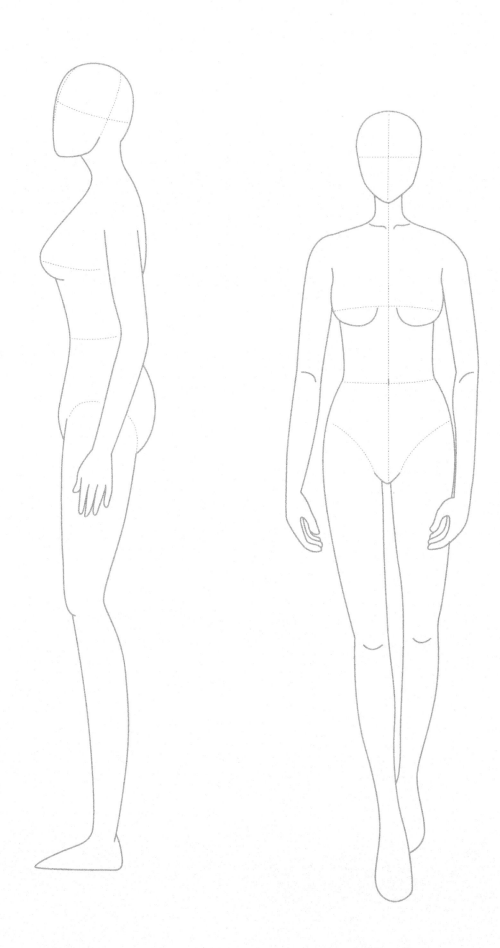

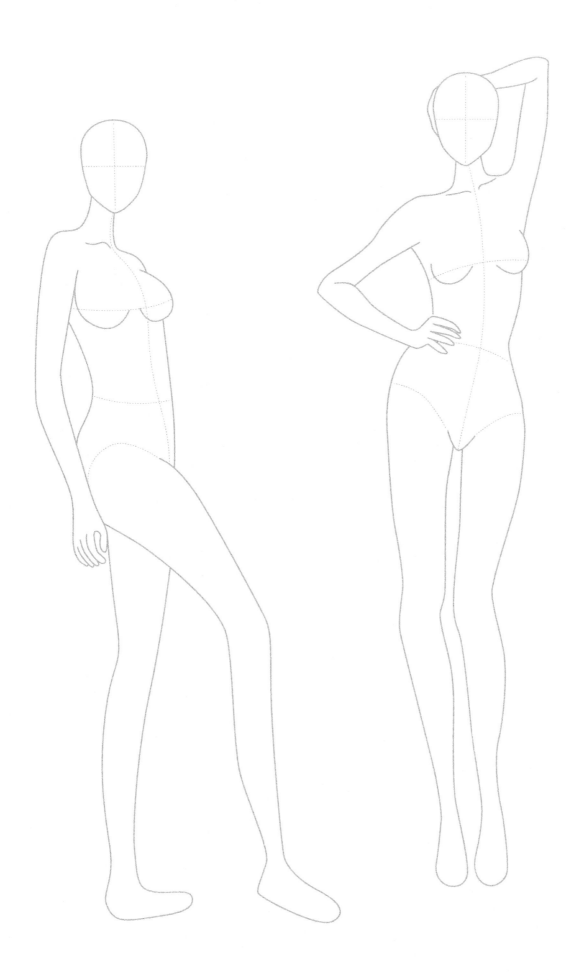

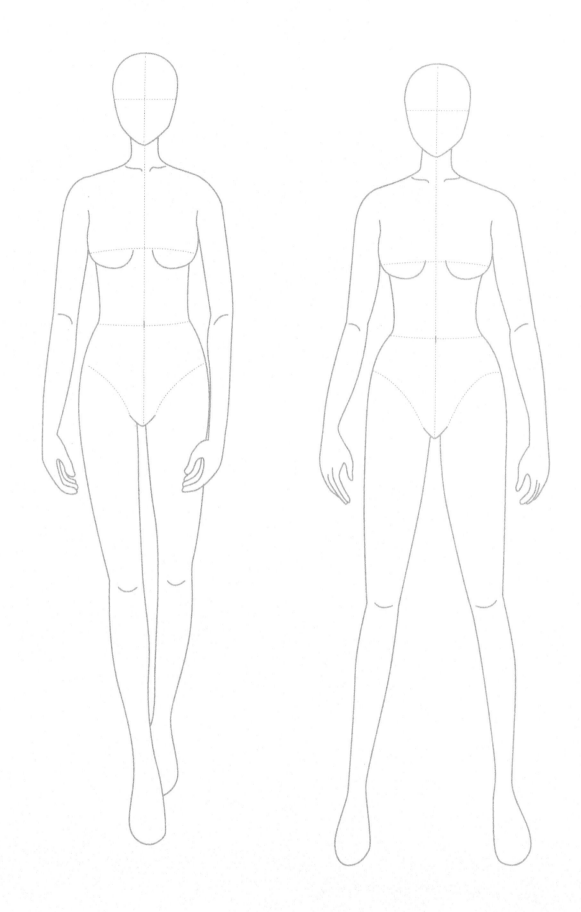

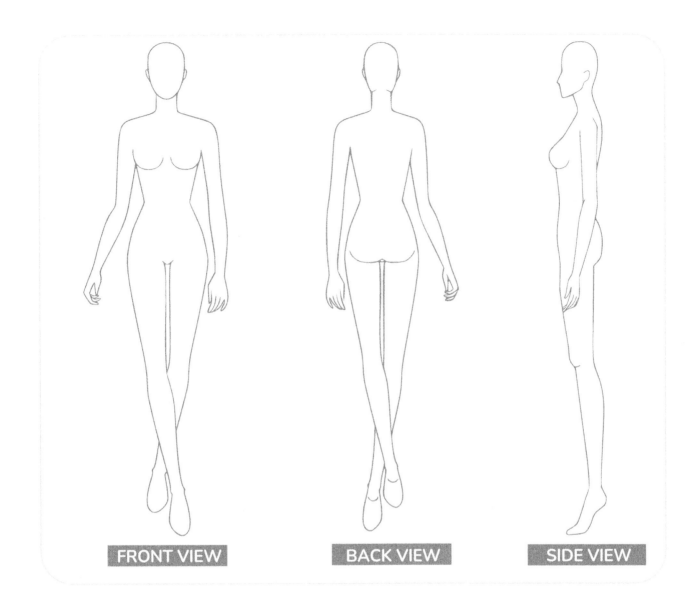

FRONT VIEW

BACK VIEW

SIDE VIEW

COLORS ◯◯◯◯◯◯◯◯◯◯◯◯◯◯◯◯

MATERIALS			PATTERNS		

ACCESSORIES

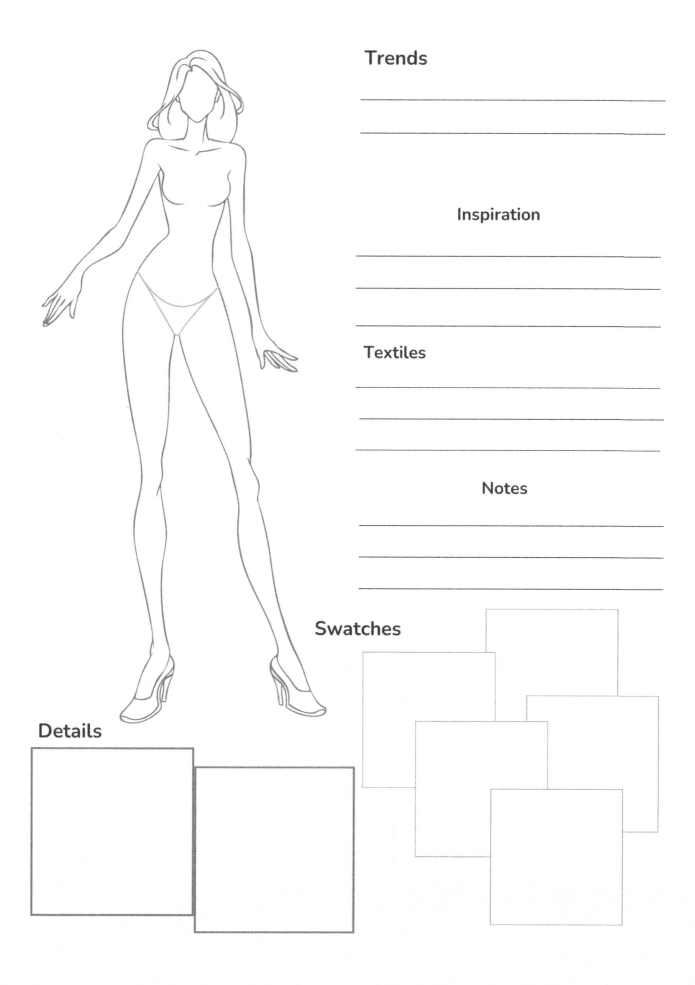

Trends

Inspiration

Textiles

Notes

Swatches

Details

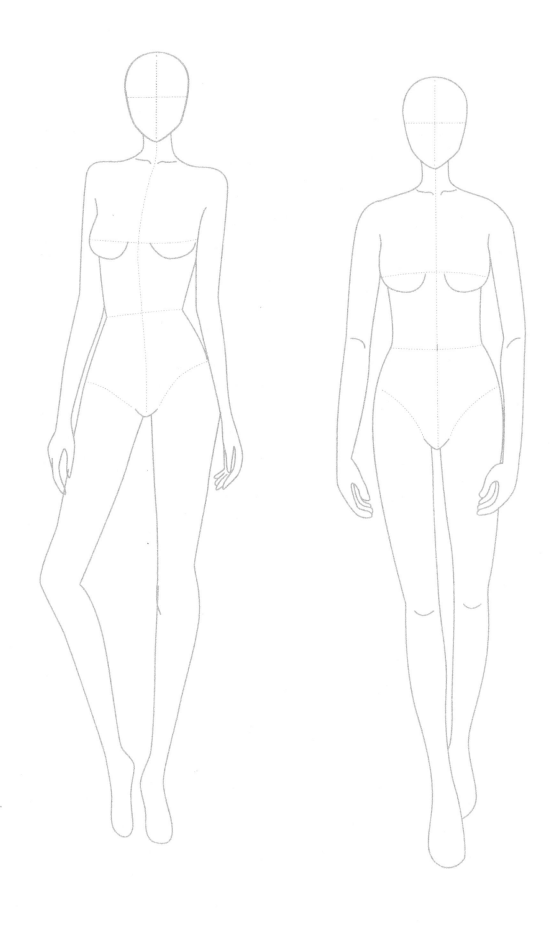

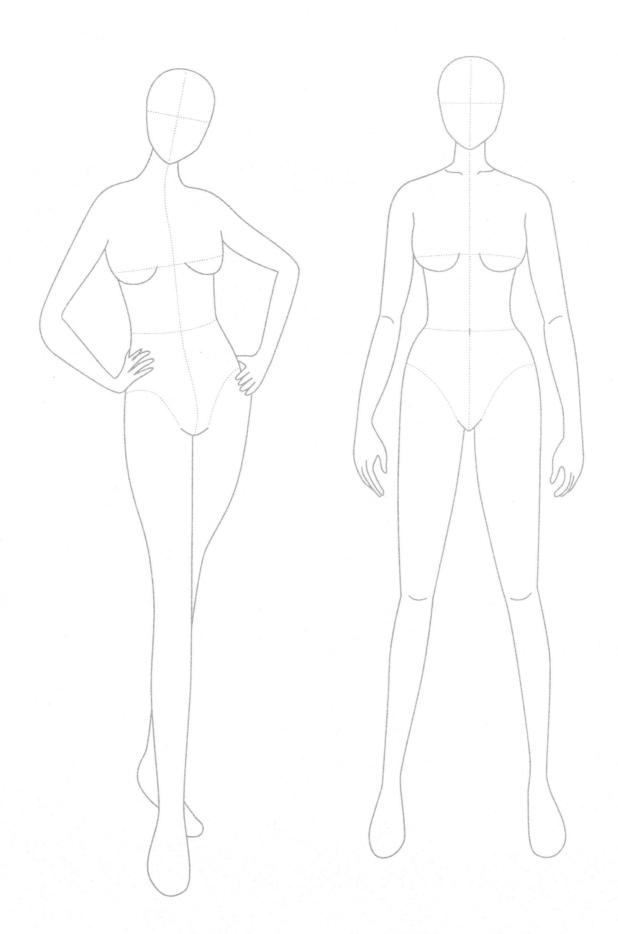

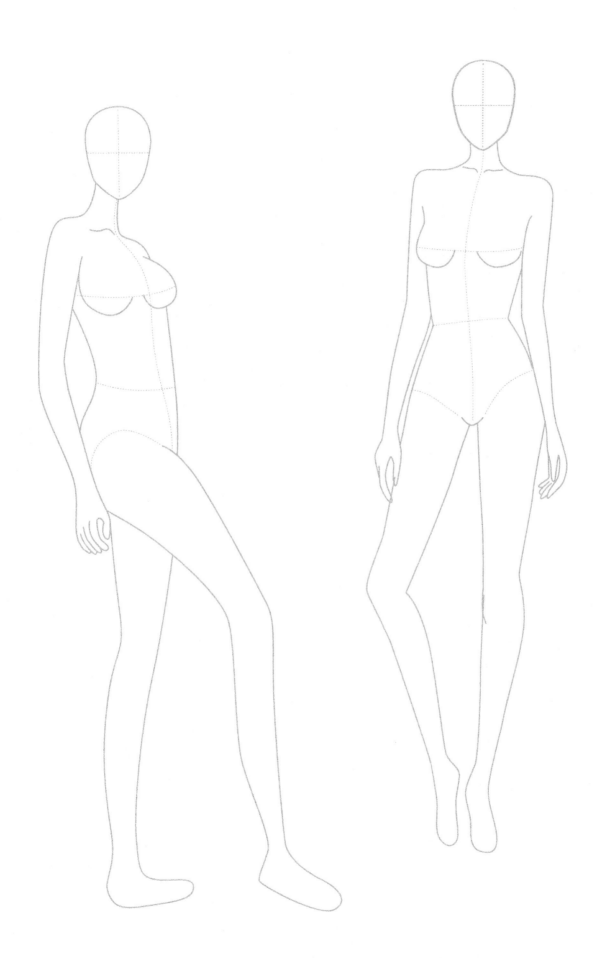

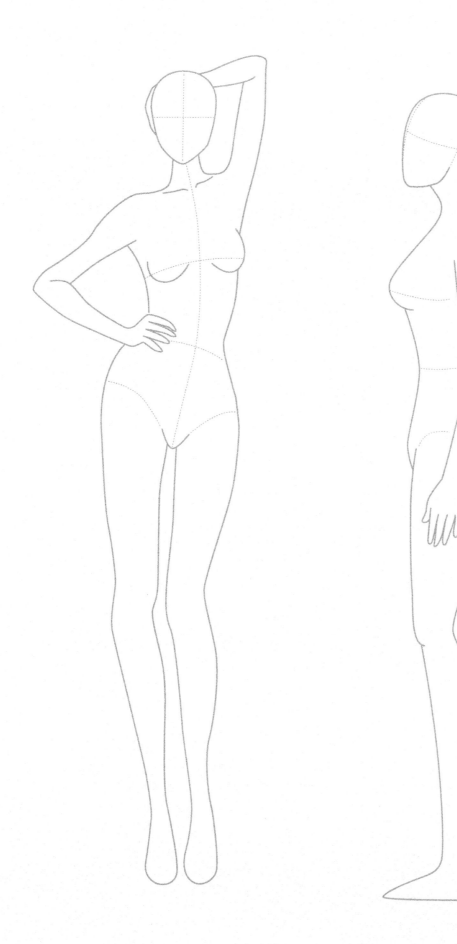

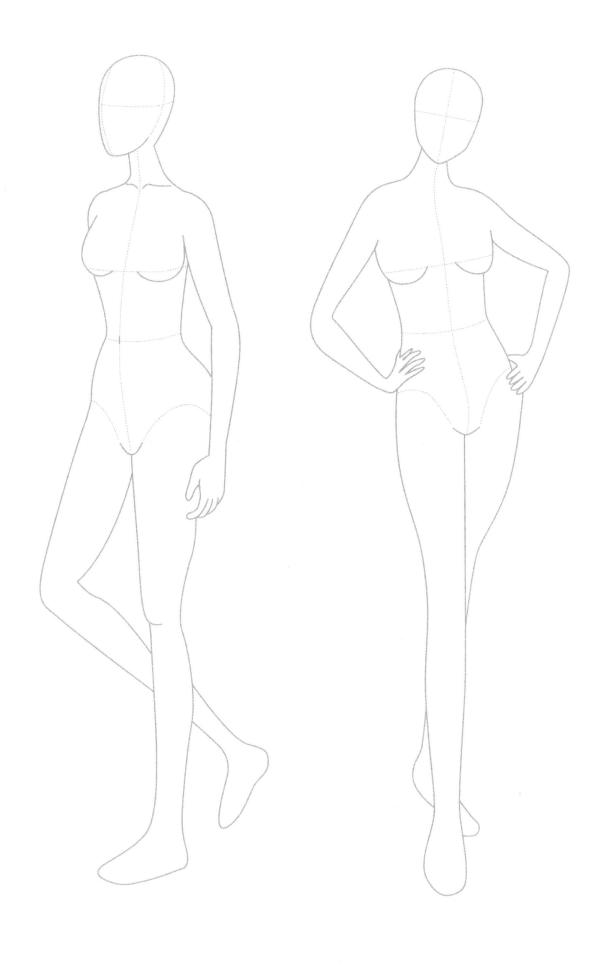

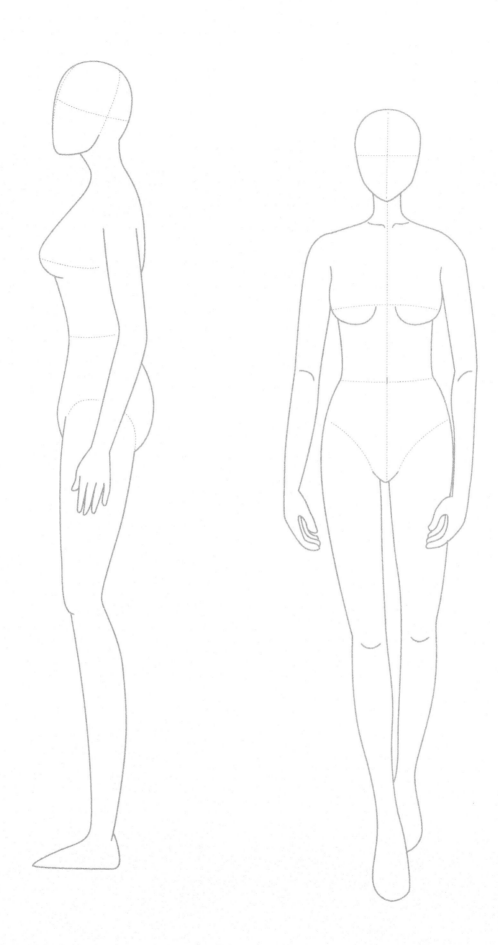

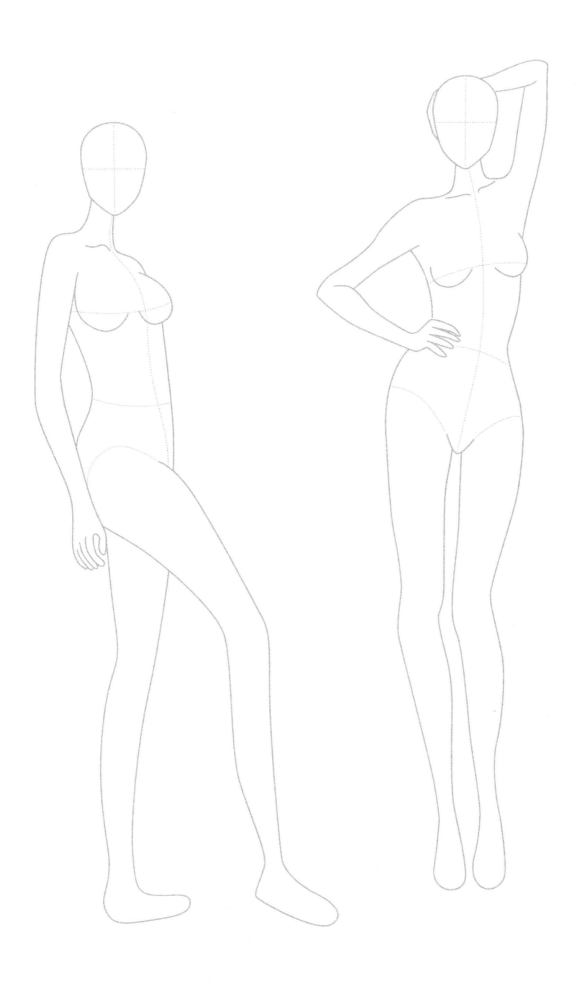

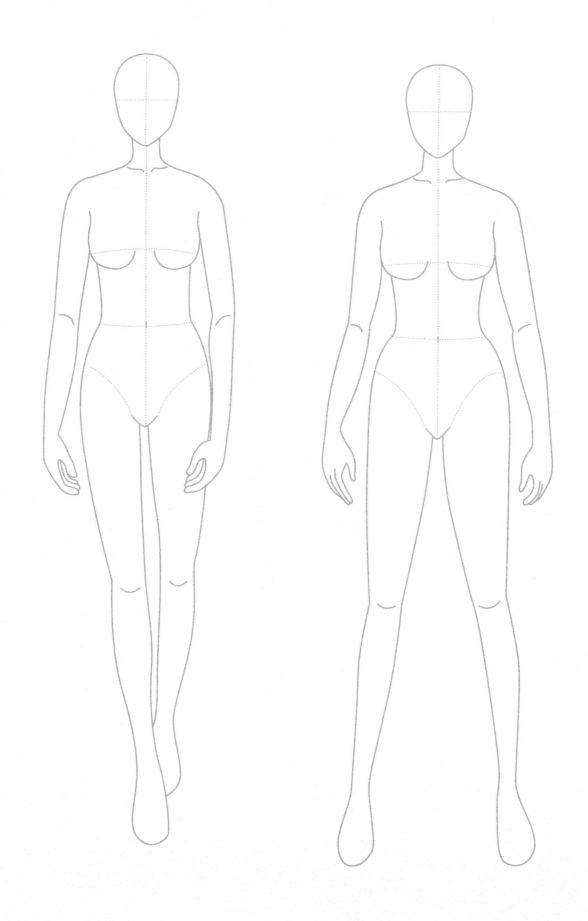

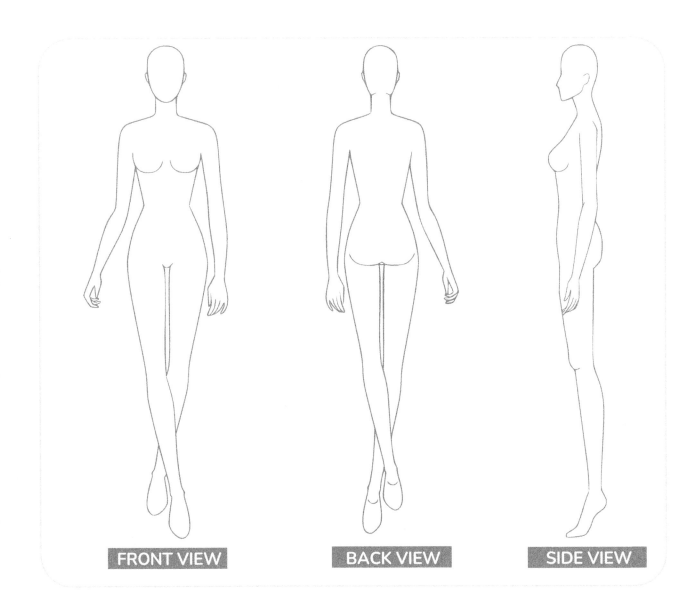

FRONT VIEW

BACK VIEW

SIDE VIEW

COLORS ○ ○ ○ ○ ○ ○ ○ ○ ○ ○ ○ ○ ○ ○ ○ ○

MATERIALS

PATTERNS

ACCESSORIES

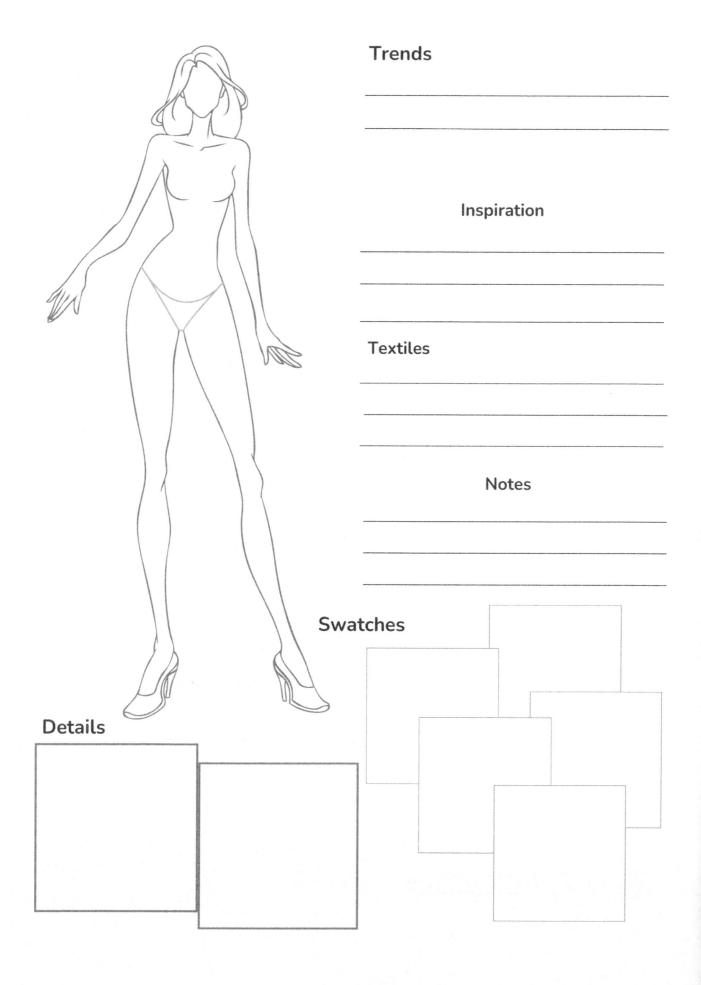

Trends

Inspiration

Textiles

Notes

Swatches

Details

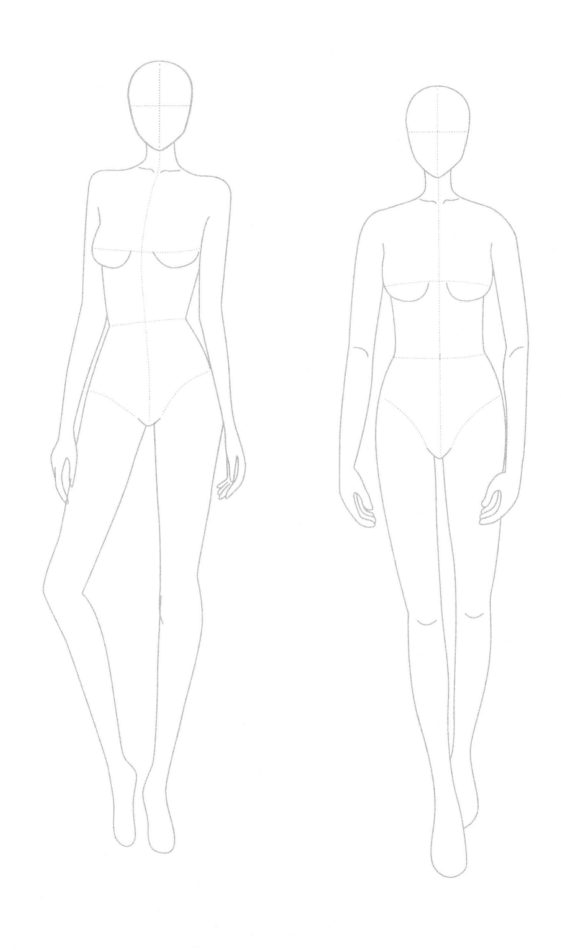

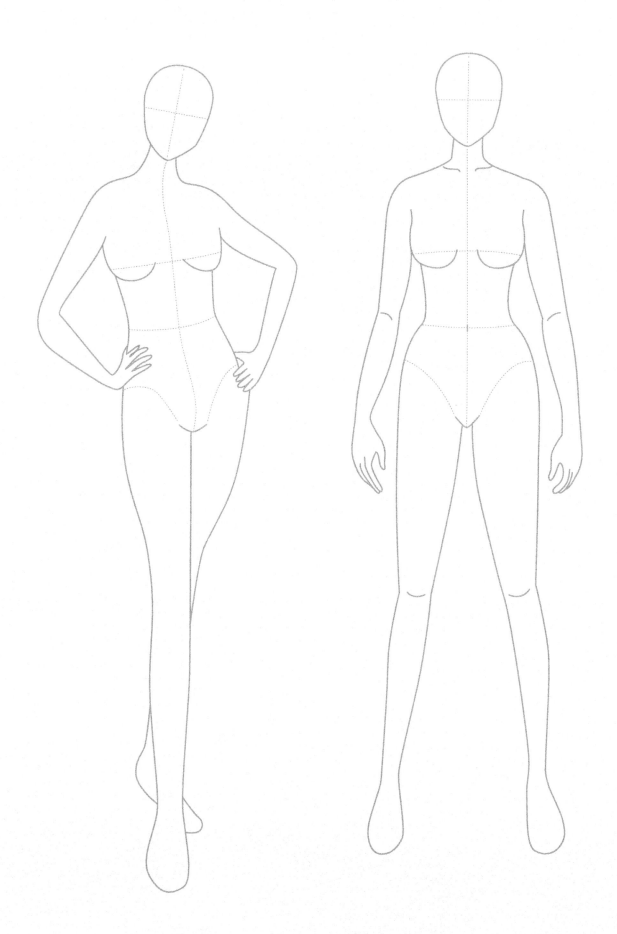

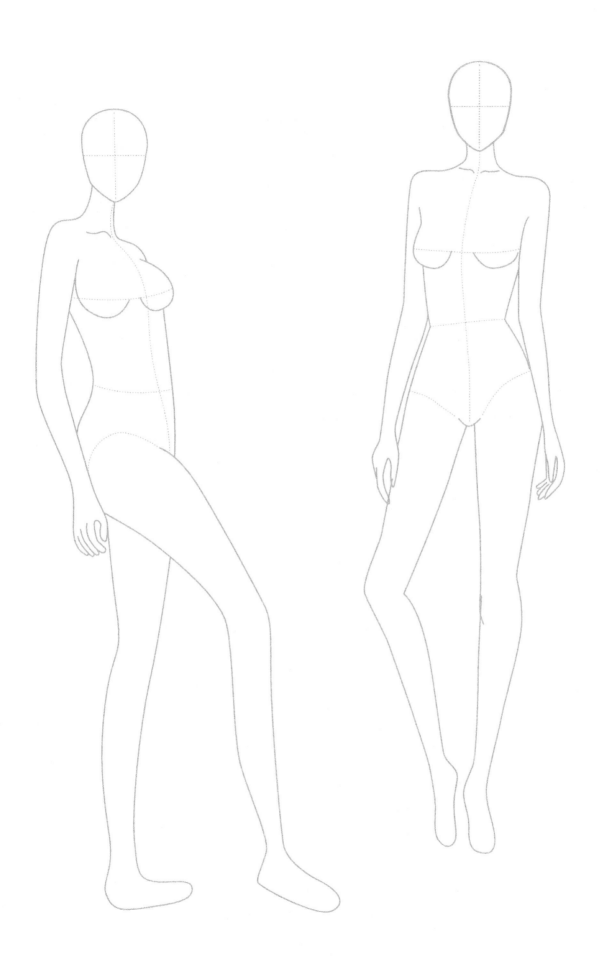

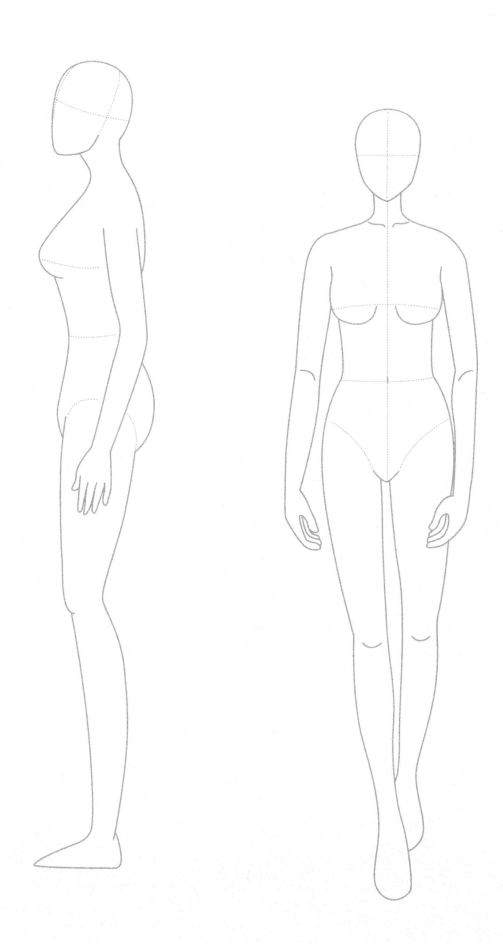

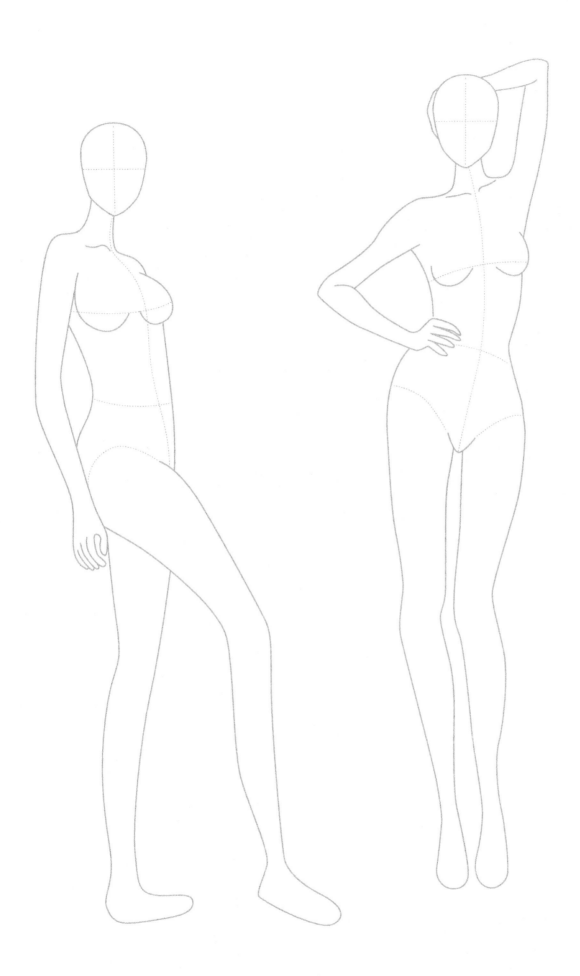

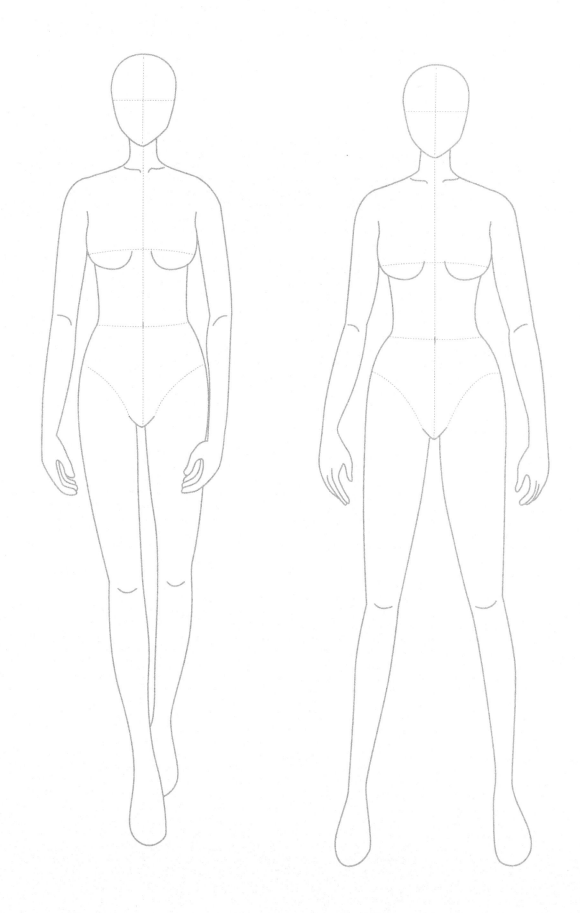

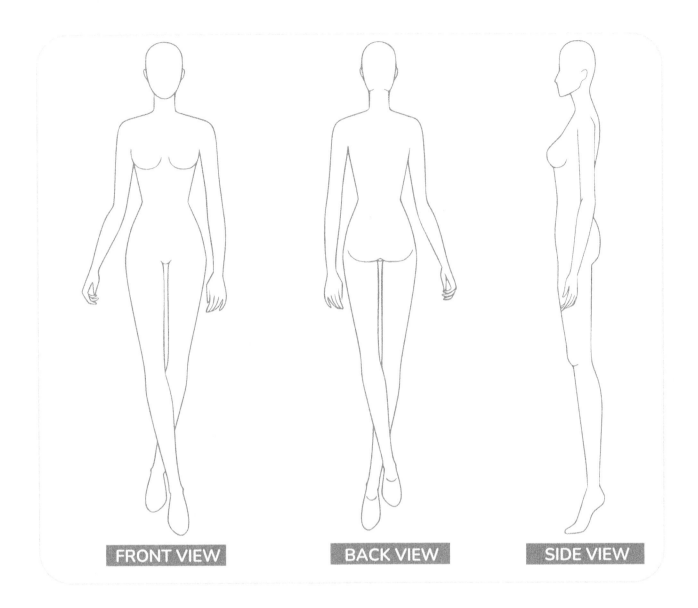

FRONT VIEW

BACK VIEW

SIDE VIEW

COLORS

MATERIALS

PATTERNS

ACCESSORIES

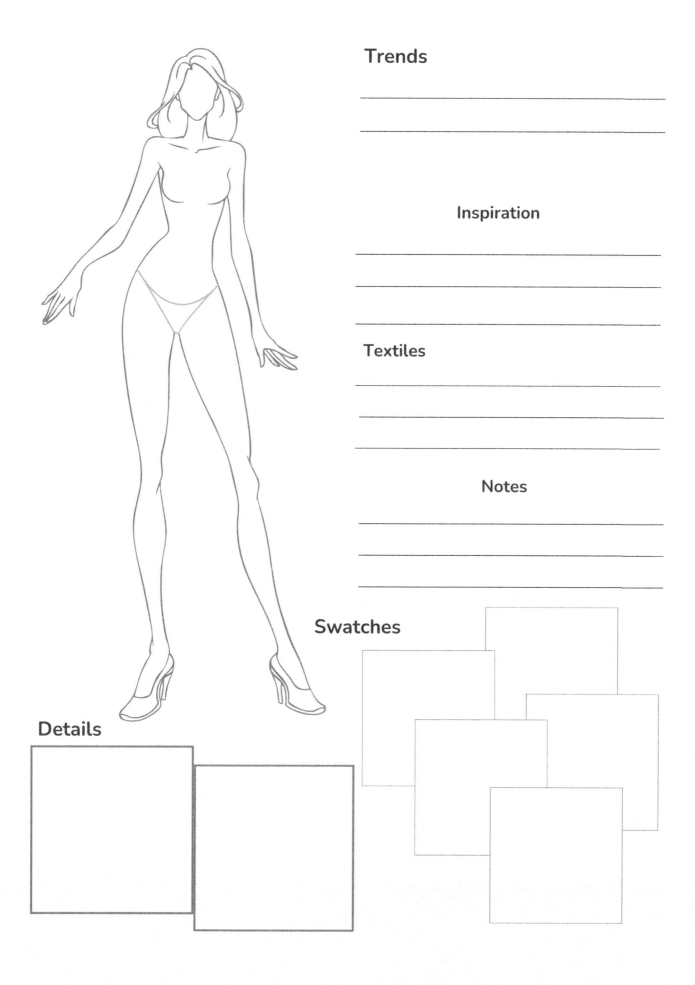

Trends

_____
_____

Inspiration

_____
_____
_____

Textiles

_____
_____

Notes

_____
_____
_____

Swatches

Details

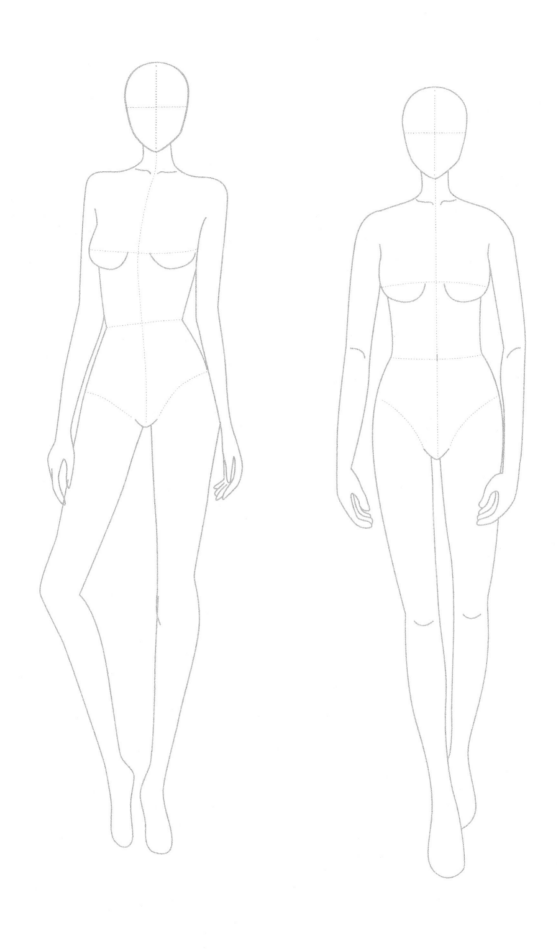

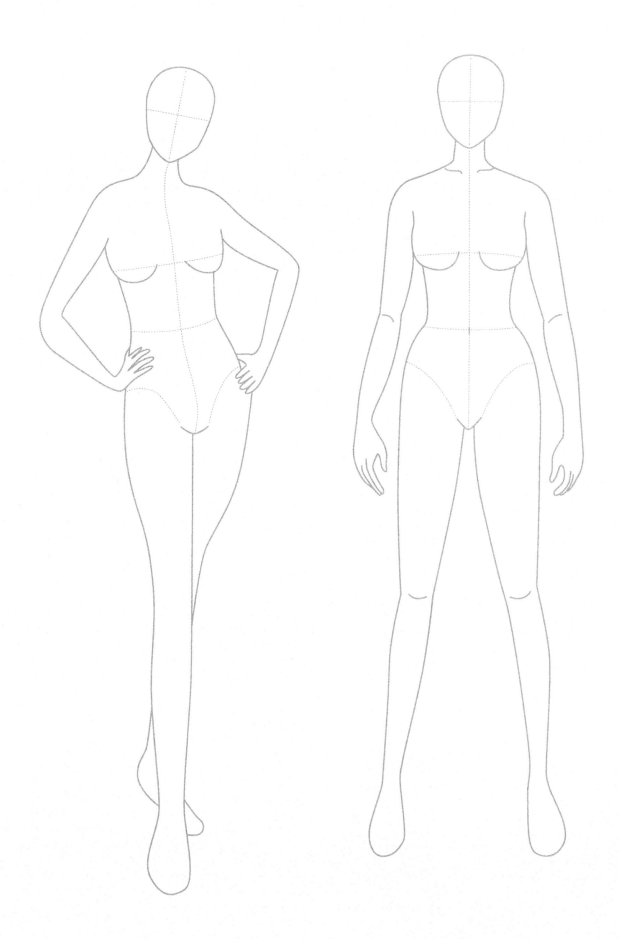

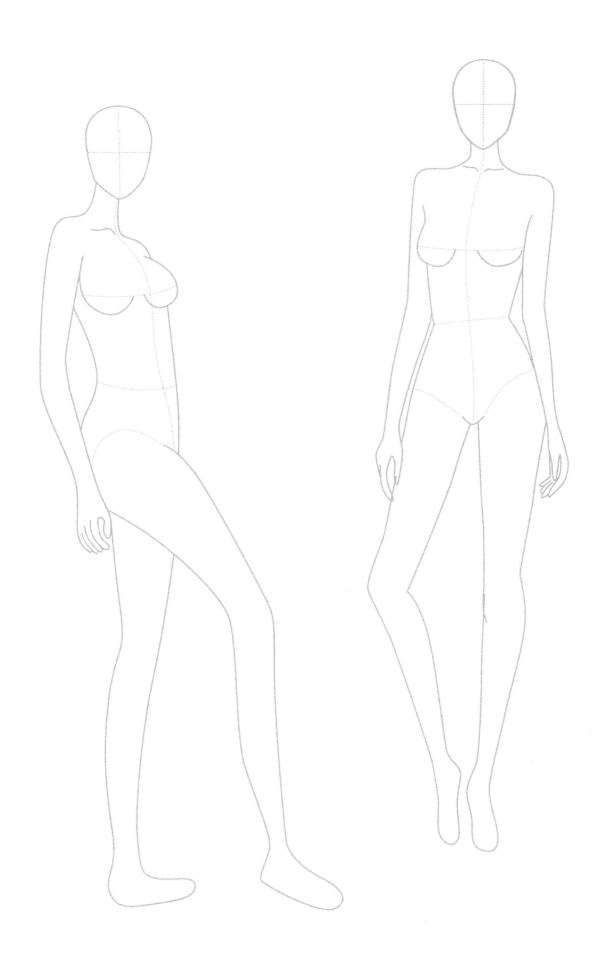

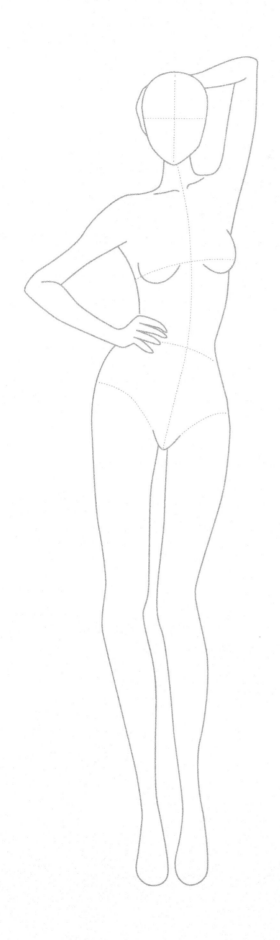
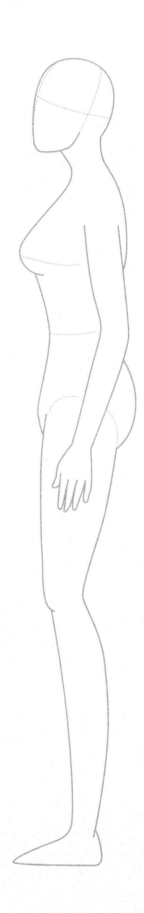

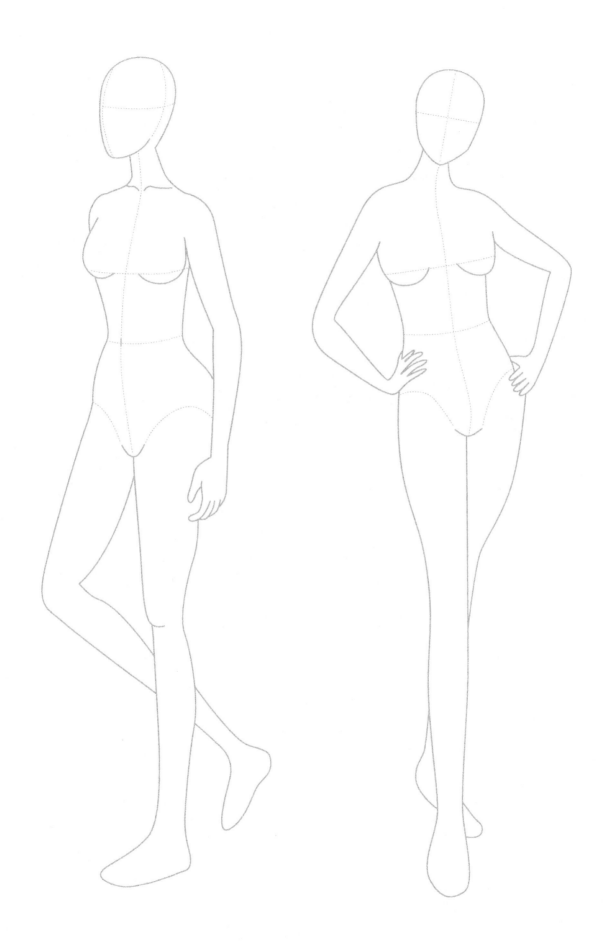

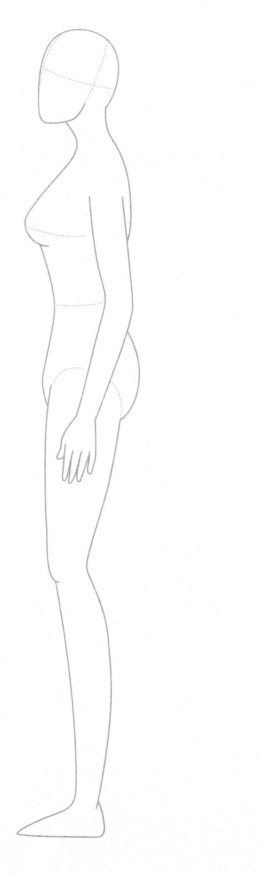
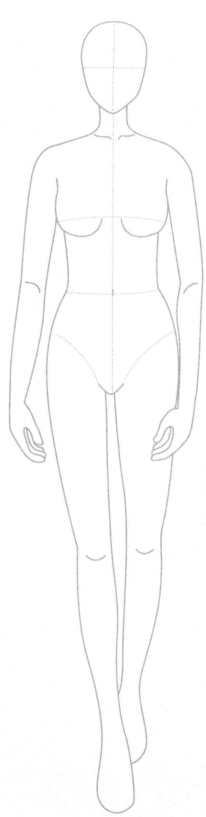

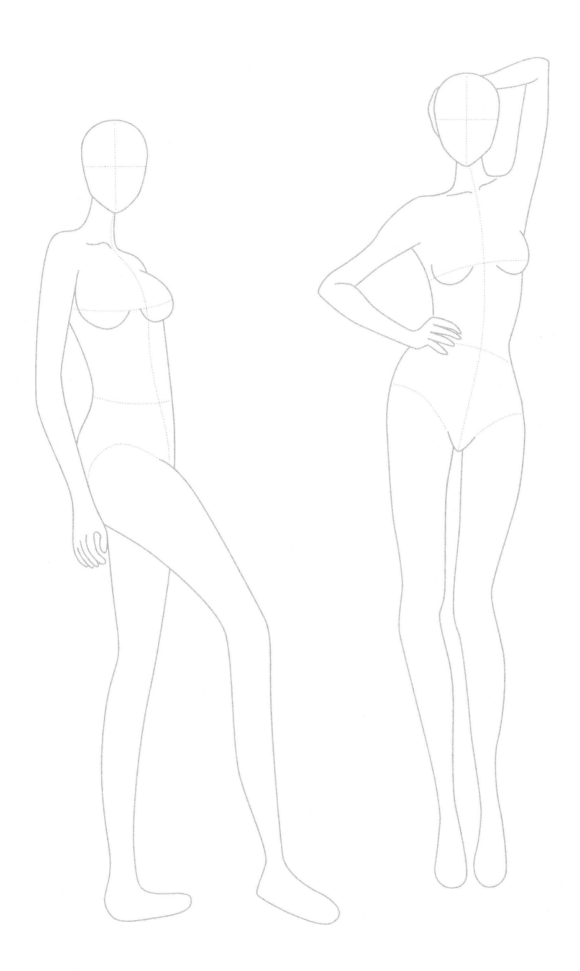

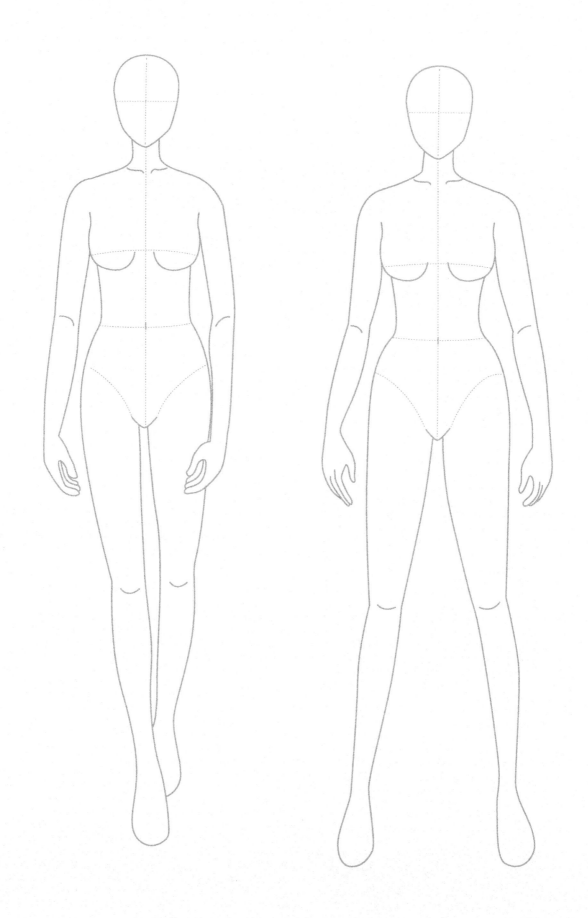

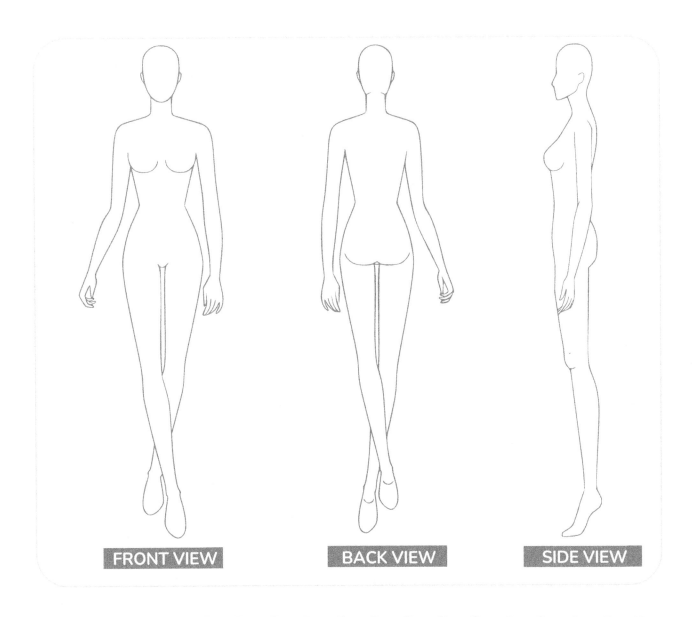

FRONT VIEW BACK VIEW SIDE VIEW

COLORS ◯ ◯ ◯ ◯ ◯ ◯ ◯ ◯ ◯ ◯ ◯ ◯ ◯ ◯ ◯

MATERIALS

PATTERNS

ACCESSORIES

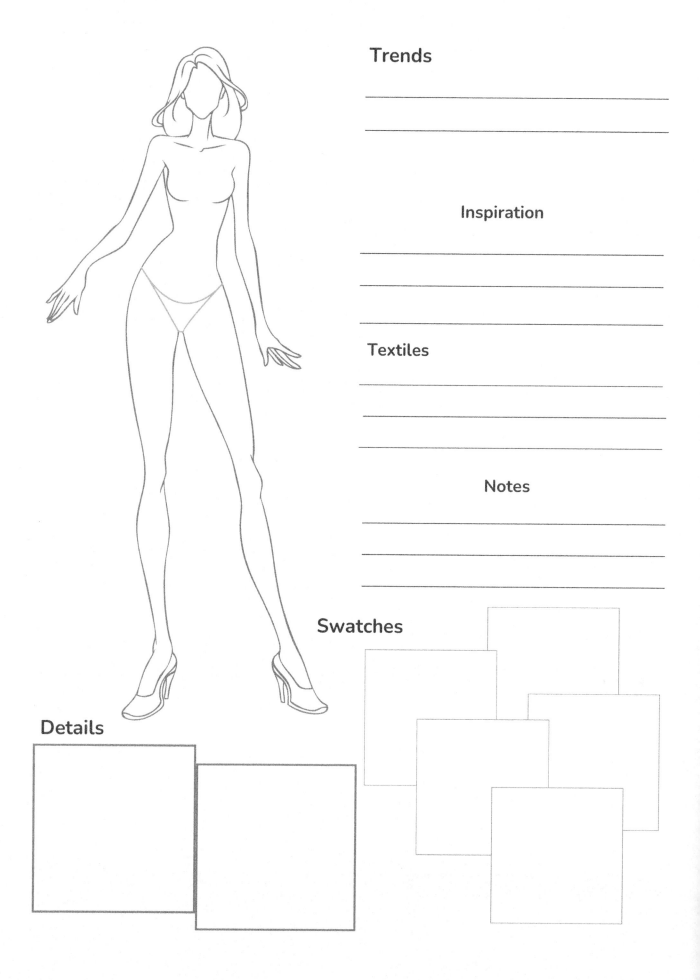

Trends

Inspiration

Textiles

Notes

Swatches

Details

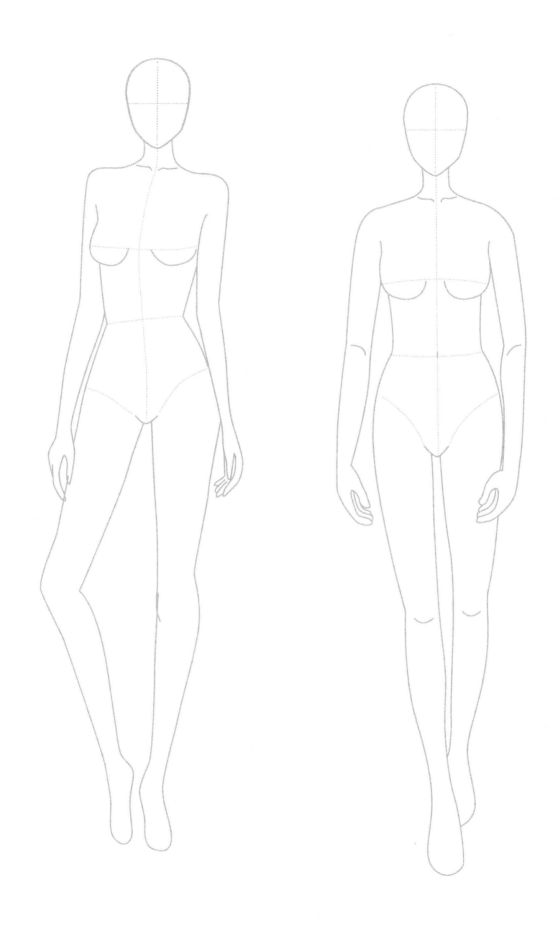

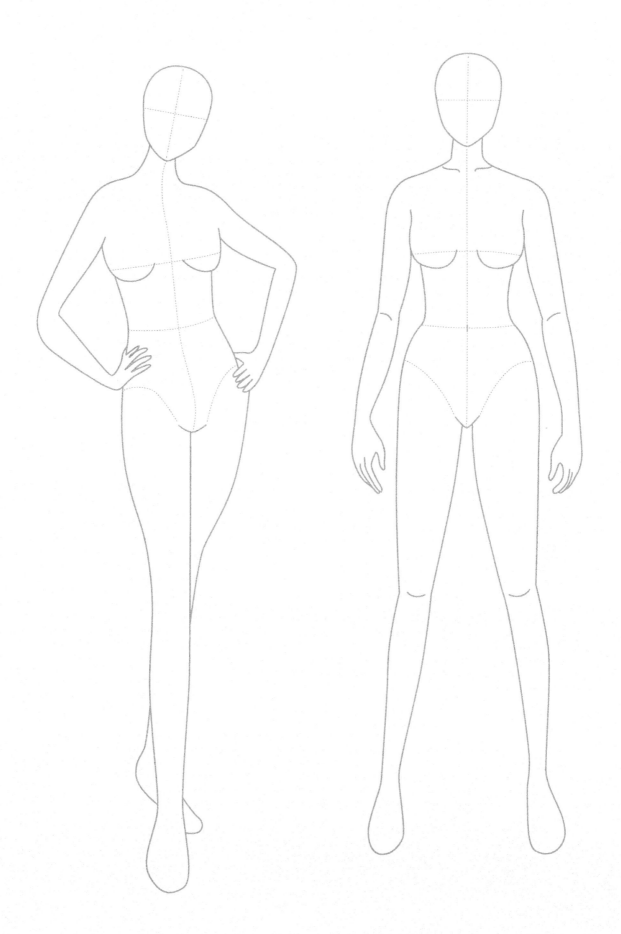

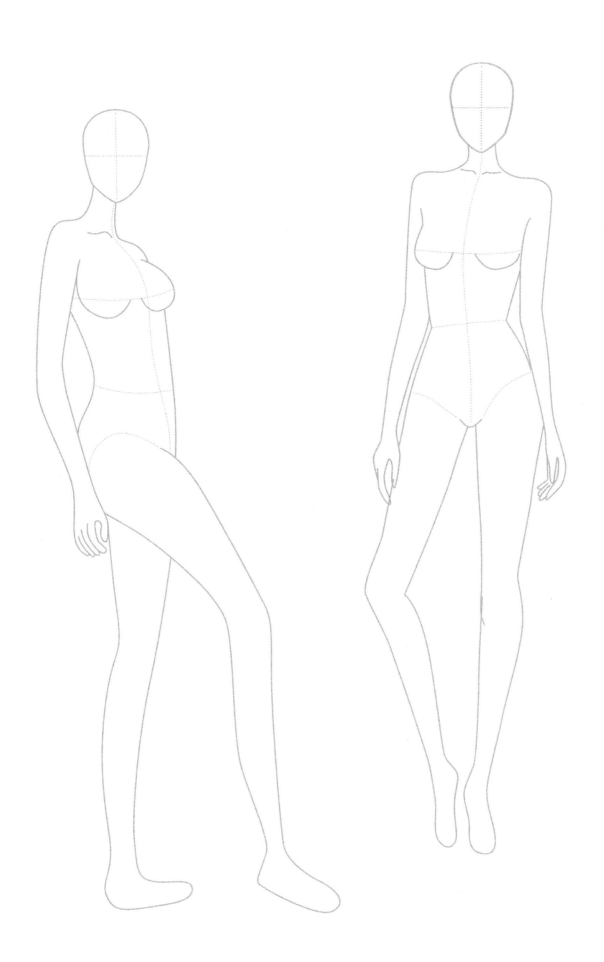

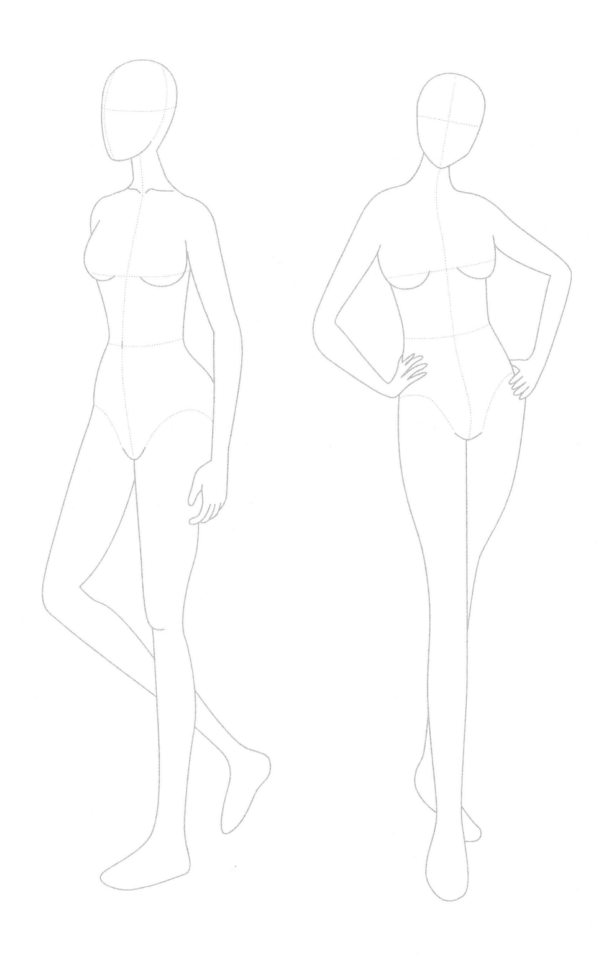

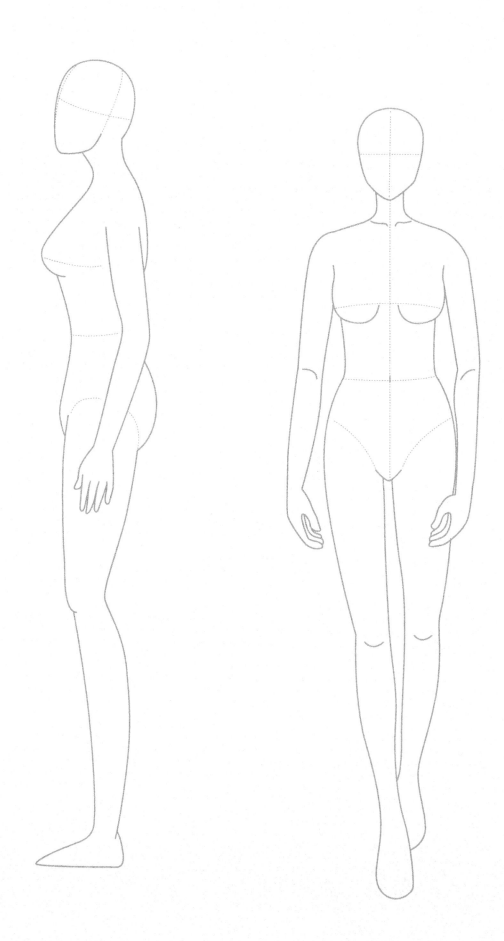

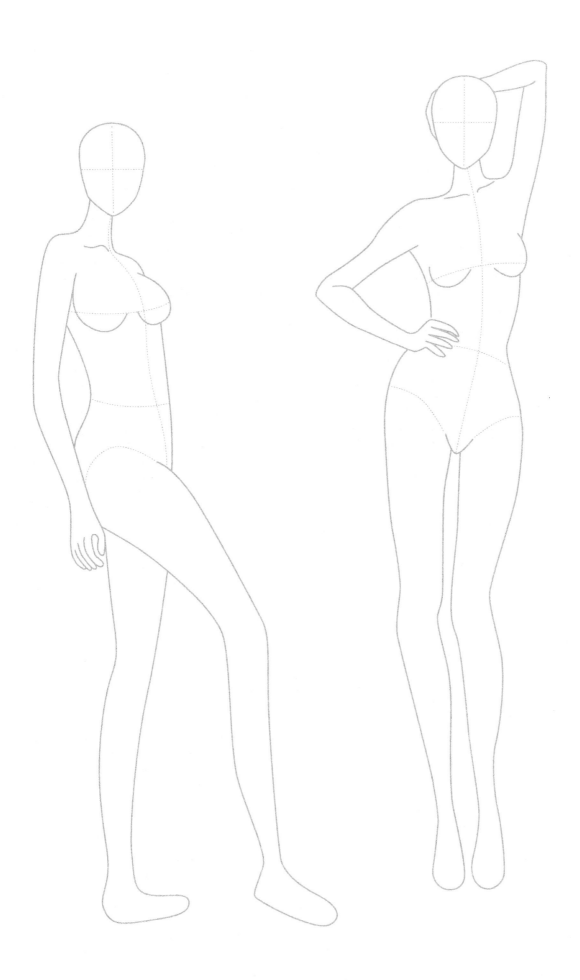

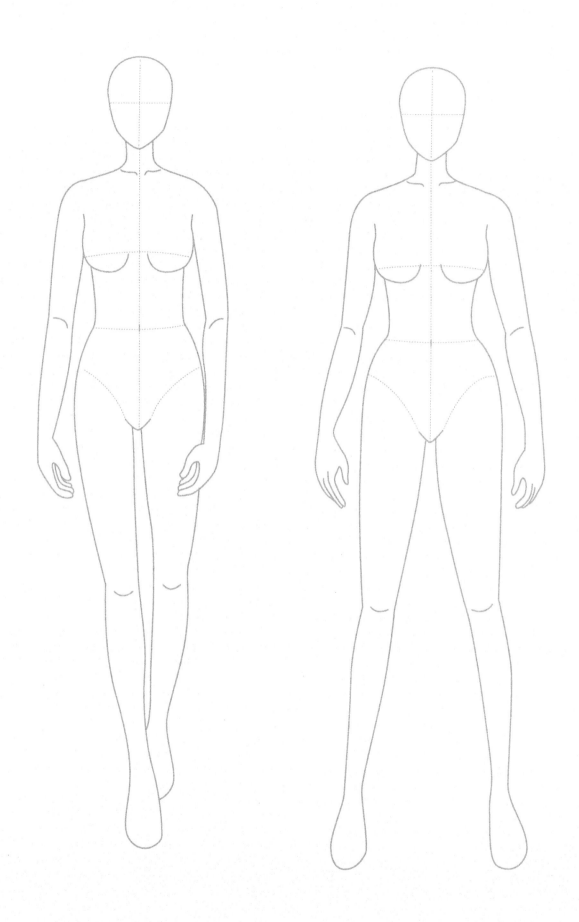

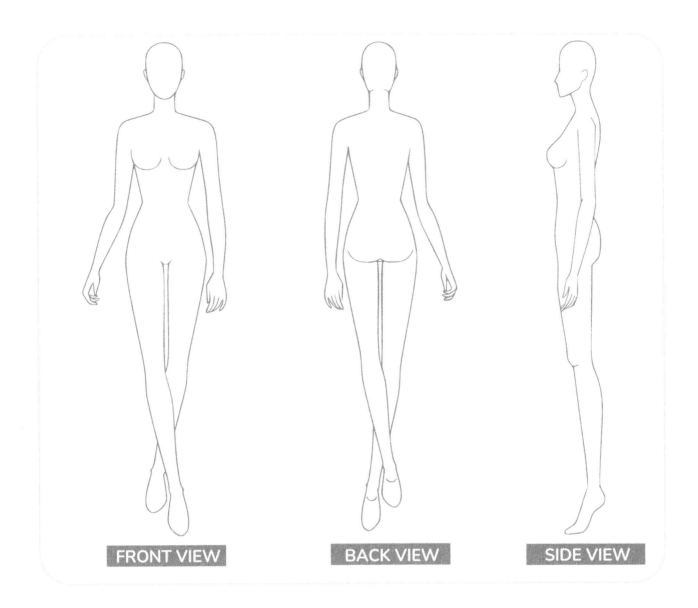

FRONT VIEW   BACK VIEW   SIDE VIEW

COLORS ◯ ◯ ◯ ◯ ◯ ◯ ◯ ◯ ◯ ◯ ◯ ◯ ◯ ◯ ◯

MATERIALS	PATTERNS

ACCESSORIES

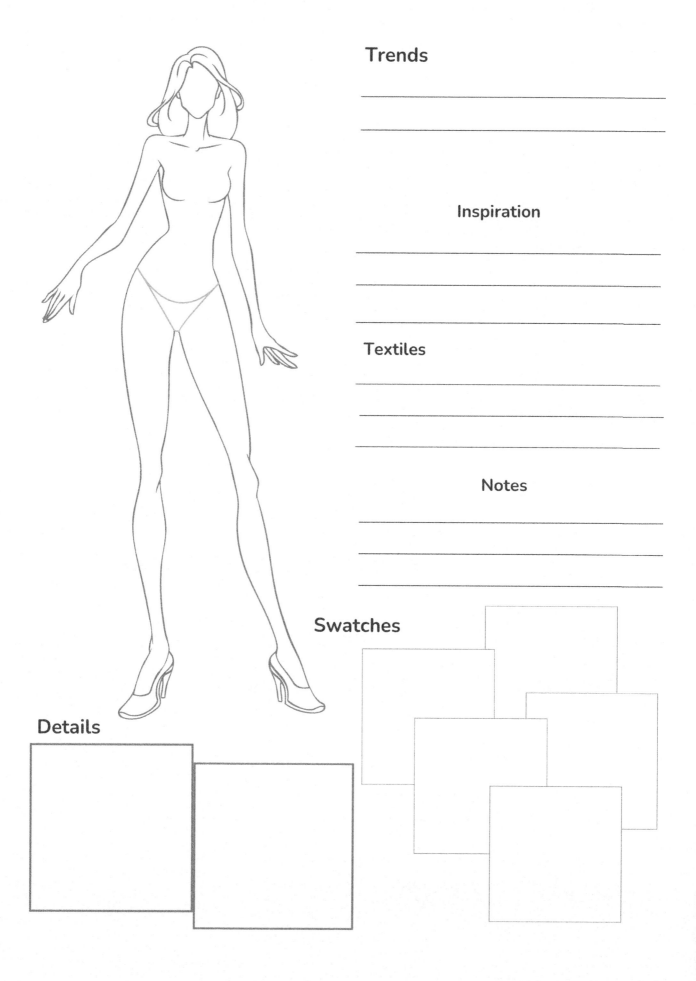

Trends

Inspiration

Textiles

Notes

Swatches

Details

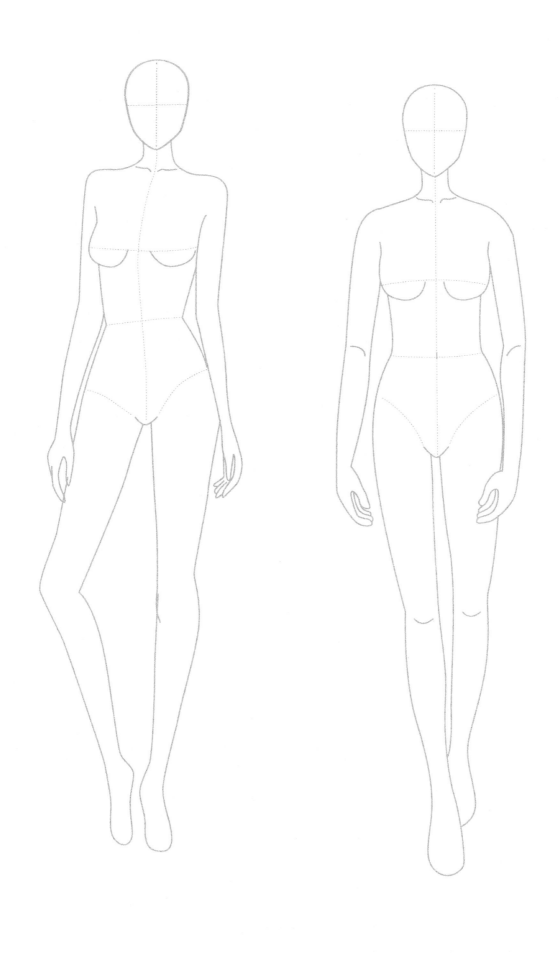

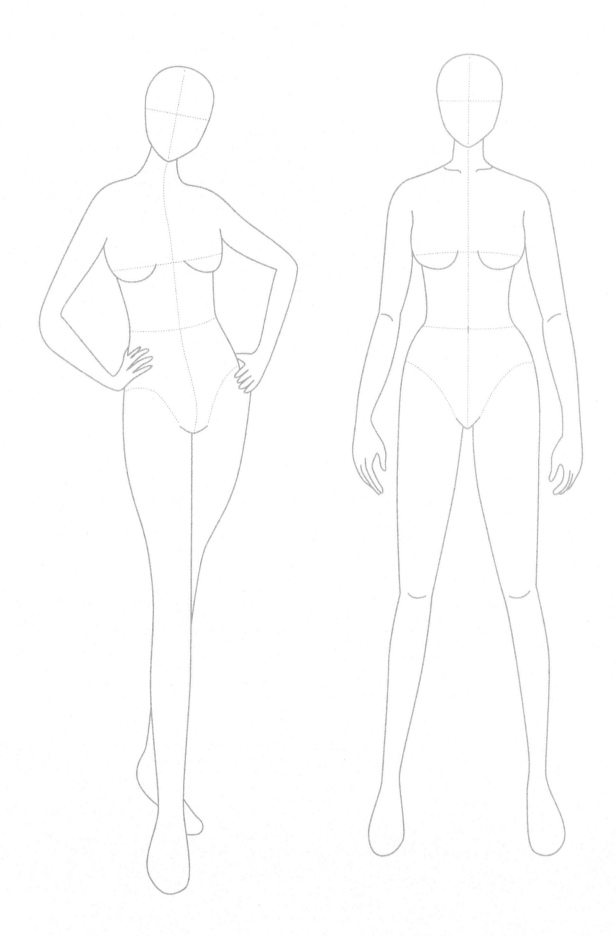

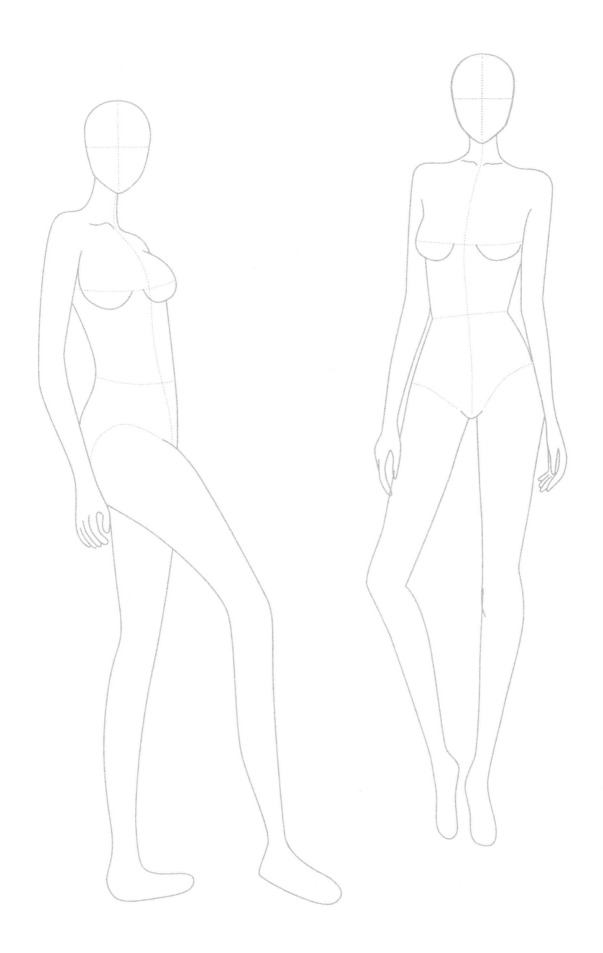

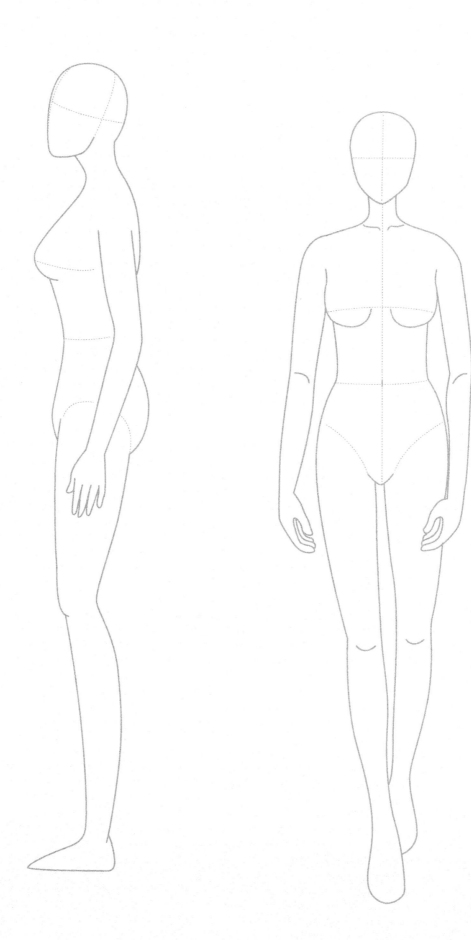

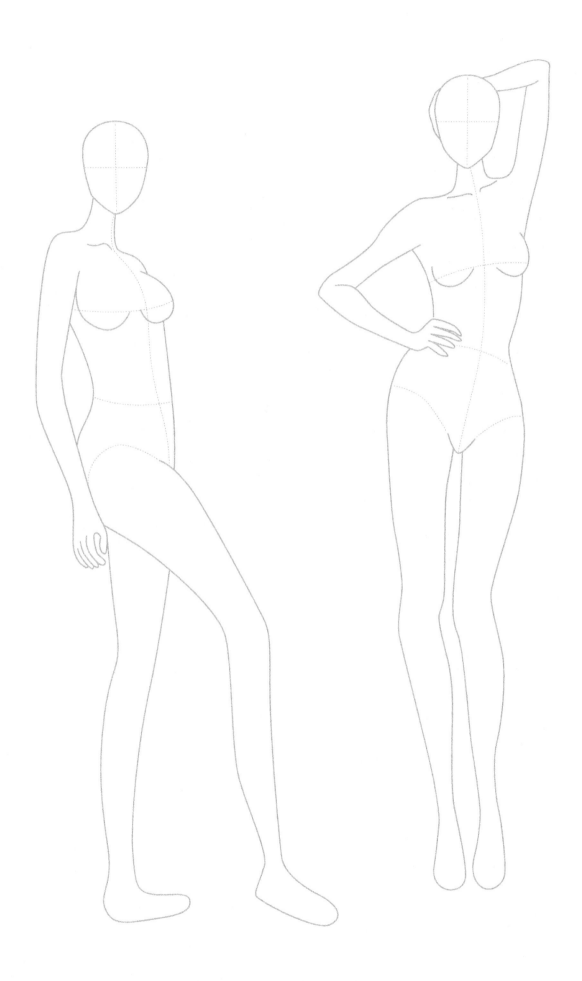

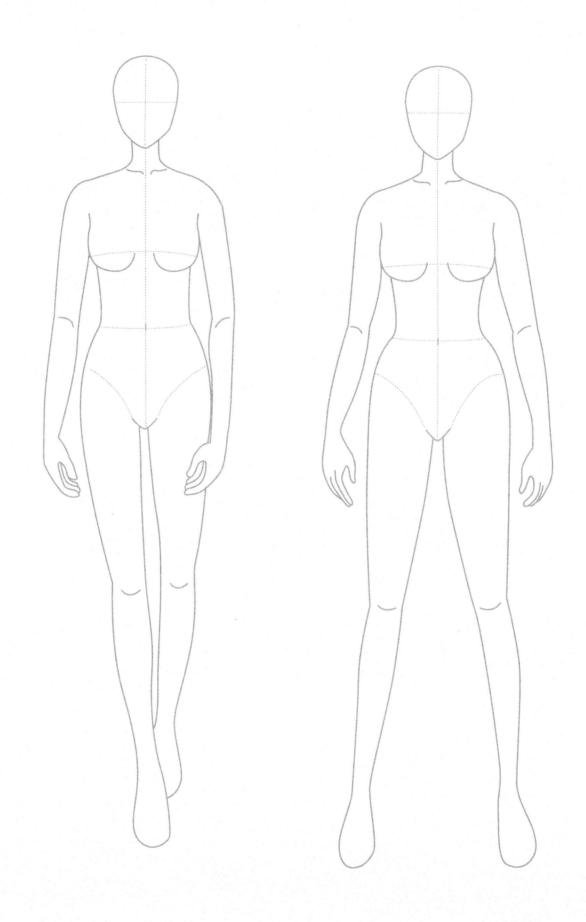

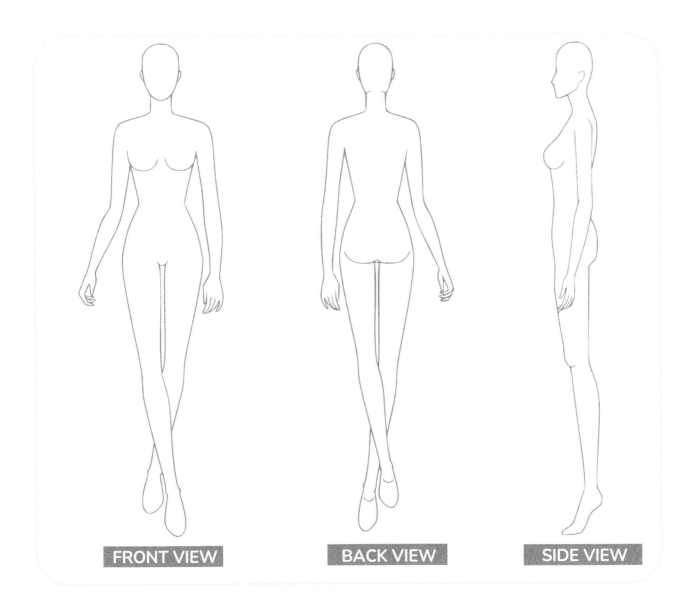

FRONT VIEW BACK VIEW SIDE VIEW

COLORS ○ ○ ○ ○ ○ ○ ○ ○ ○ ○ ○ ○ ○ ○ ○

MATERIALS PATTERNS

ACCESSORIES

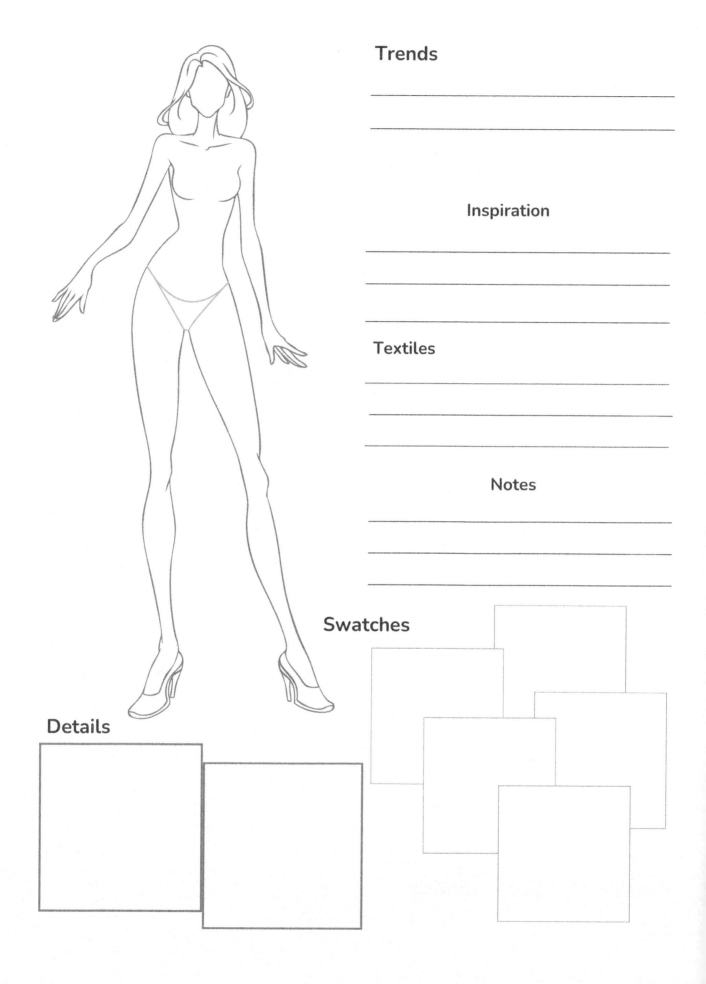

Trends

_____

_____

Inspiration

_____

_____

_____

Textiles

_____

_____

_____

Notes

_____

_____

_____

Swatches

Details

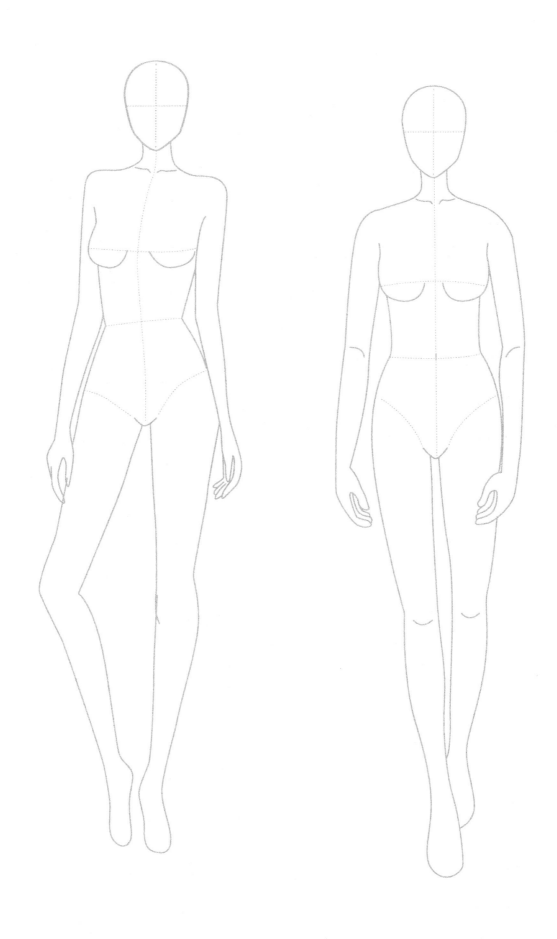

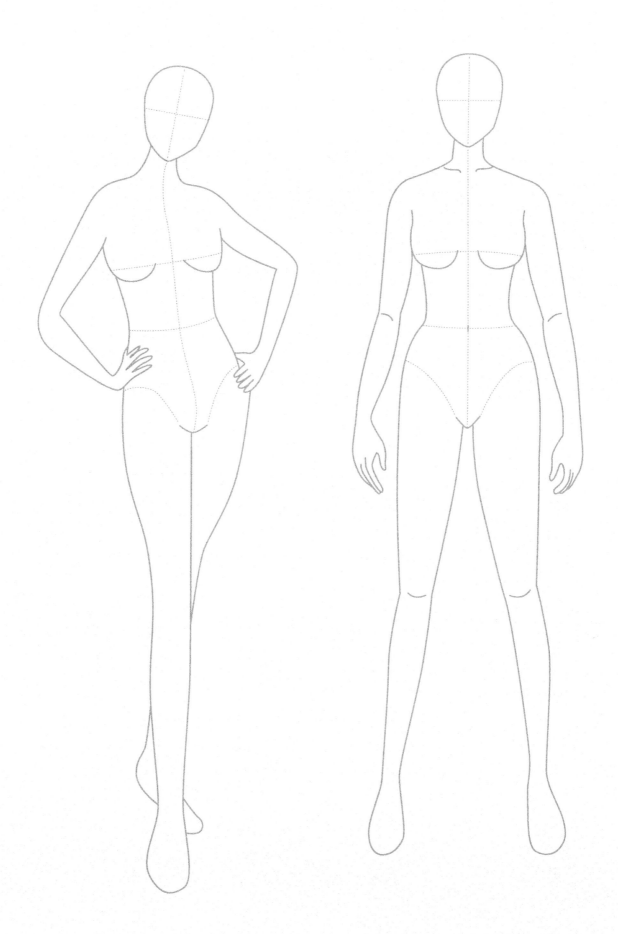

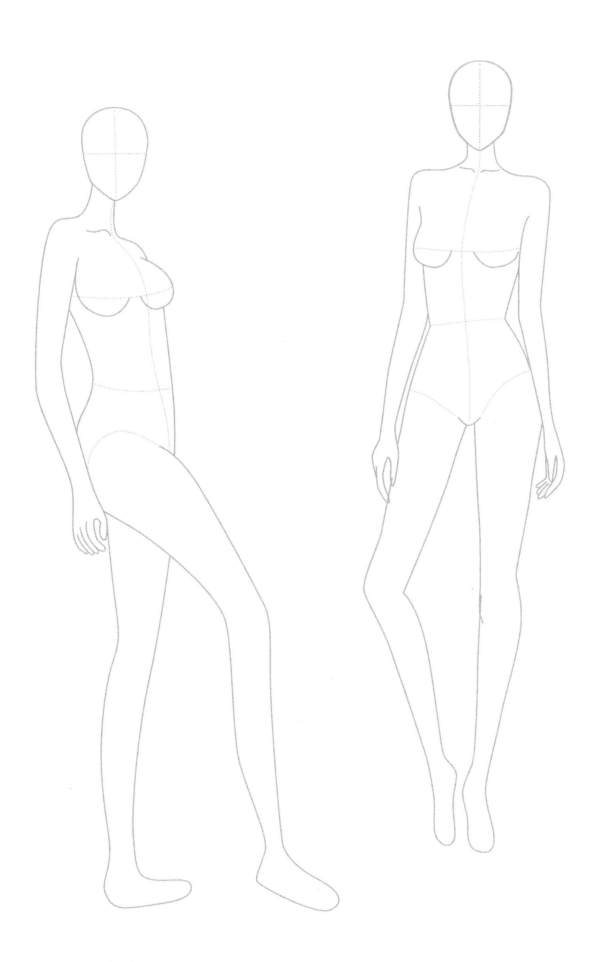

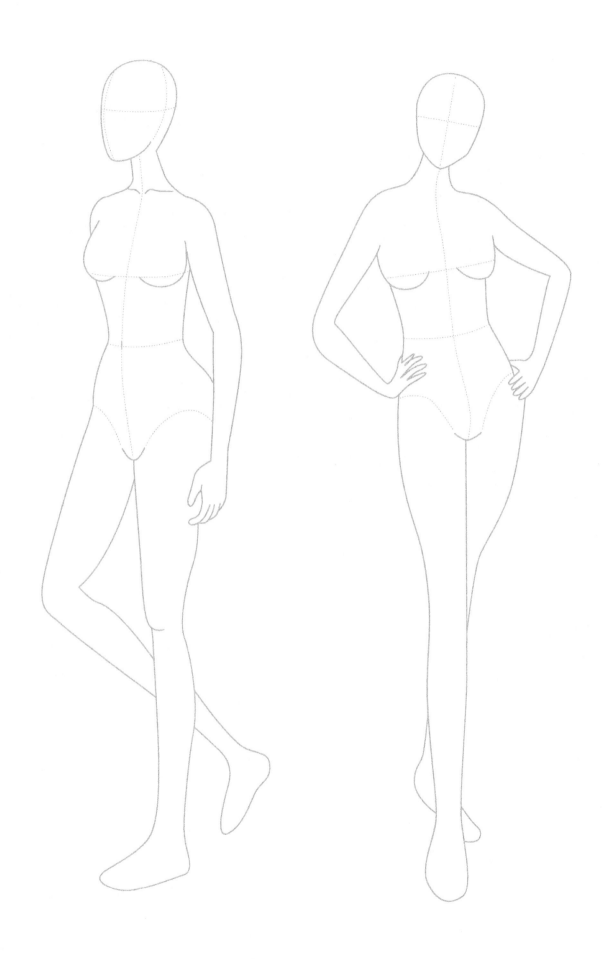

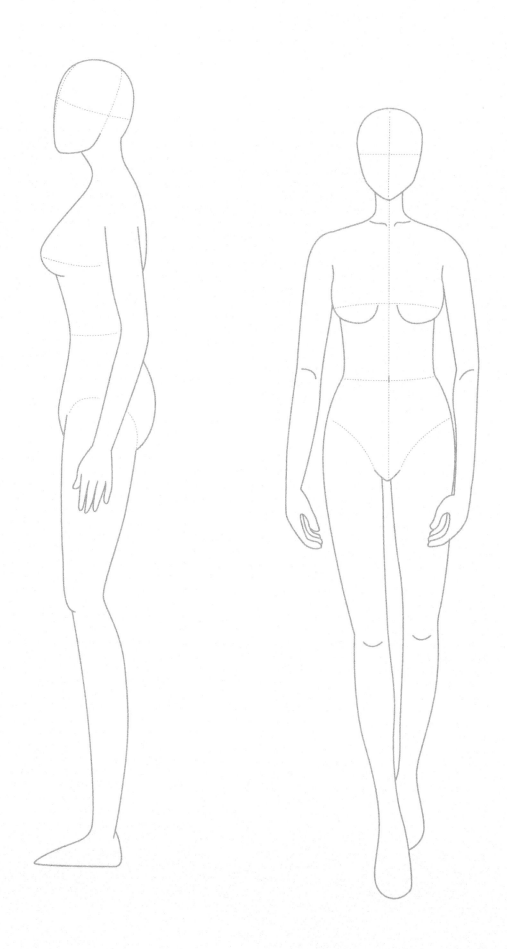

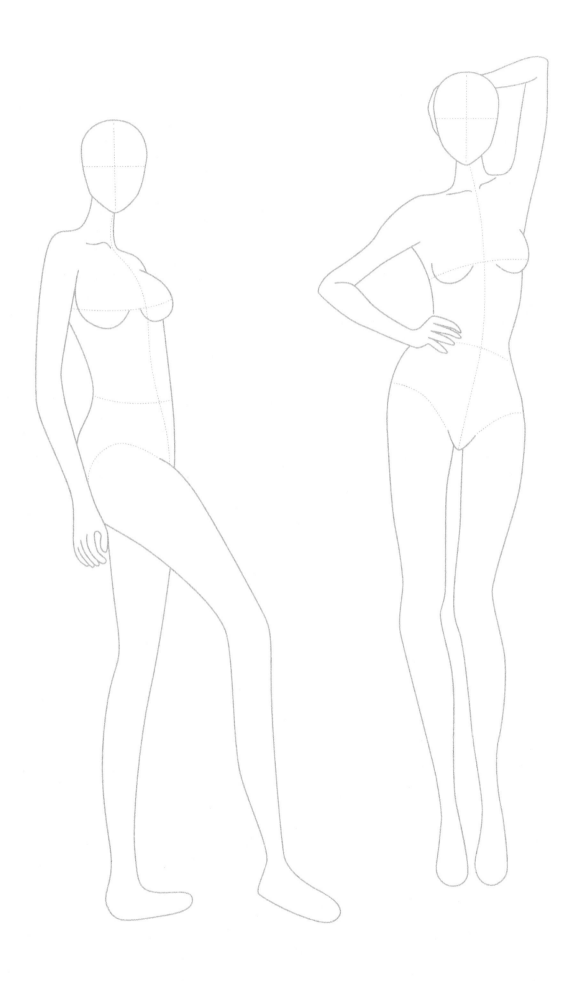

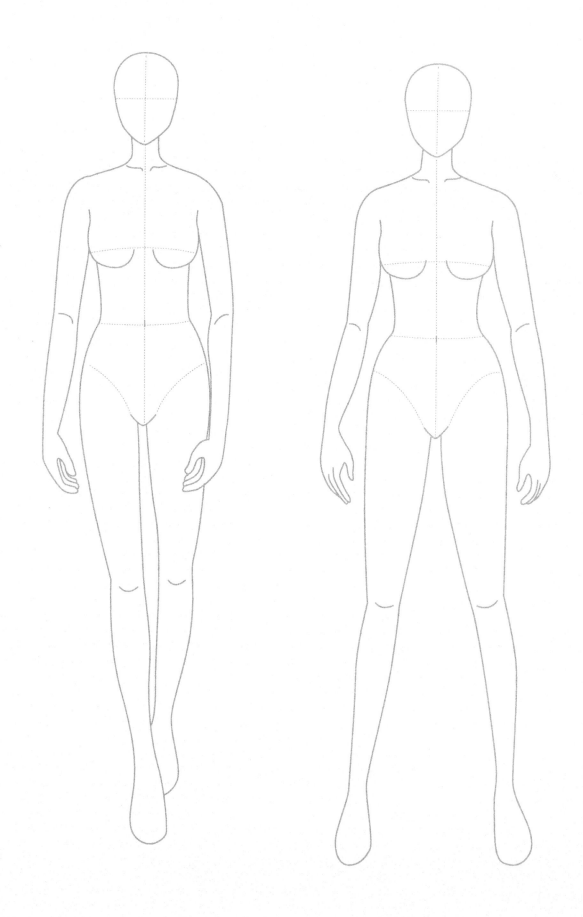

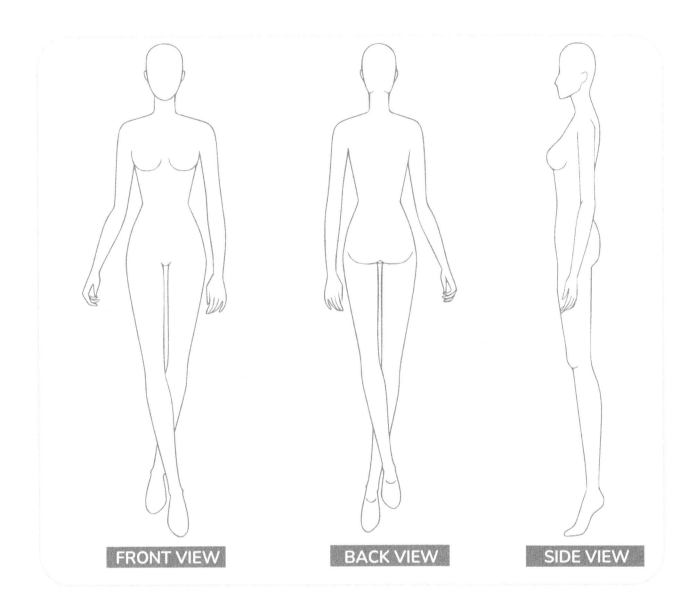

FRONT VIEW　　　BACK VIEW　　　SIDE VIEW

COLORS ◯ ◯ ◯ ◯ ◯ ◯ ◯ ◯ ◯ ◯ ◯ ◯ ◯ ◯ ◯

MATERIALS	PATTERNS

ACCESSORIES

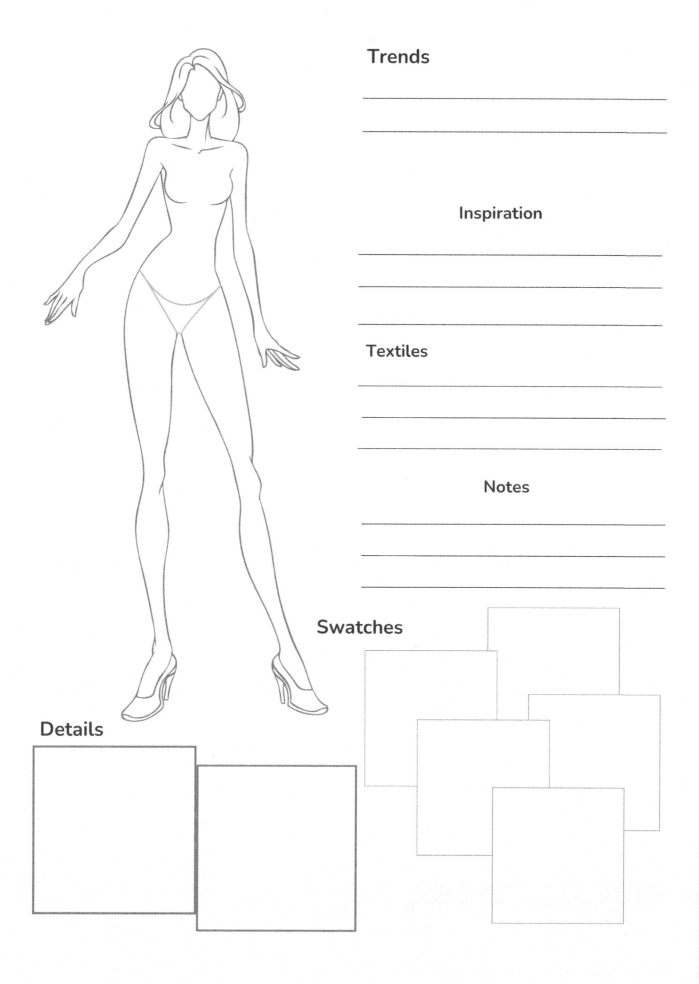

Trends

_____

_____

Inspiration

_____

_____

_____

Textiles

_____

_____

_____

Notes

_____

_____

_____

_____

Swatches

Details

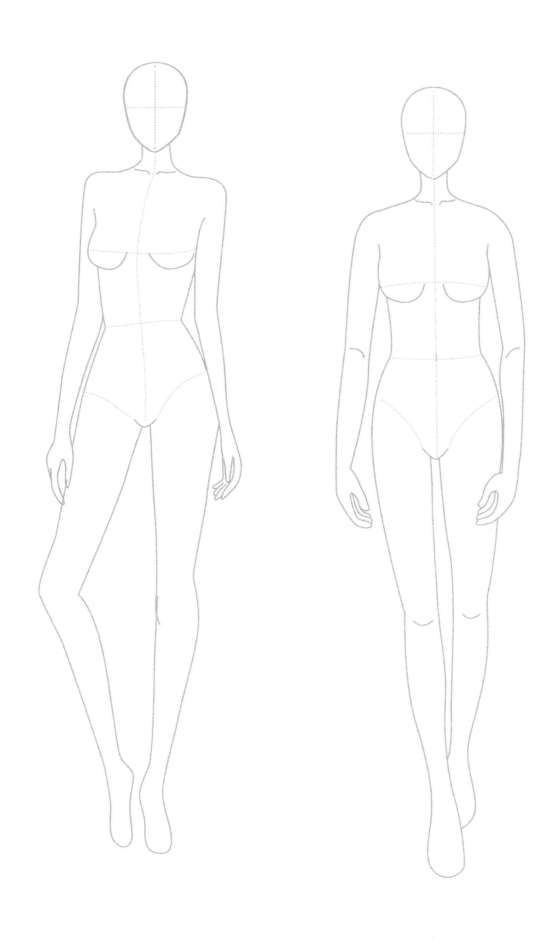

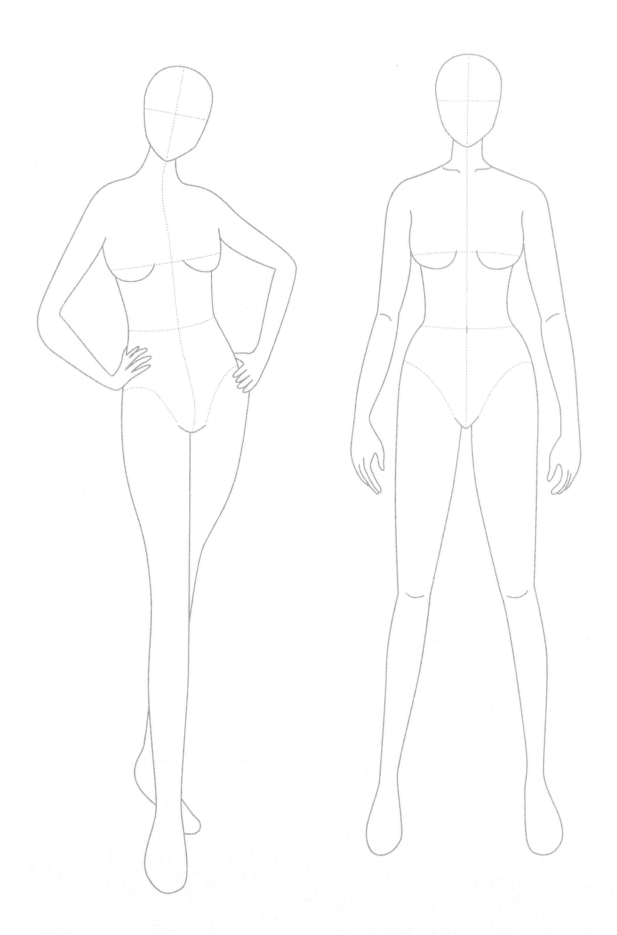

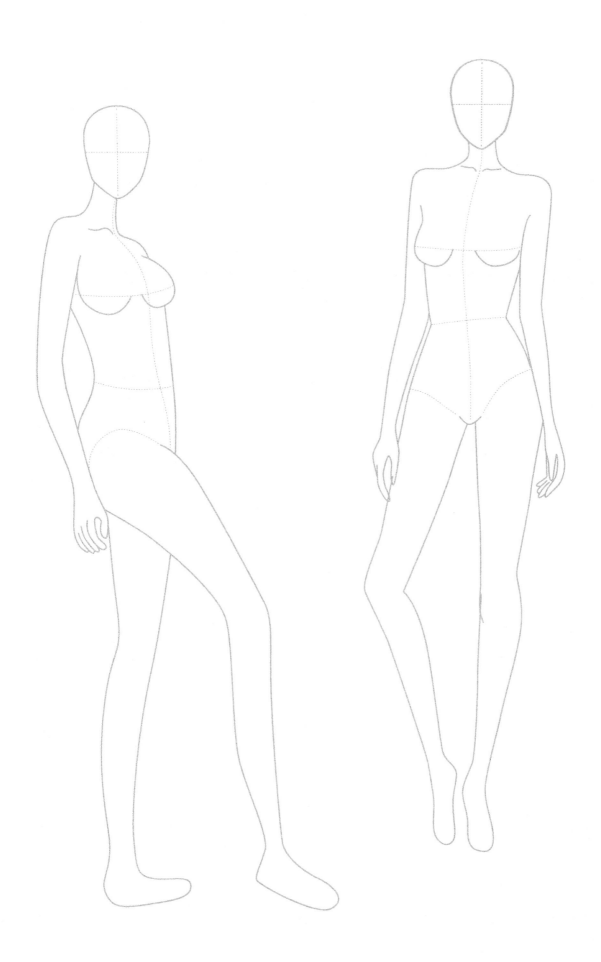

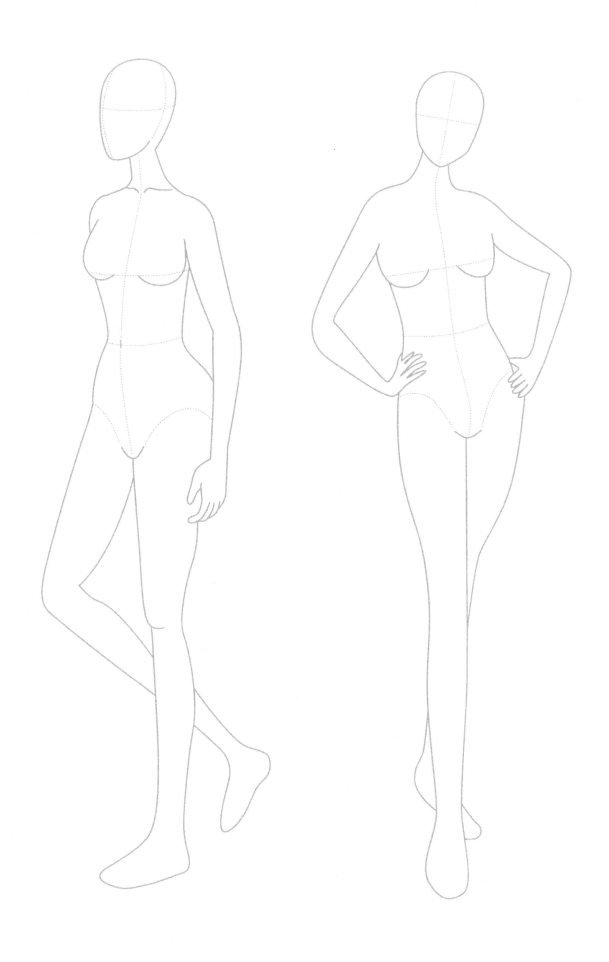

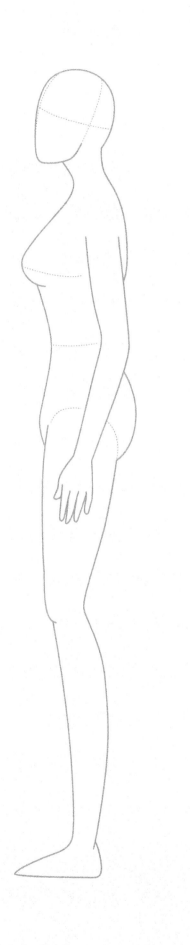
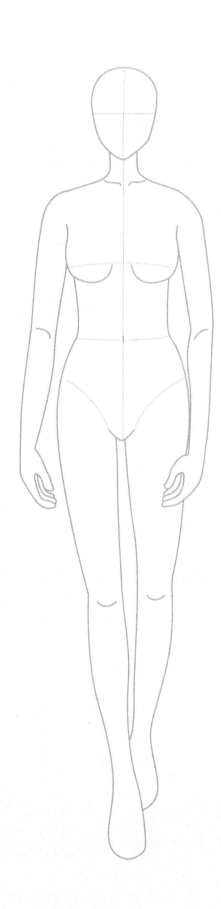

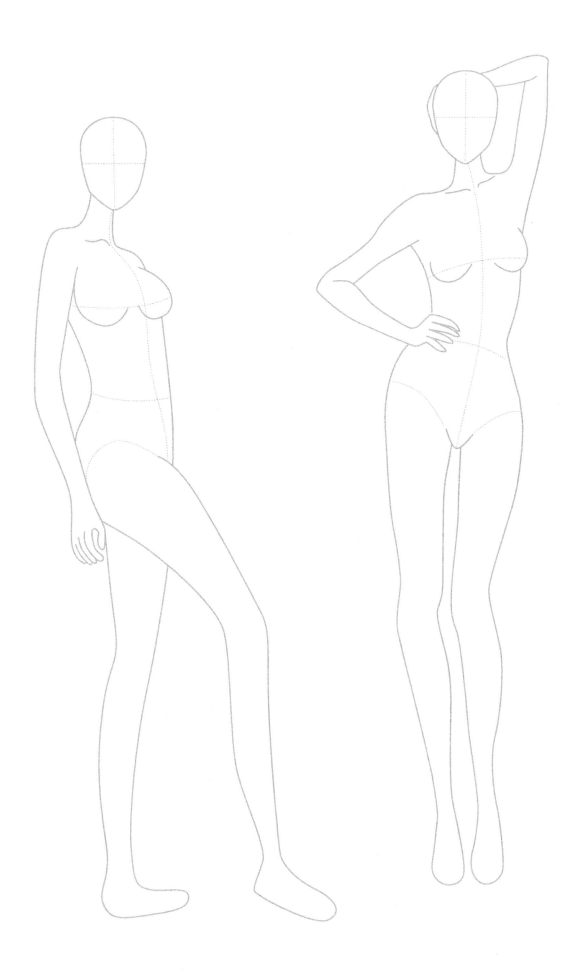

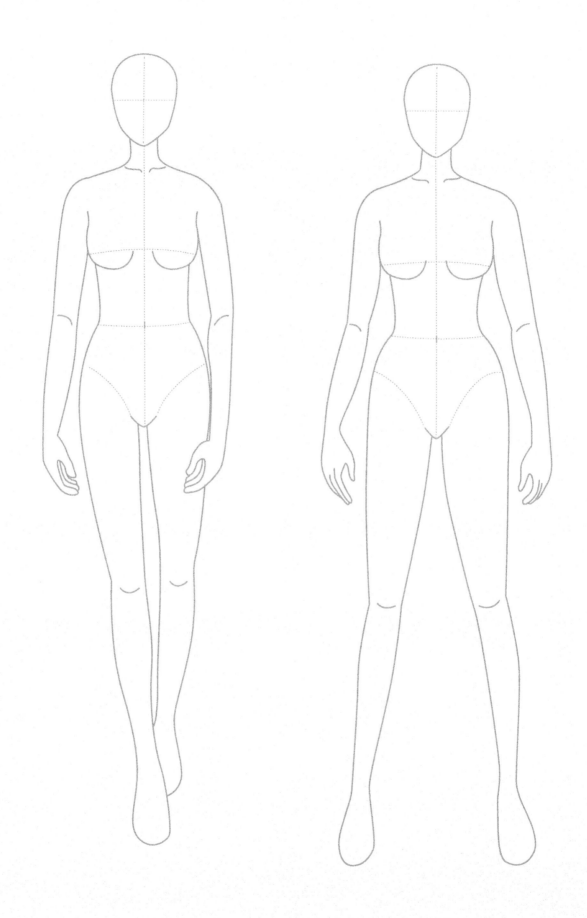

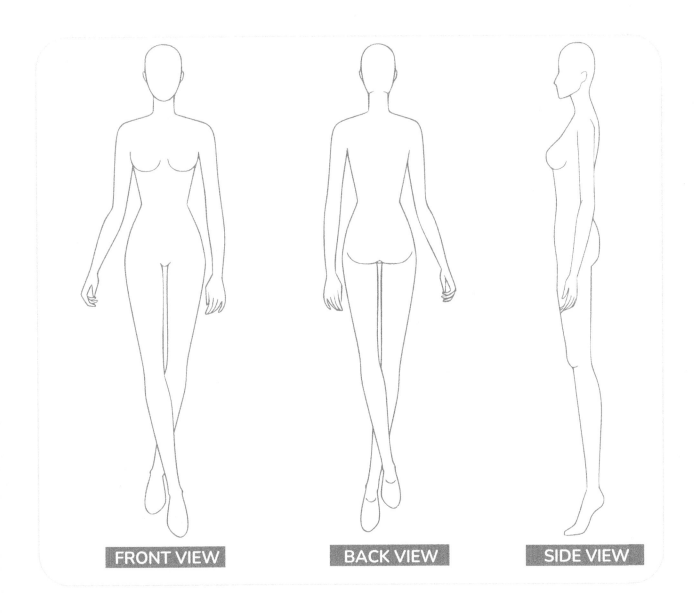

FRONT VIEW   BACK VIEW   SIDE VIEW

COLORS ◯◯◯◯◯◯◯◯◯◯◯◯◯◯◯

MATERIALS   PATTERNS

ACCESSORIES

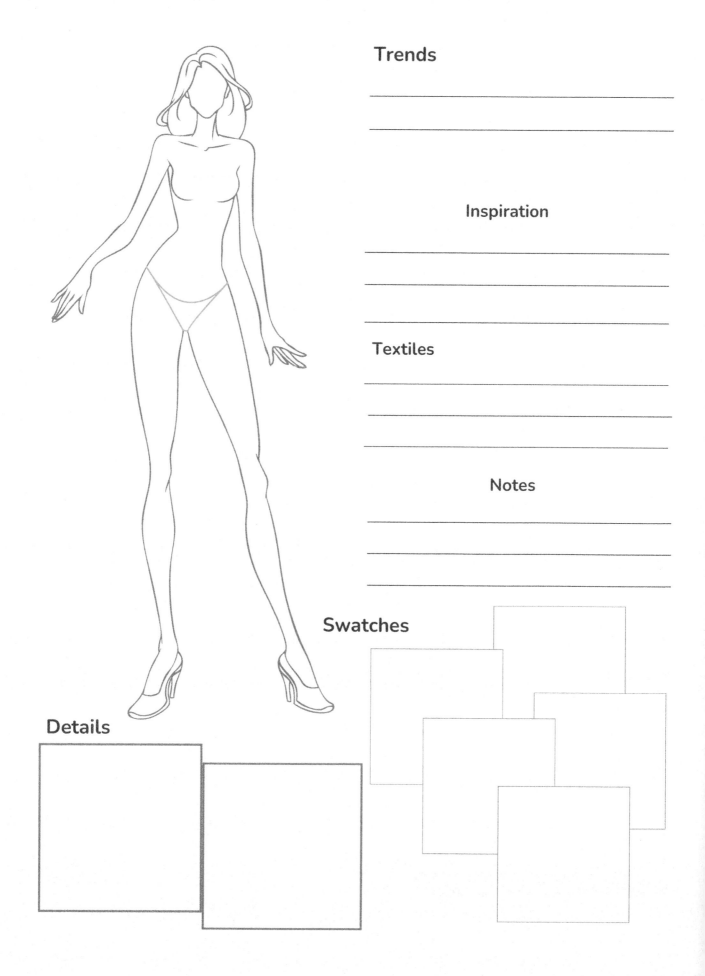

Trends

Inspiration

Textiles

Notes

Swatches

Details

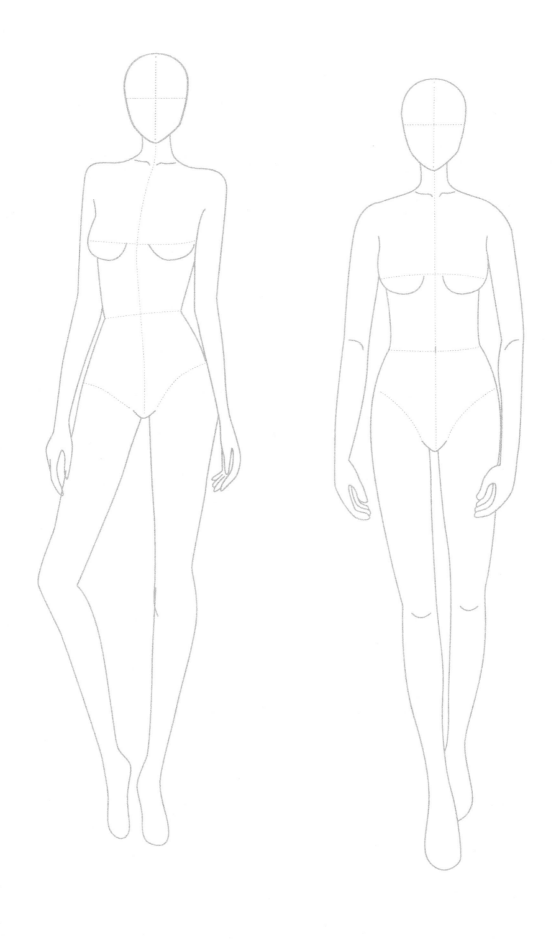

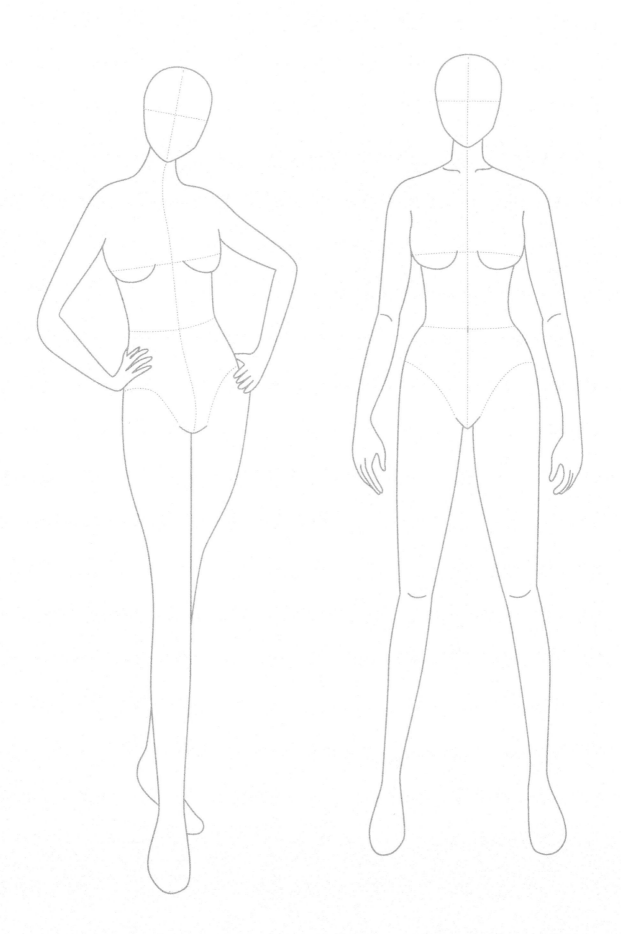

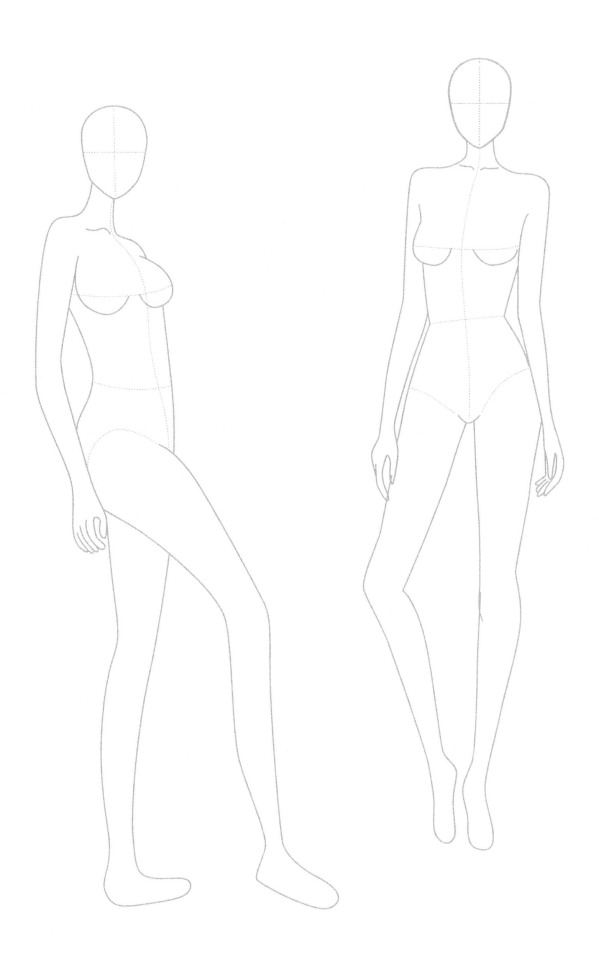

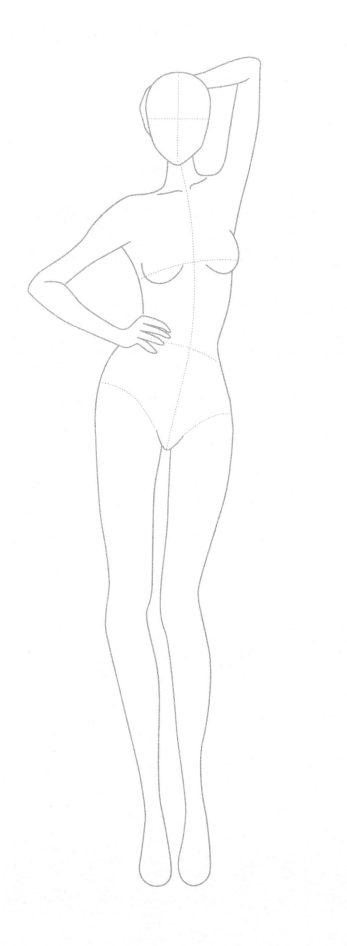

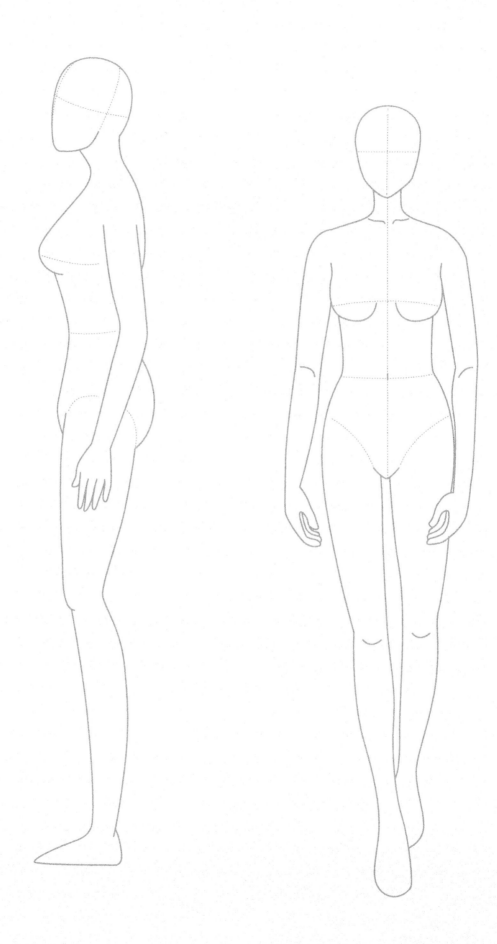

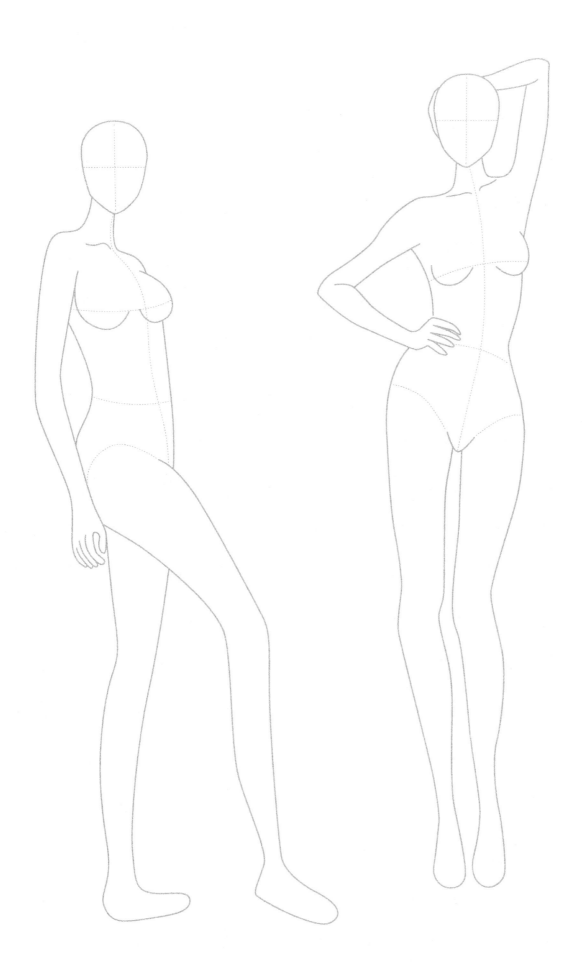

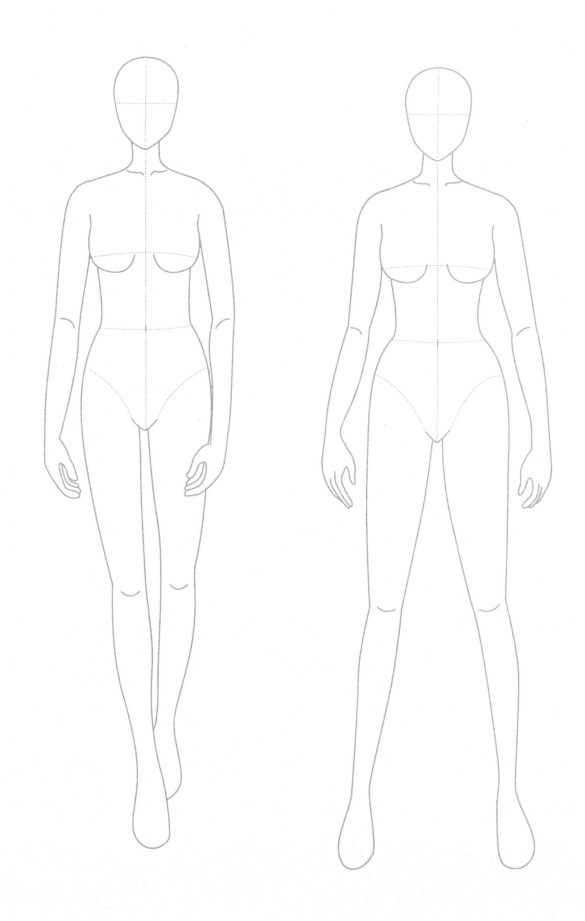

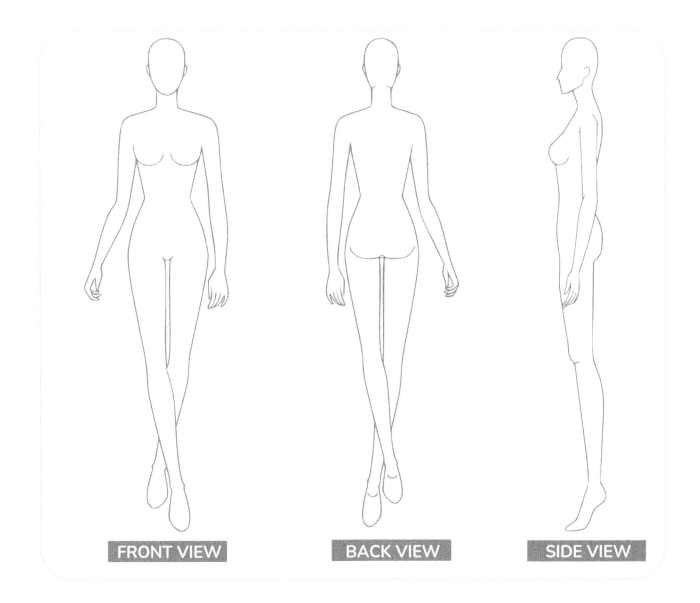

FRONT VIEW   BACK VIEW   SIDE VIEW

COLORS ○ ○ ○ ○ ○ ○ ○ ○ ○ ○ ○ ○ ○ ○ ○

MATERIALS   PATTERNS

ACCESSORIES

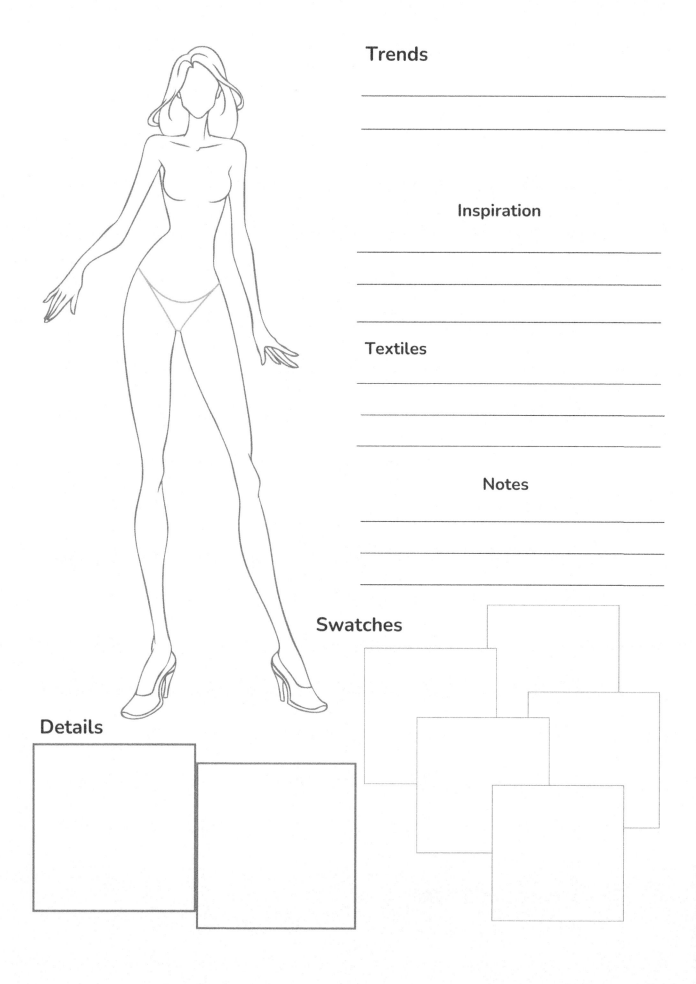

Trends

Inspiration

Textiles

Notes

Swatches

Details

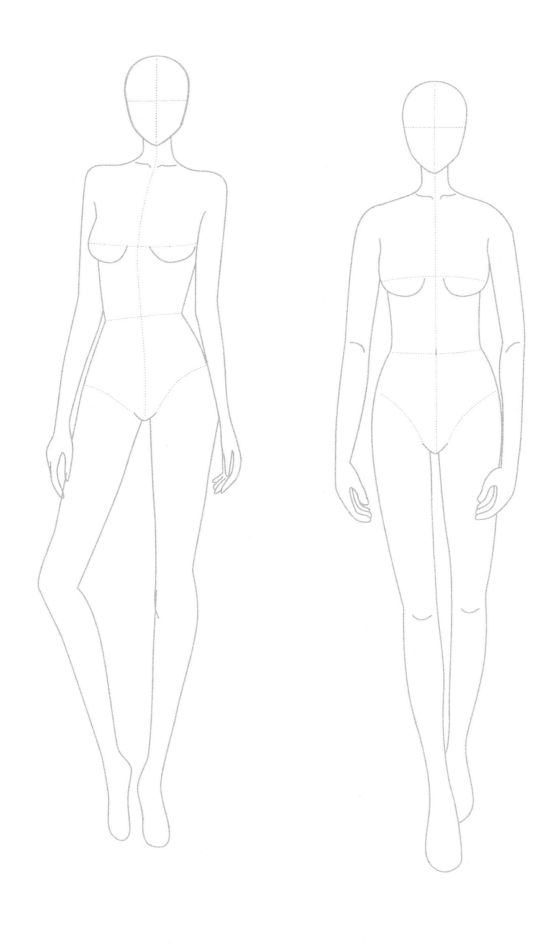

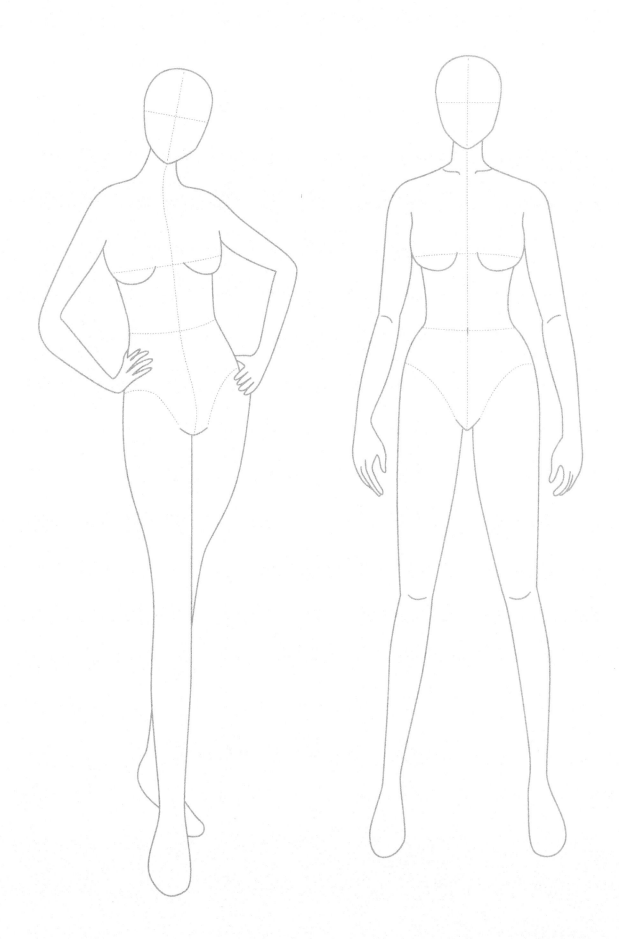

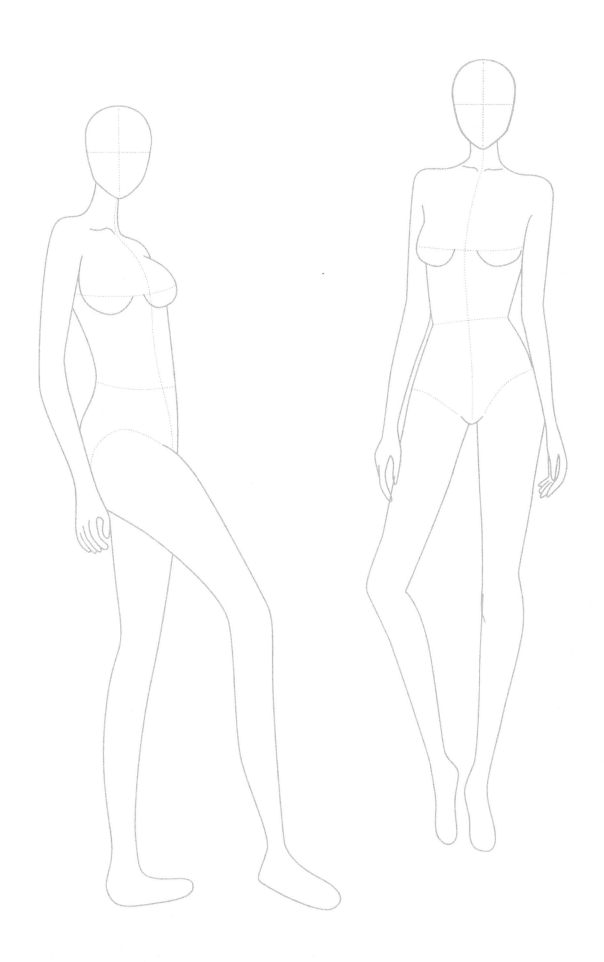

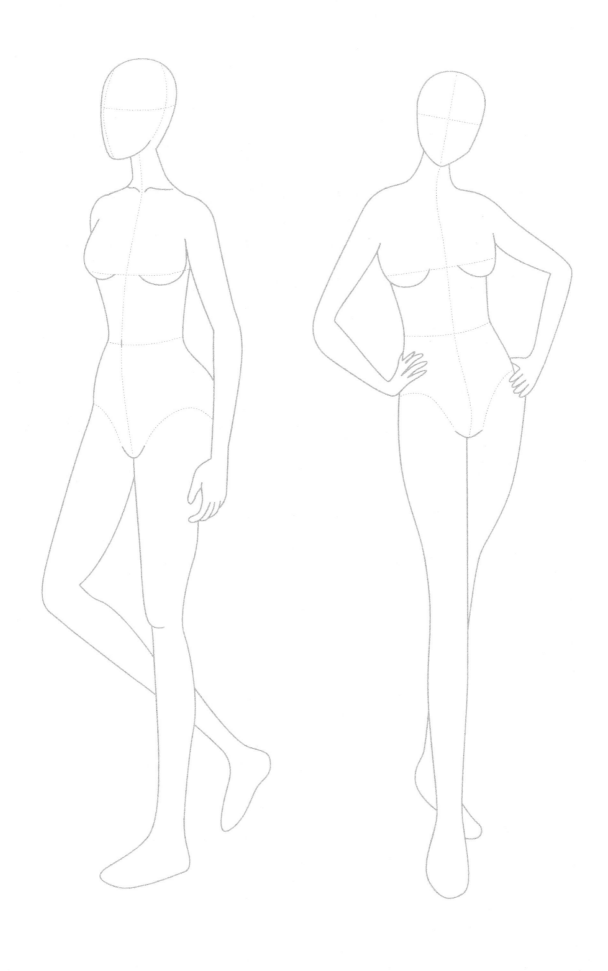

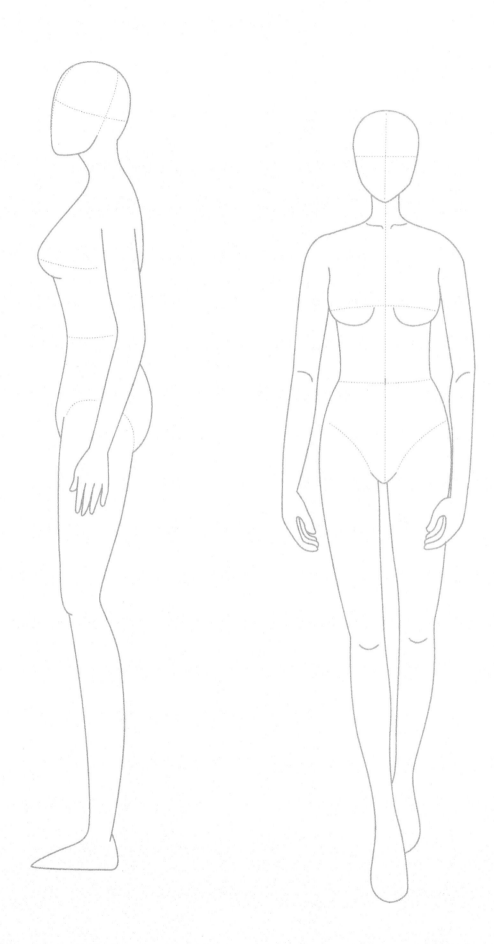

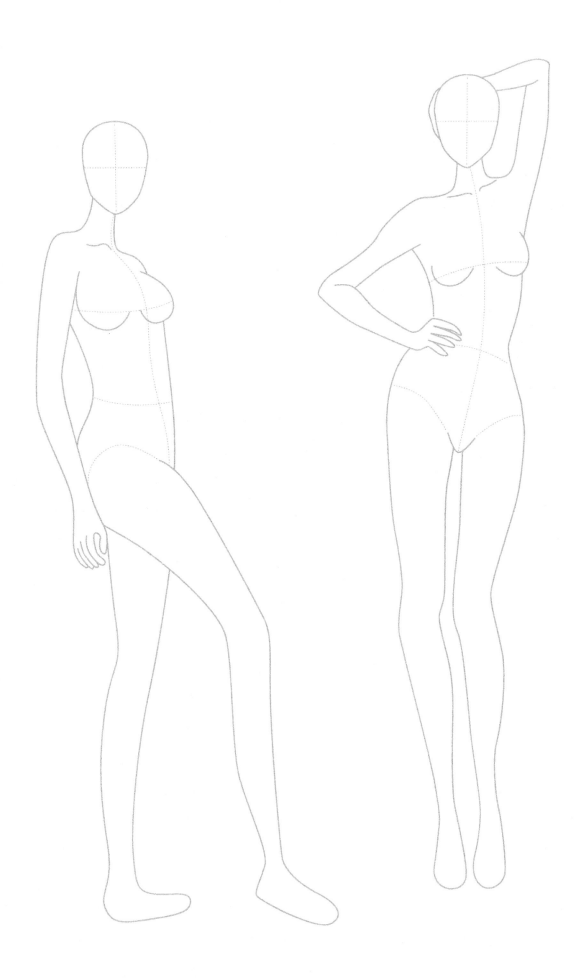

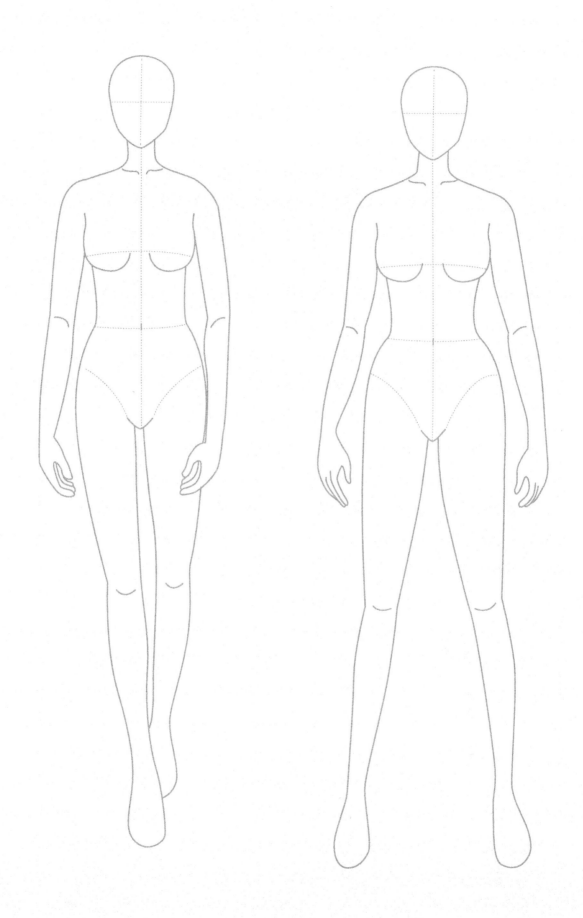

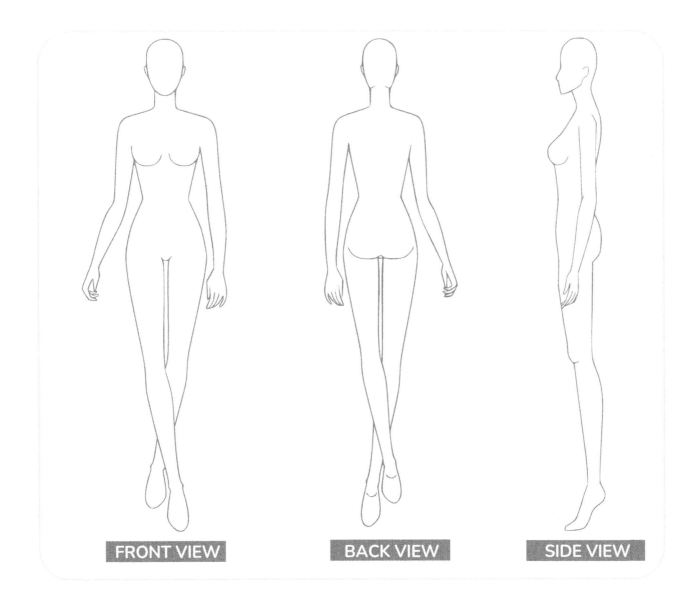

FRONT VIEW BACK VIEW SIDE VIEW

COLORS ○ ○ ○ ○ ○ ○ ○ ○ ○ ○ ○ ○ ○ ○ ○ ○

MATERIALS

PATTERNS

ACCESSORIES

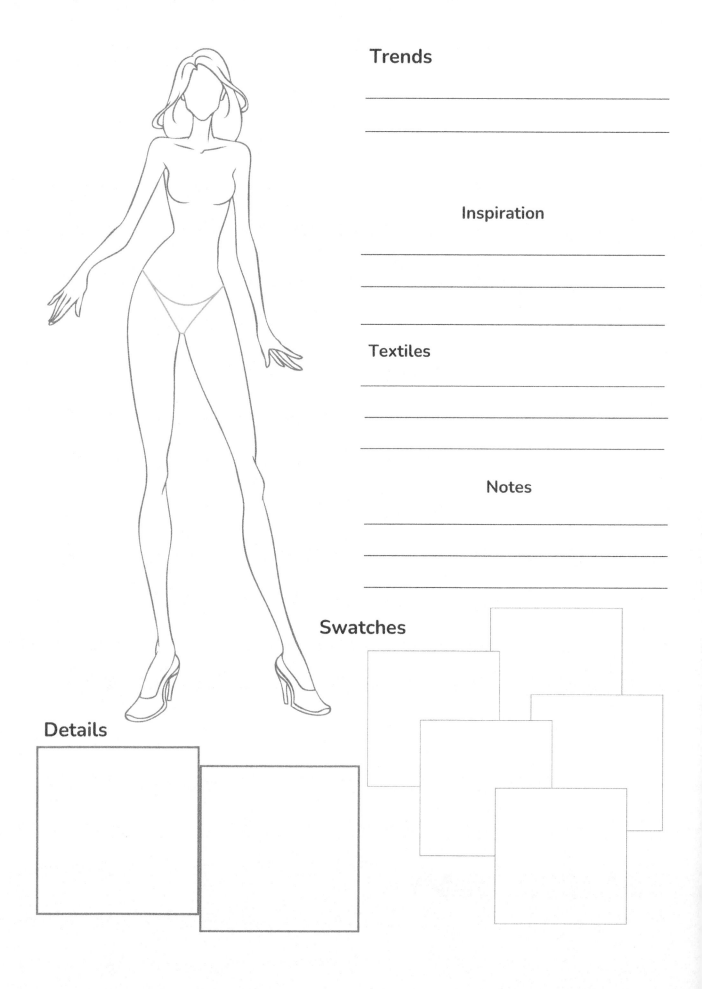

Trends

Inspiration

Textiles

Notes

Swatches

Details

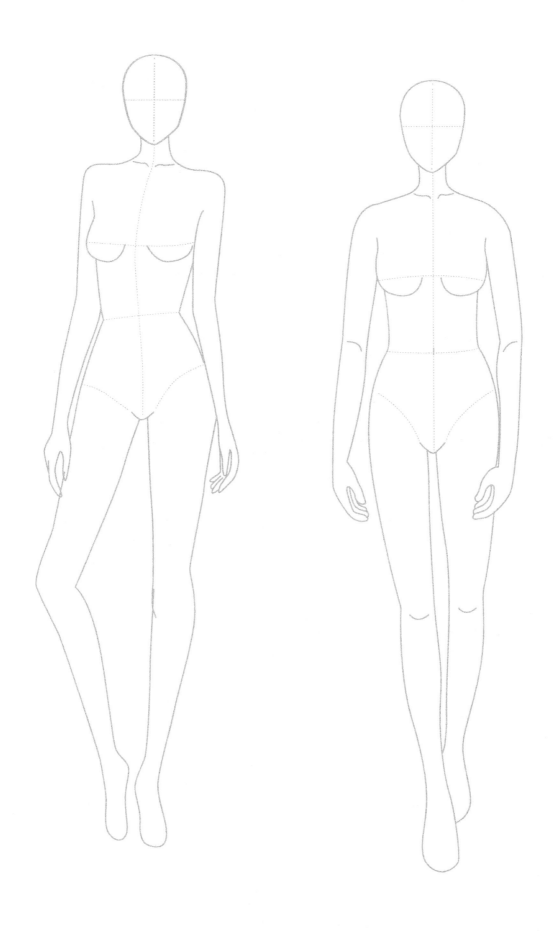

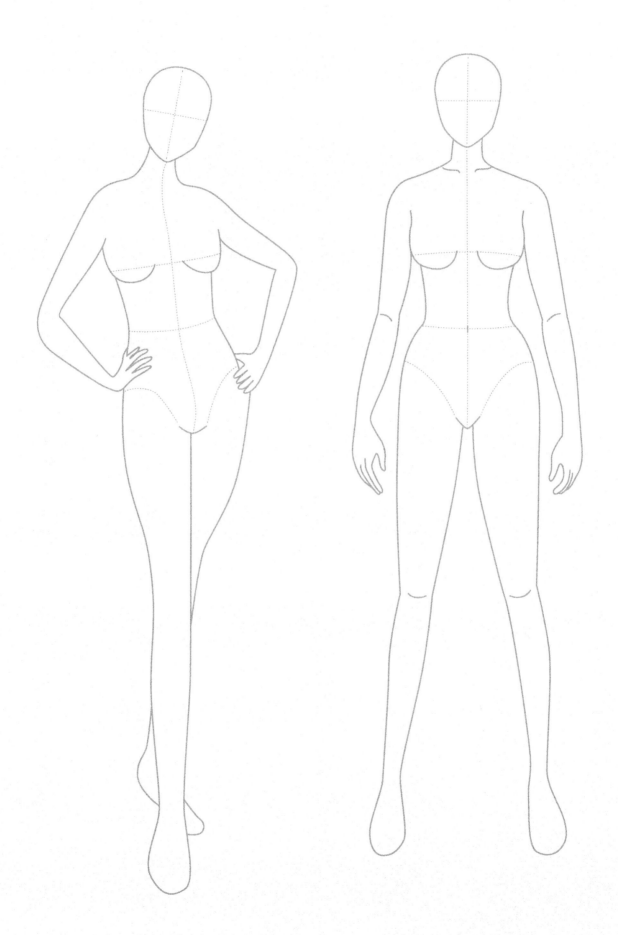

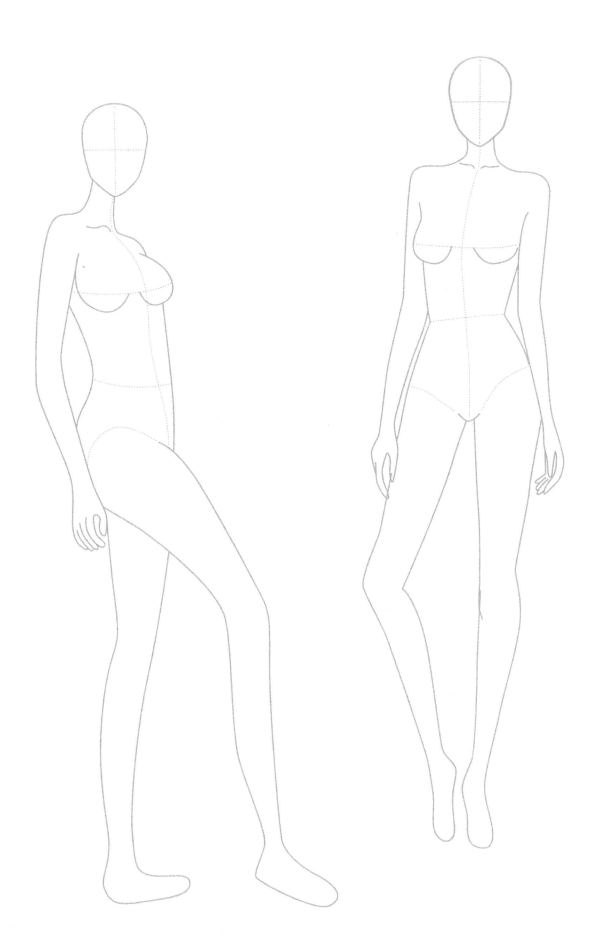

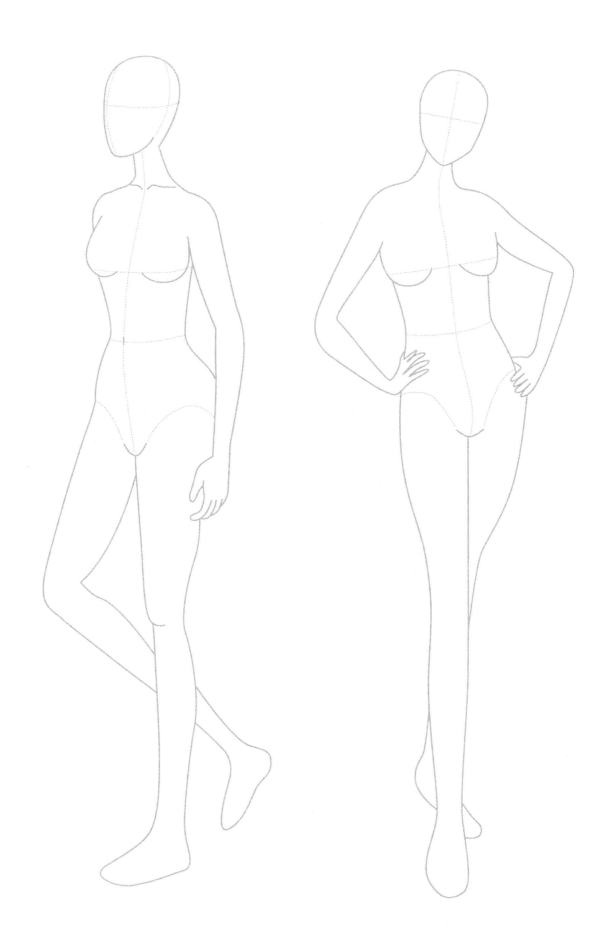

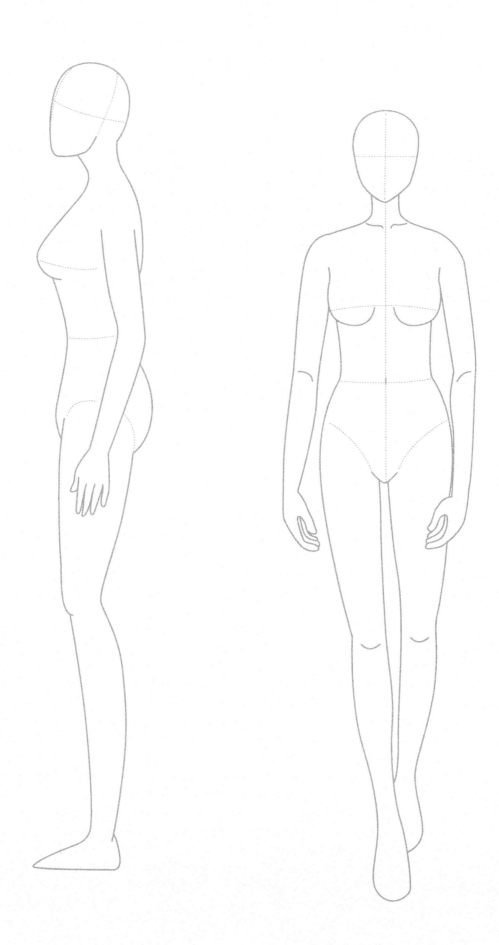

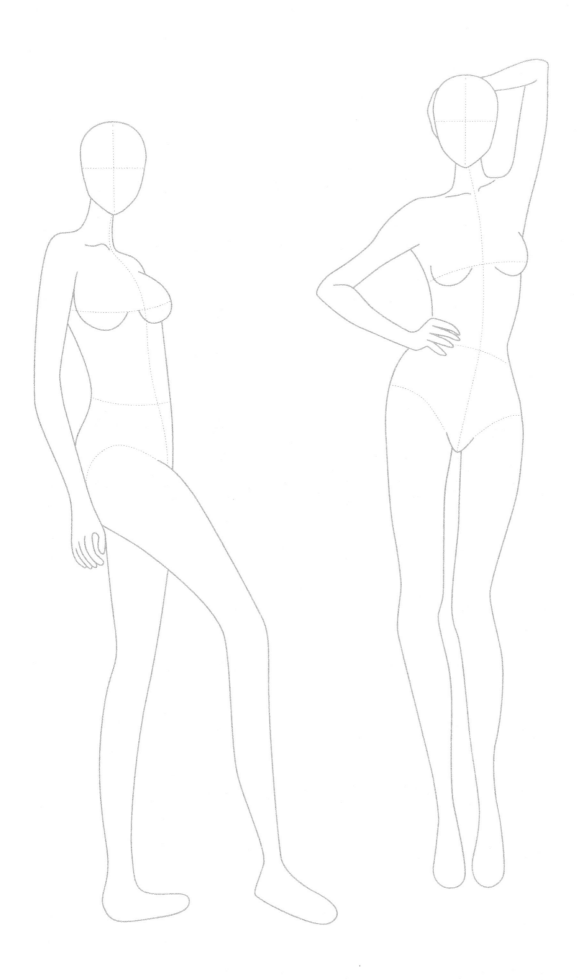

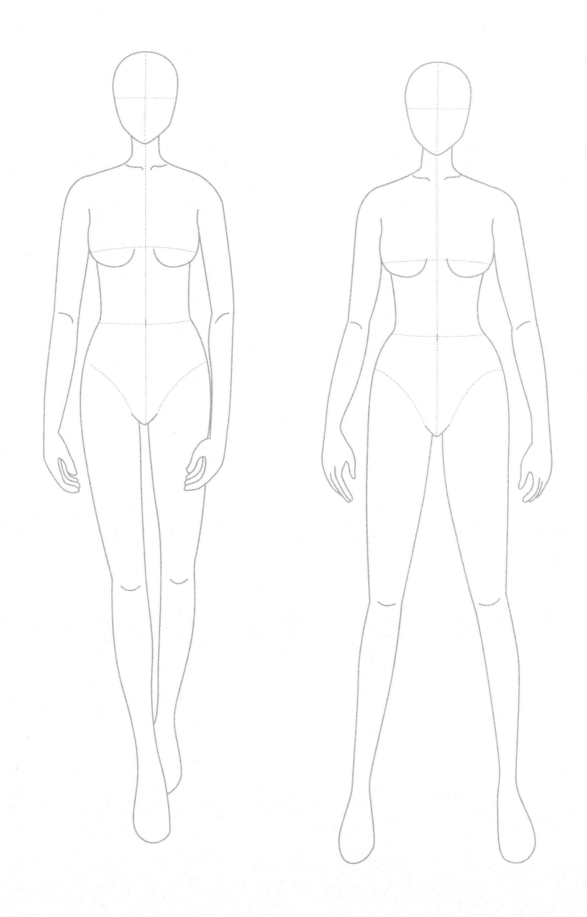

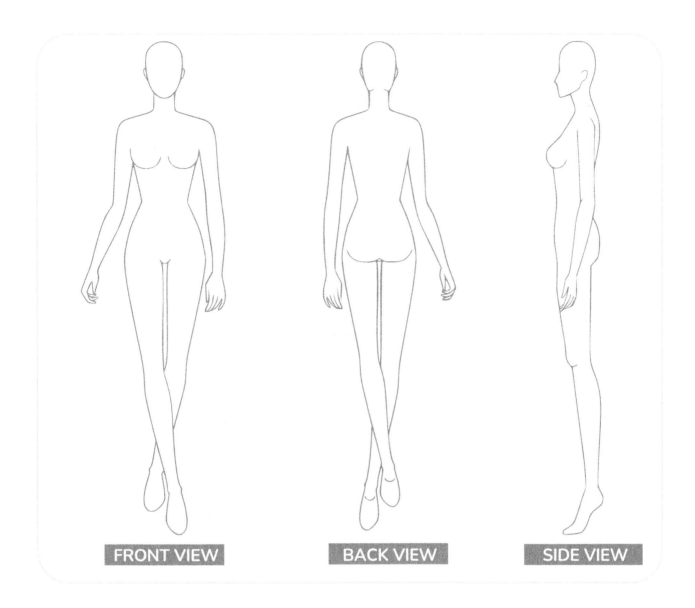

FRONT VIEW   BACK VIEW   SIDE VIEW

COLORS

○ ○ ○ ○ ○ ○ ○ ○ ○ ○ ○ ○ ○ ○ ○

MATERIALS	PATTERNS

ACCESSORIES

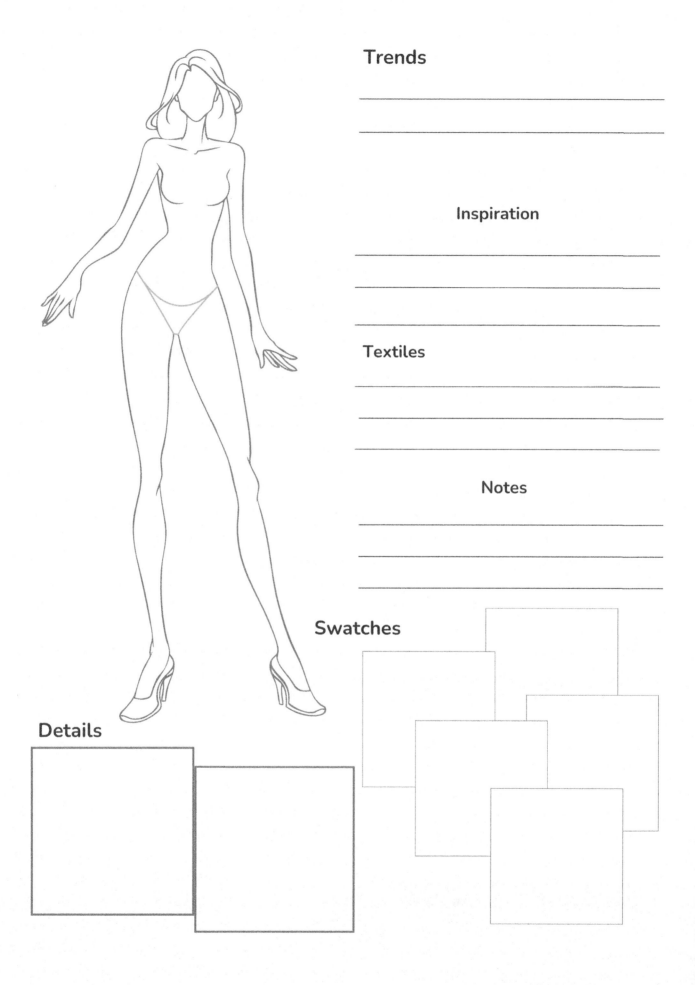

Trends

Inspiration

Textiles

Notes

Swatches

Details

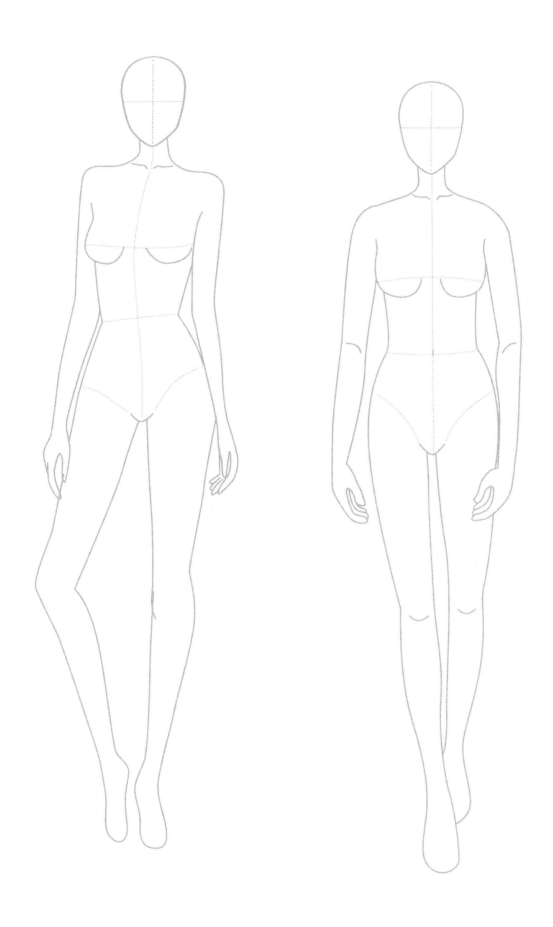

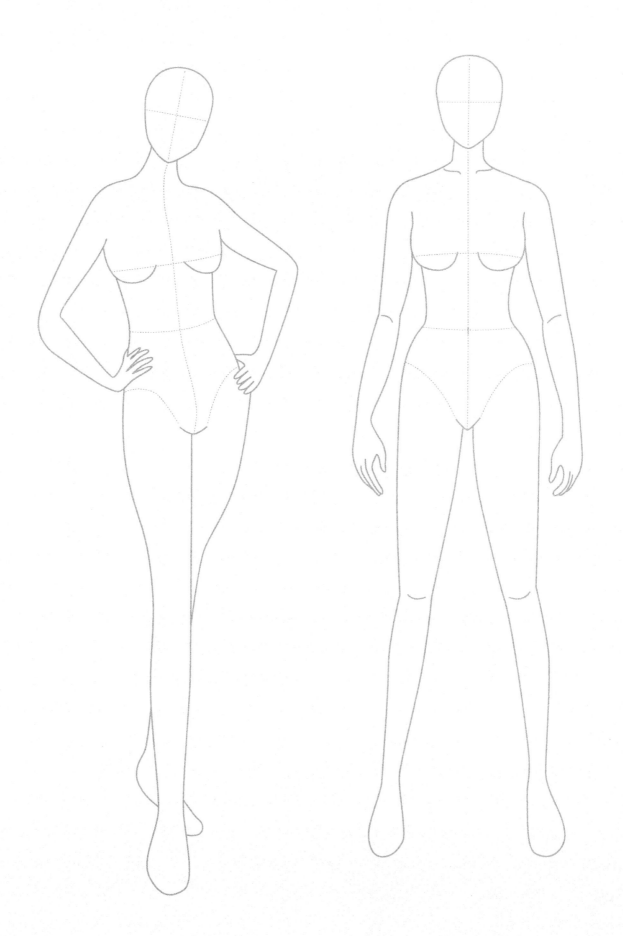

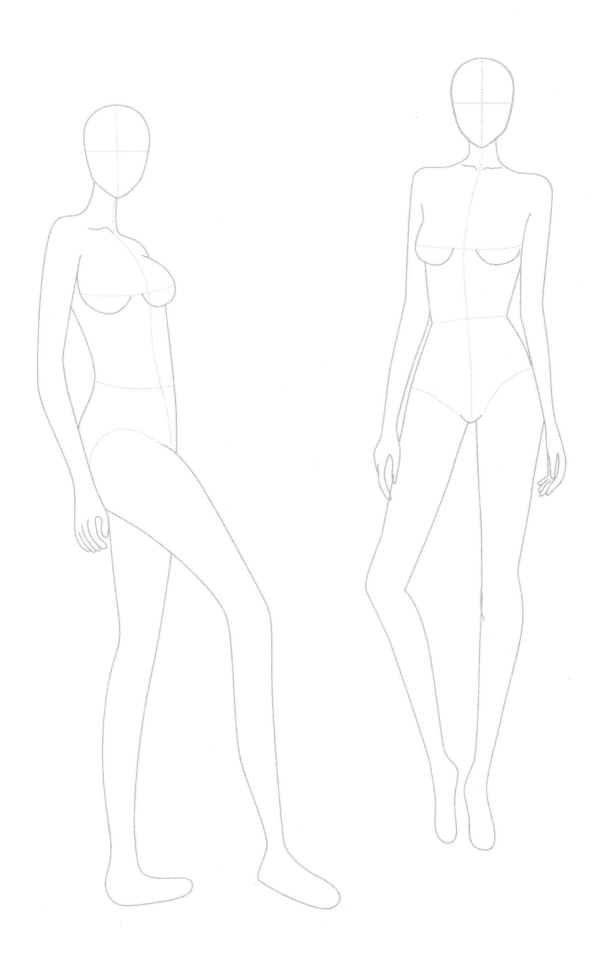

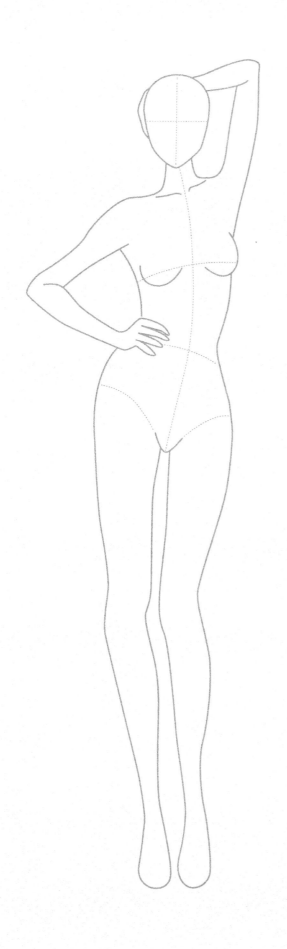

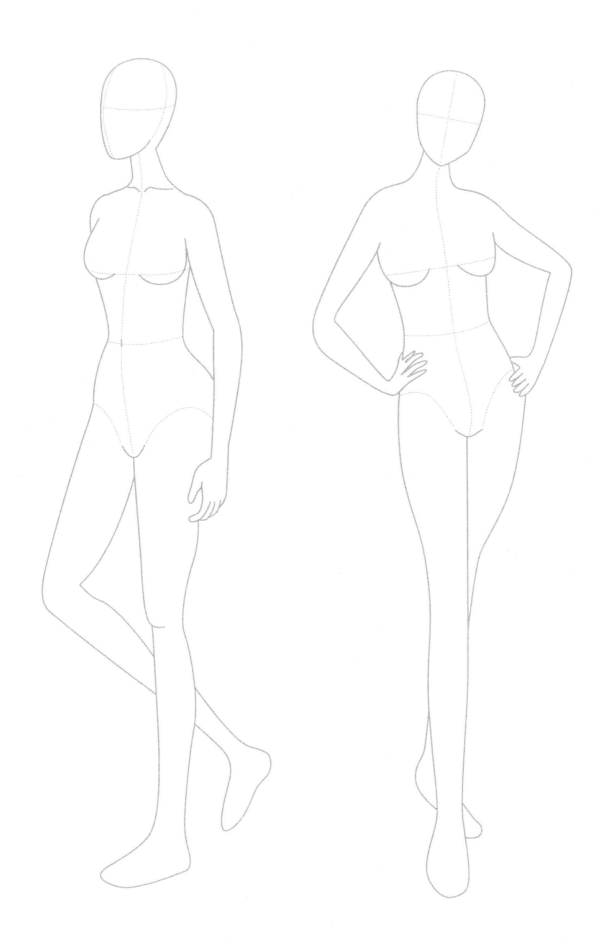

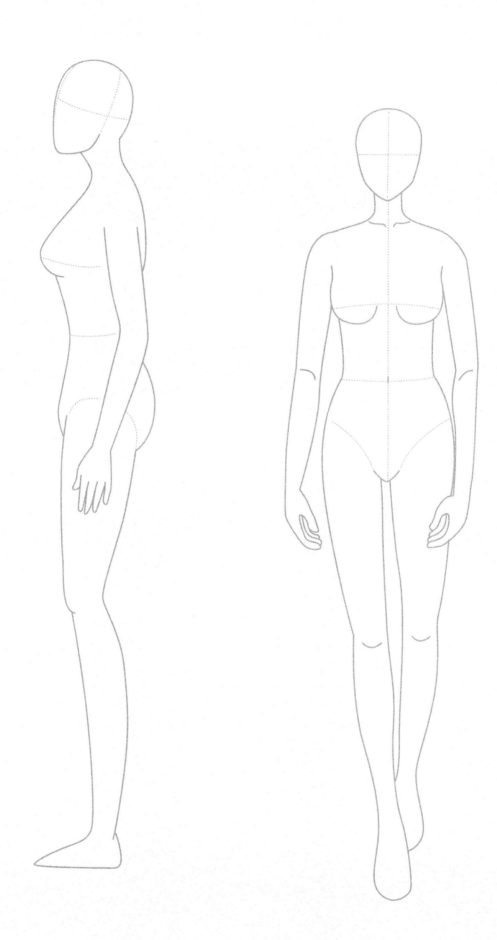

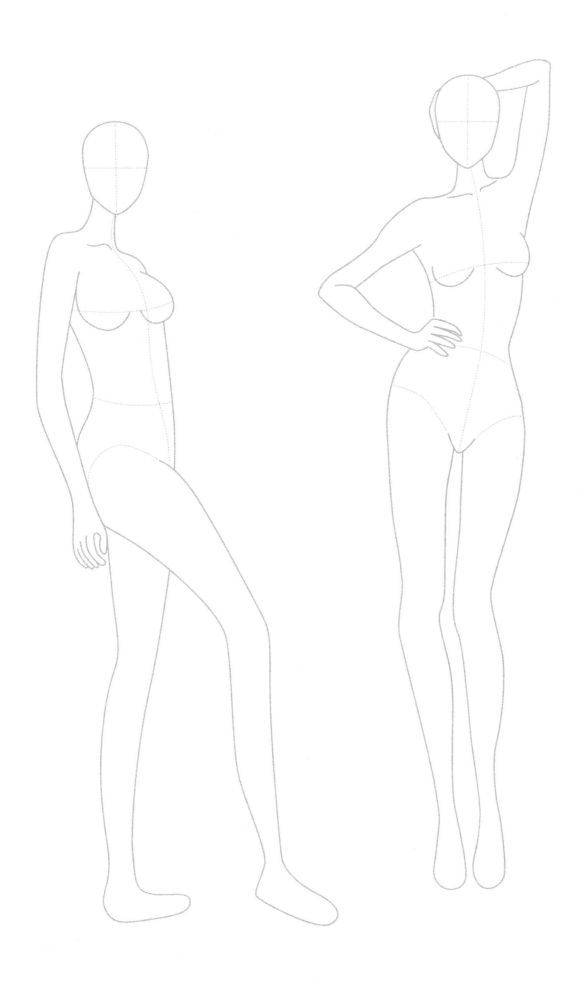

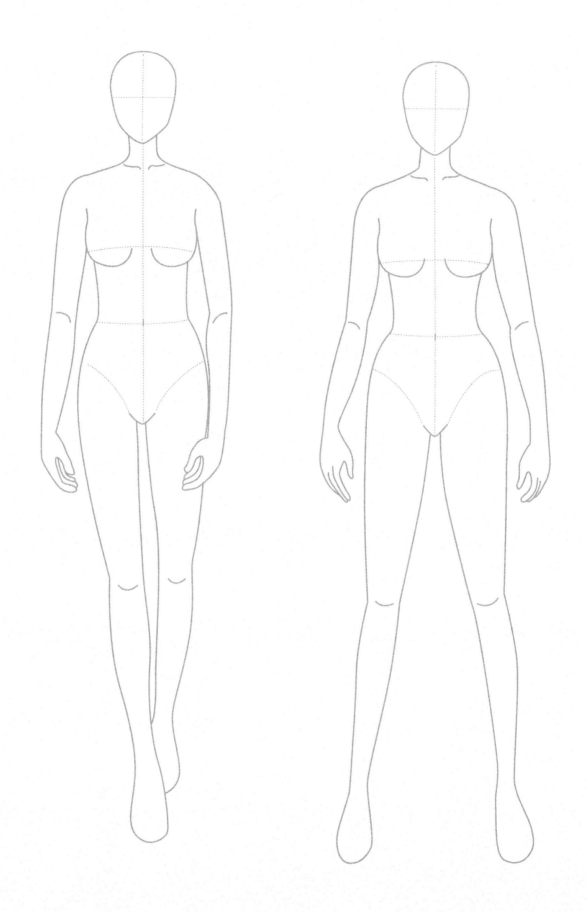

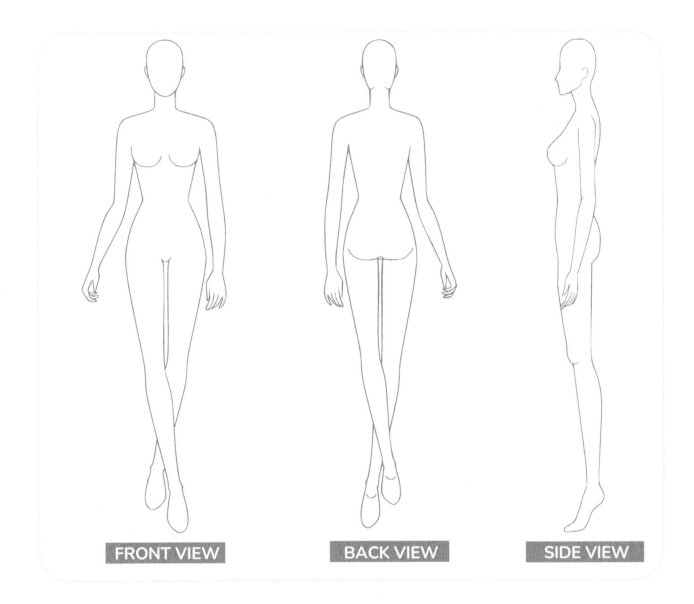

FRONT VIEW   BACK VIEW   SIDE VIEW

COLORS ○ ○ ○ ○ ○ ○ ○ ○ ○ ○ ○ ○ ○ ○ ○

MATERIALS   PATTERNS

ACCESSORIES

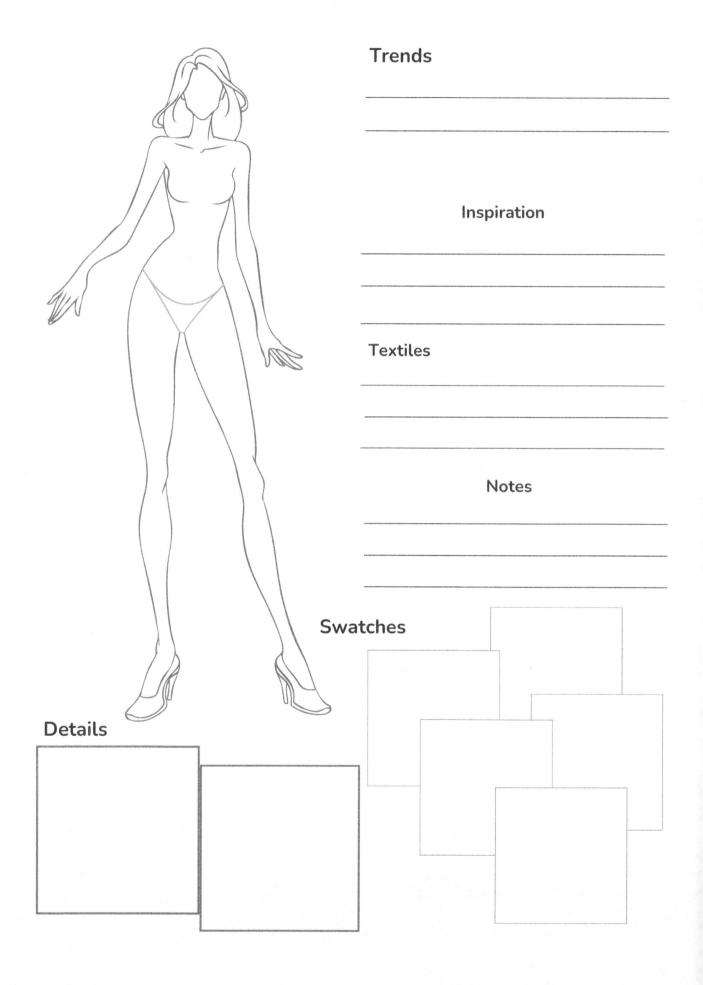

Trends

_____
_____

Inspiration

_____
_____
_____

Textiles

_____
_____
_____

Notes

_____
_____
_____

Swatches

Details

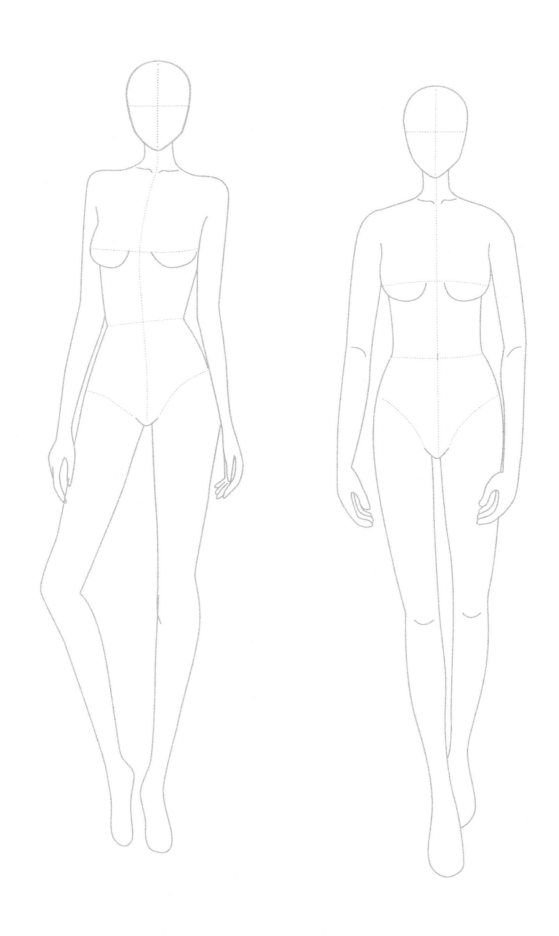

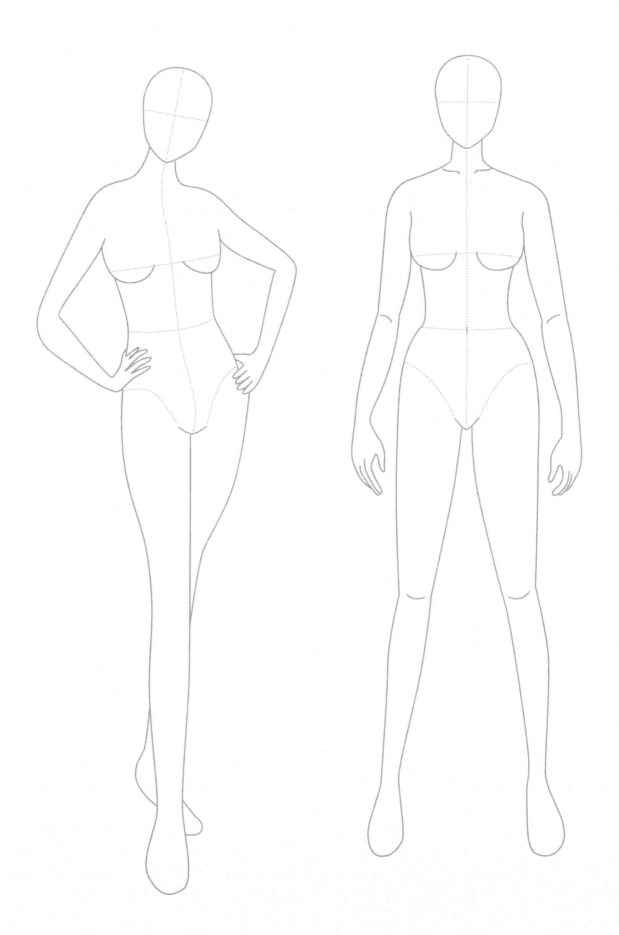

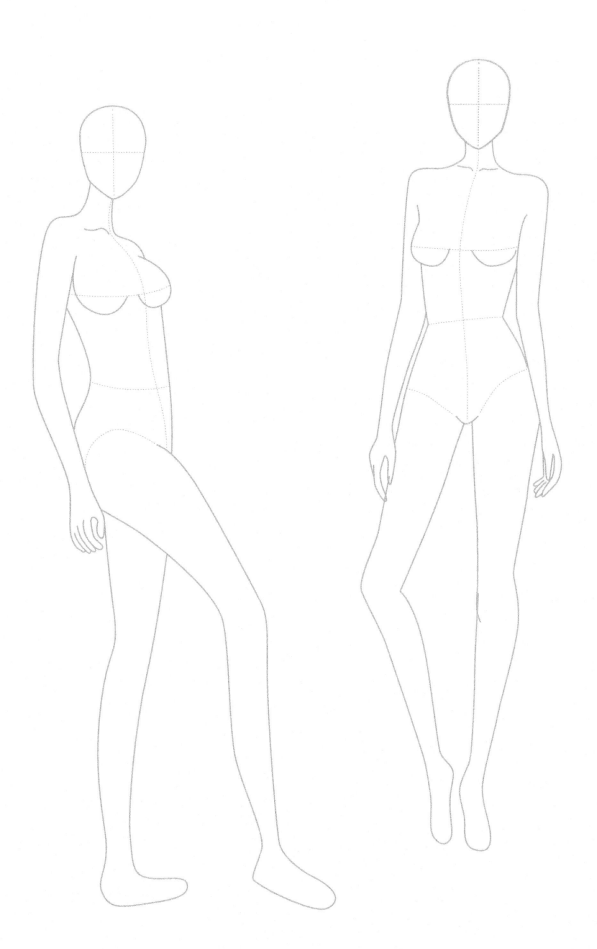

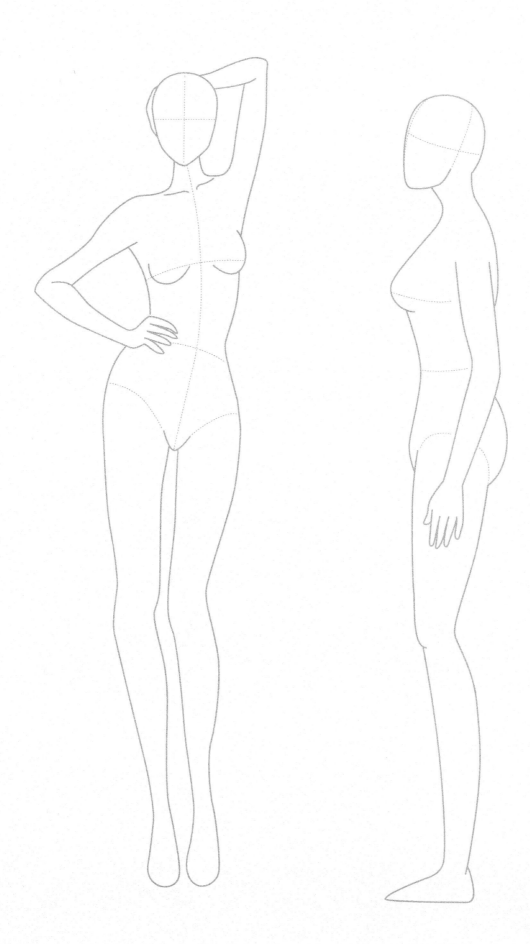

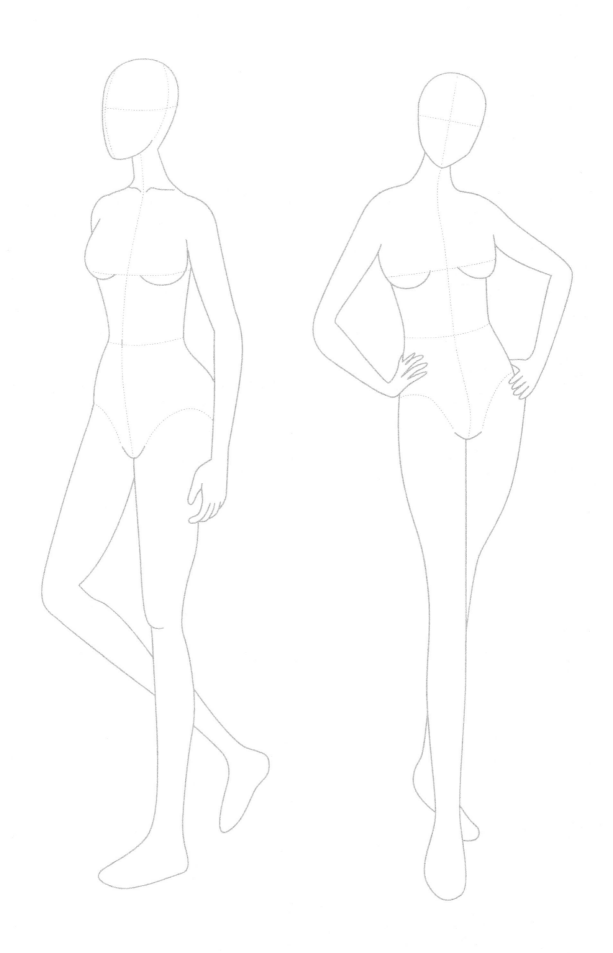

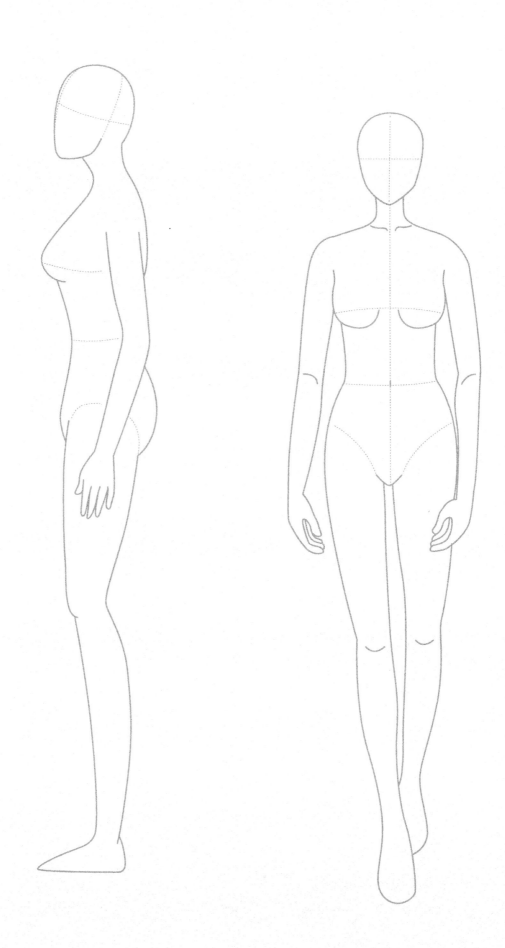

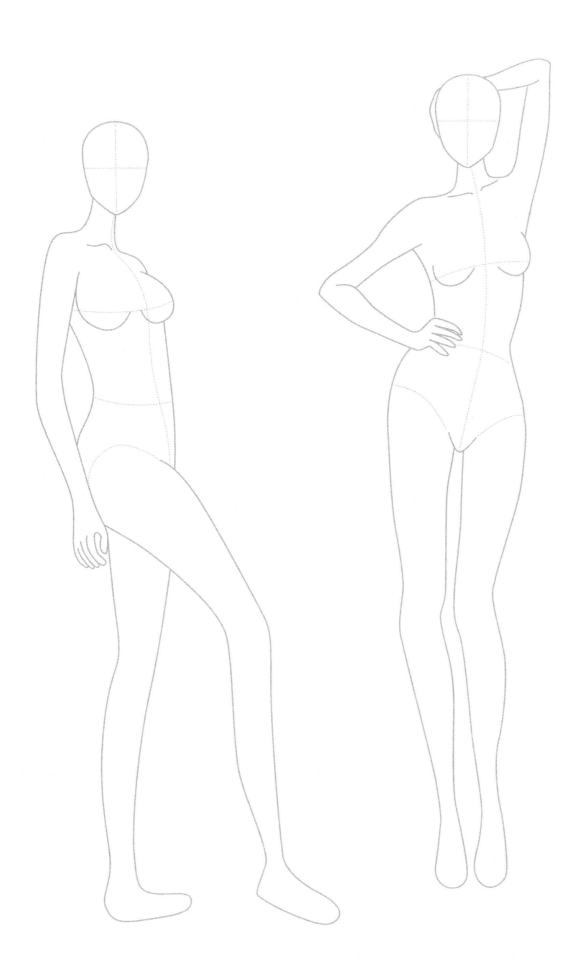

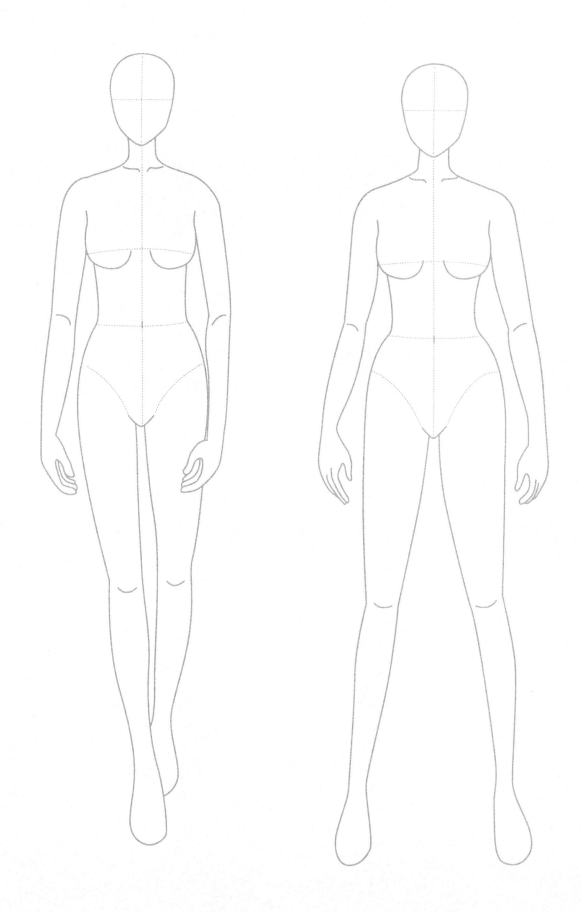

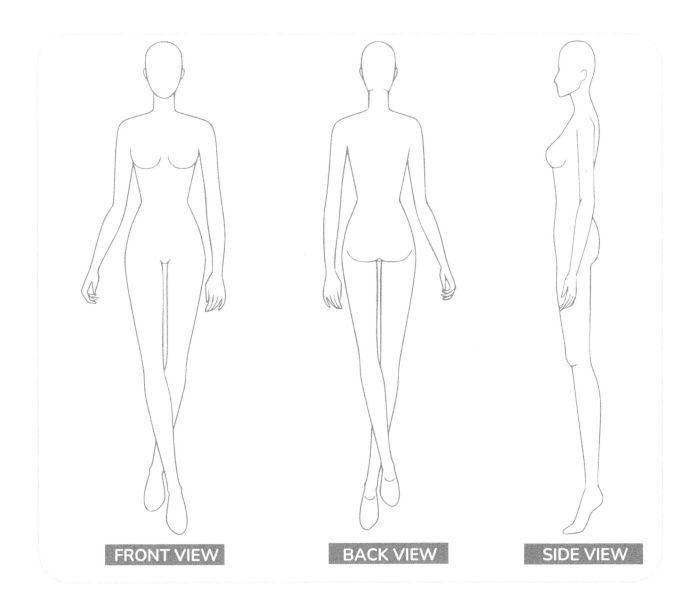

FRONT VIEW   BACK VIEW   SIDE VIEW

COLORS ◯ ◯ ◯ ◯ ◯ ◯ ◯ ◯ ◯ ◯ ◯ ◯ ◯ ◯

MATERIALS   PATTERNS

ACCESSORIES

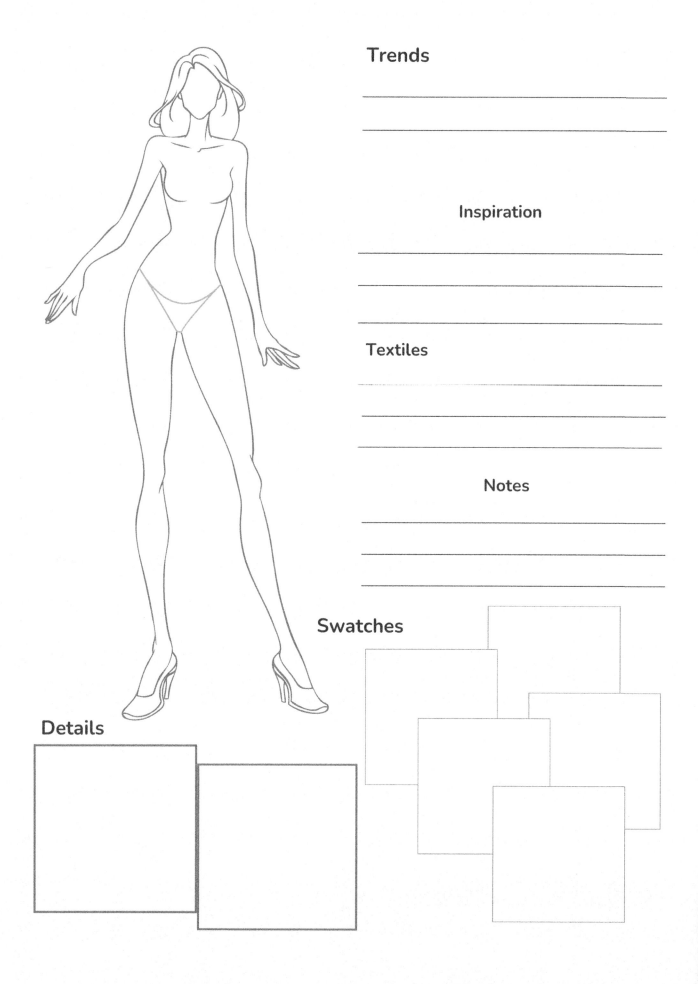

Trends

Inspiration

Textiles

Notes

Swatches

Details

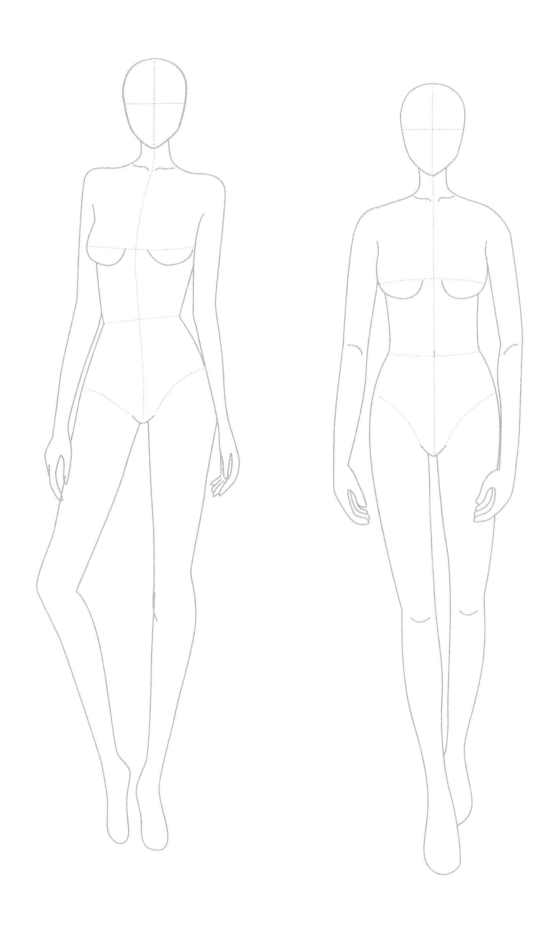

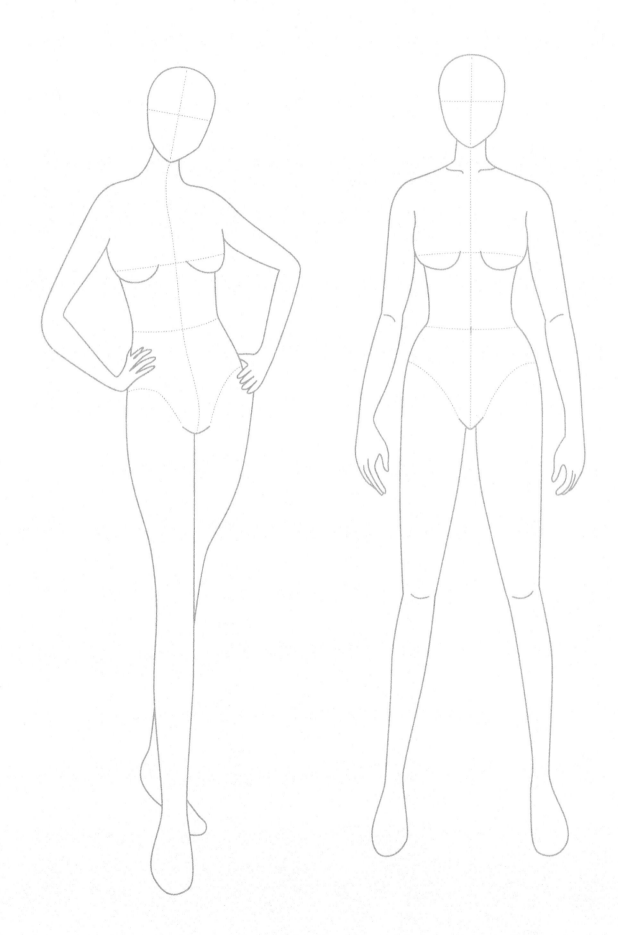

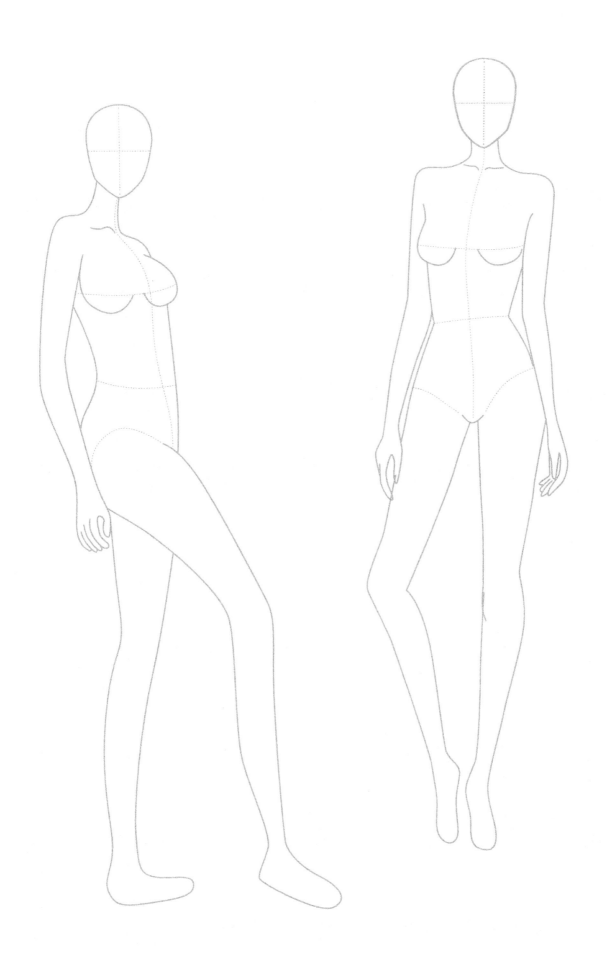

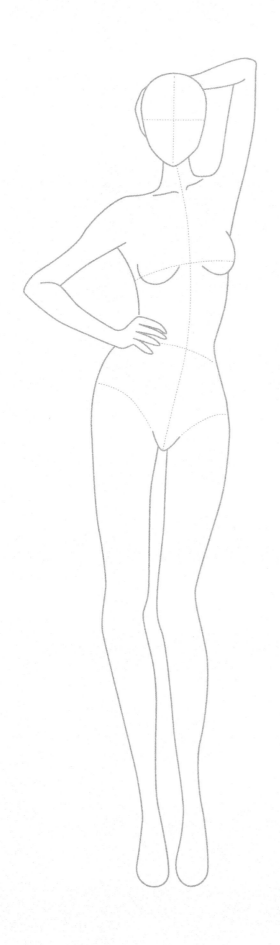

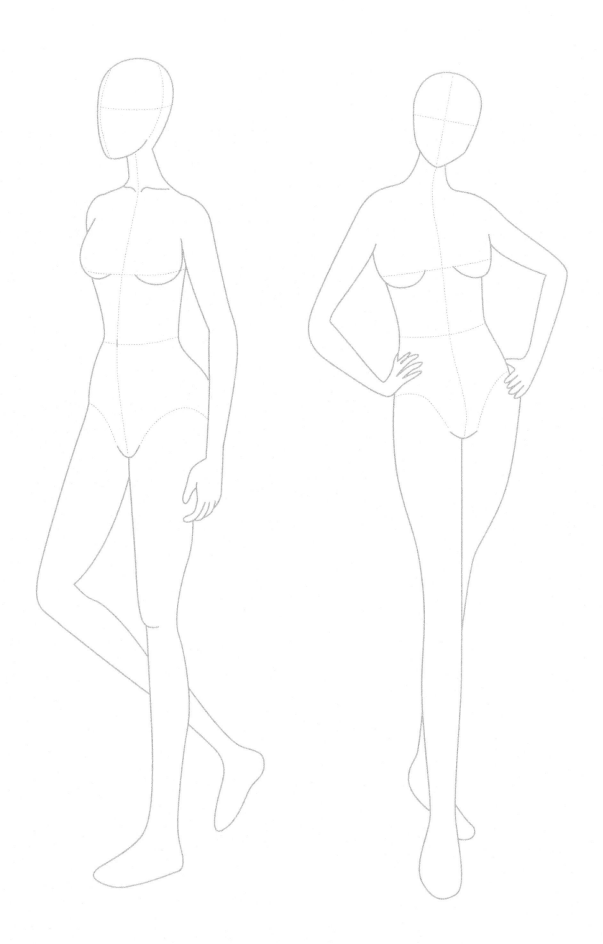

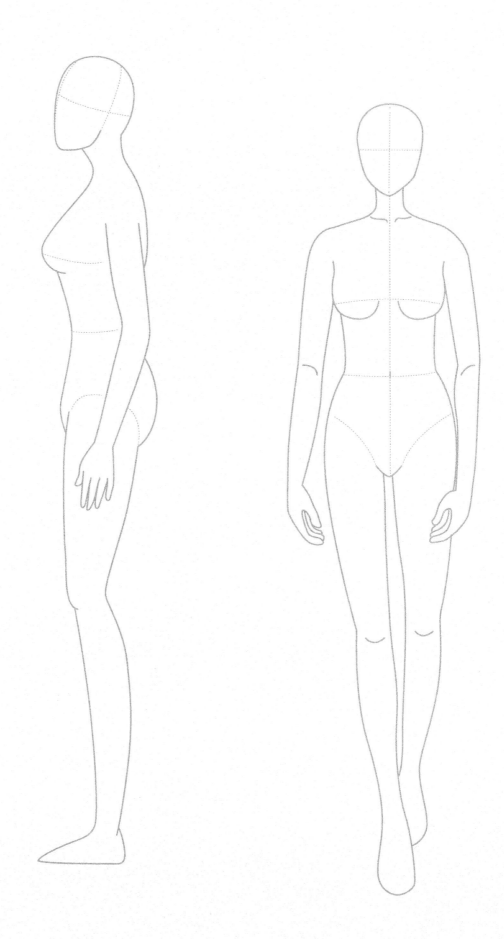

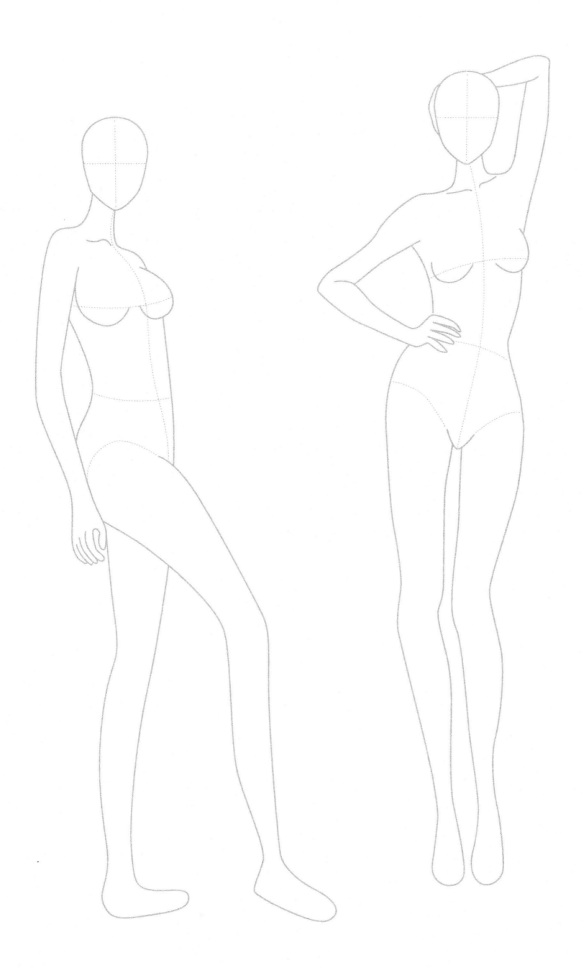

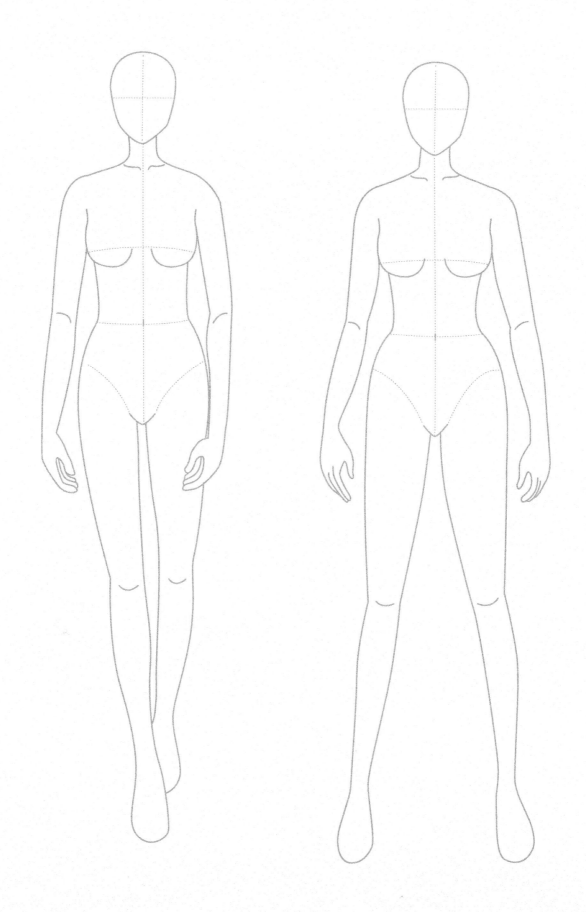

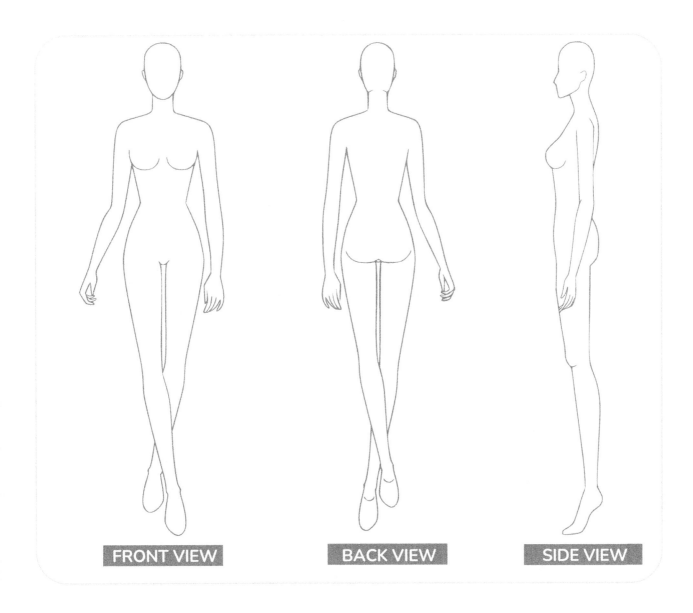

FRONT VIEW   BACK VIEW   SIDE VIEW

COLORS ◯◯◯◯◯◯◯◯◯◯◯◯◯◯◯◯

MATERIALS	PATTERNS

ACCESSORIES

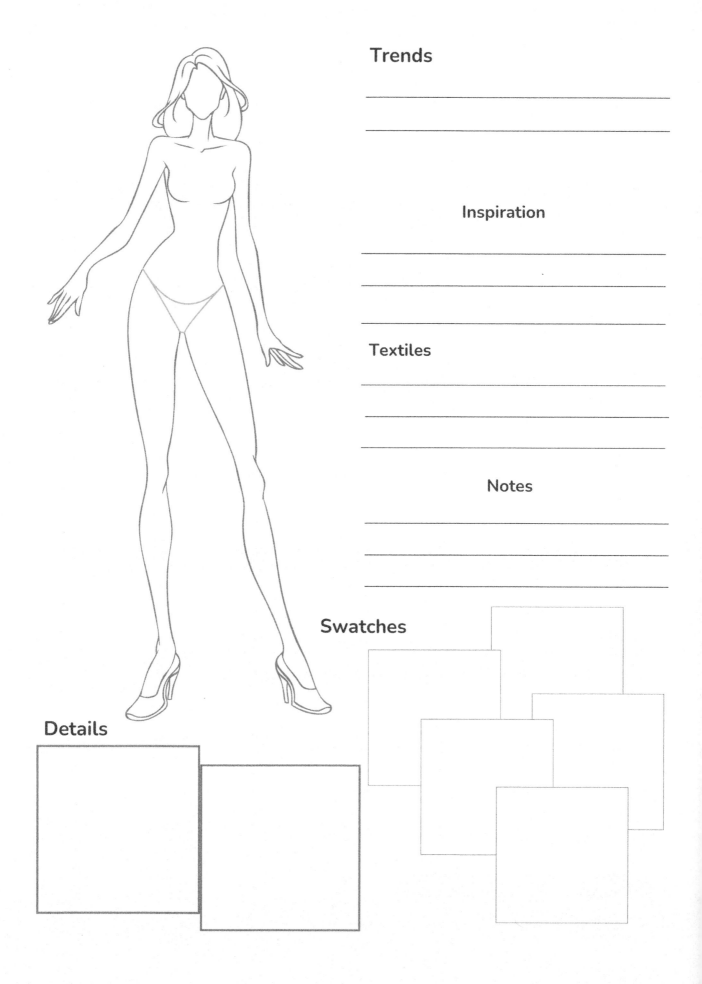

Trends

Inspiration

Textiles

Notes

Swatches

Details

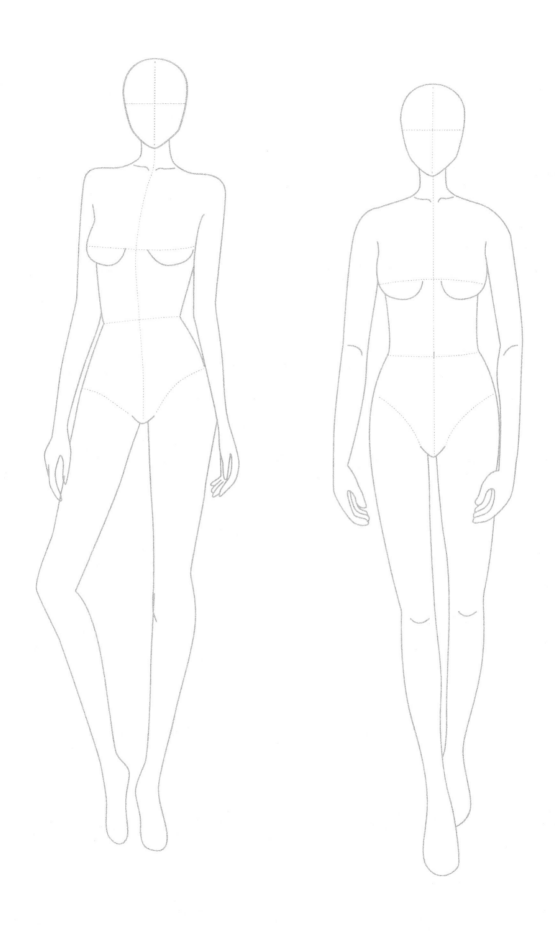

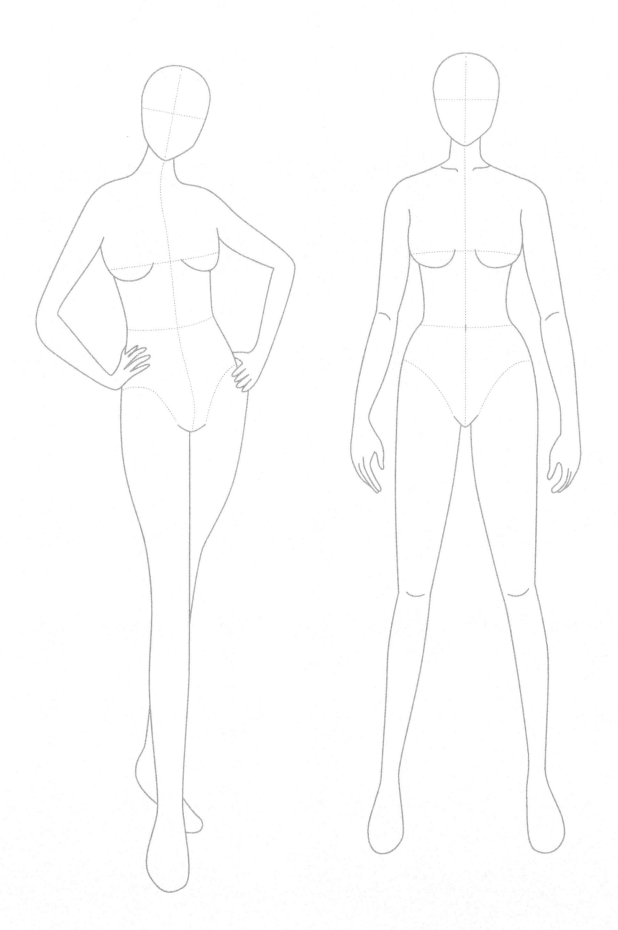

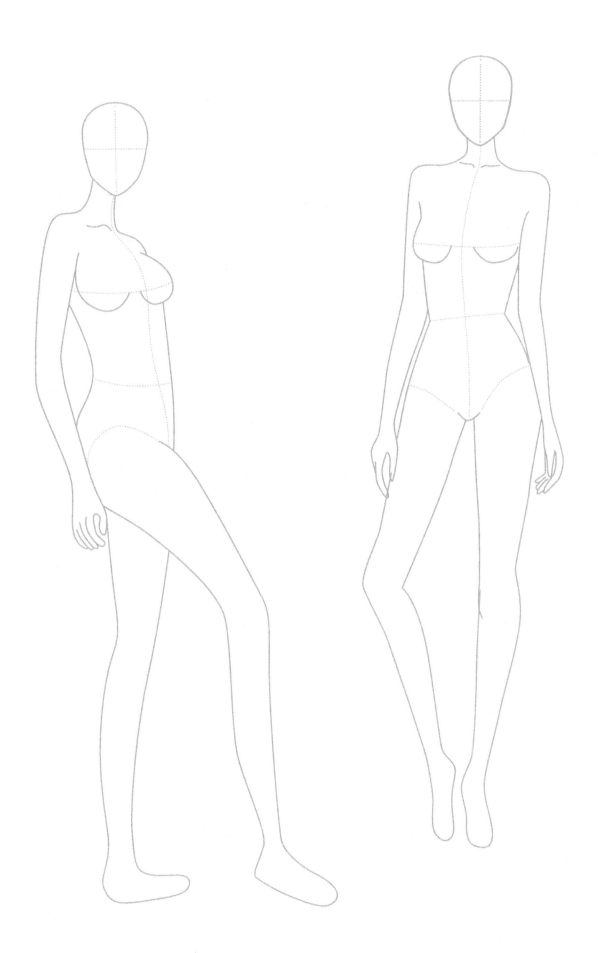

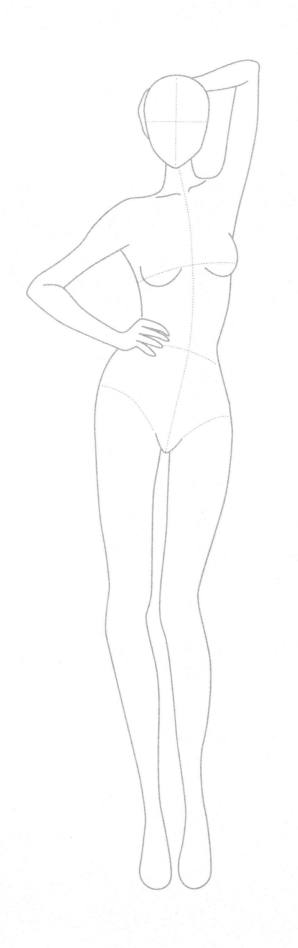

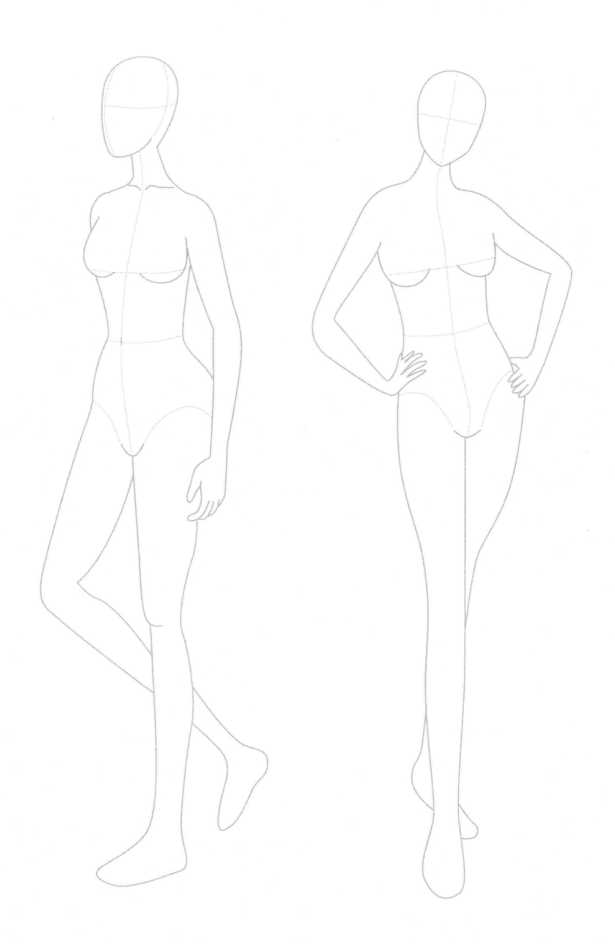

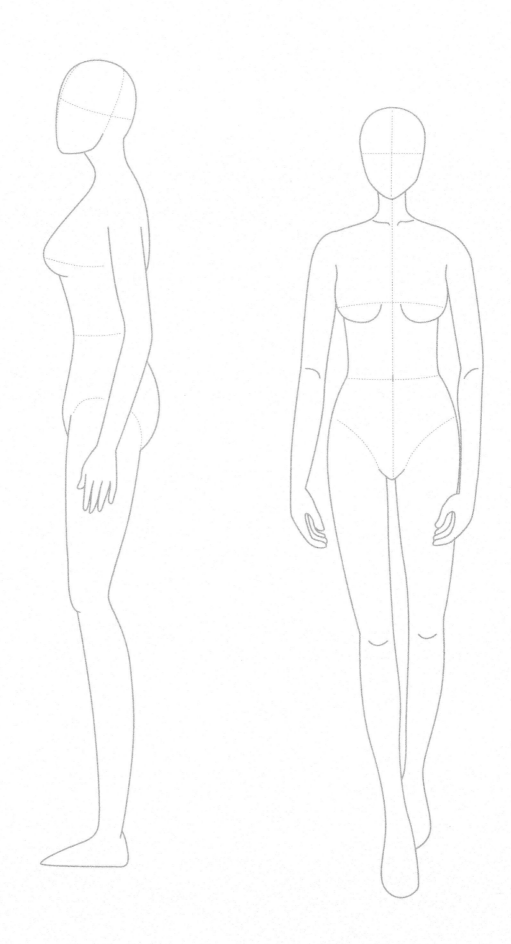

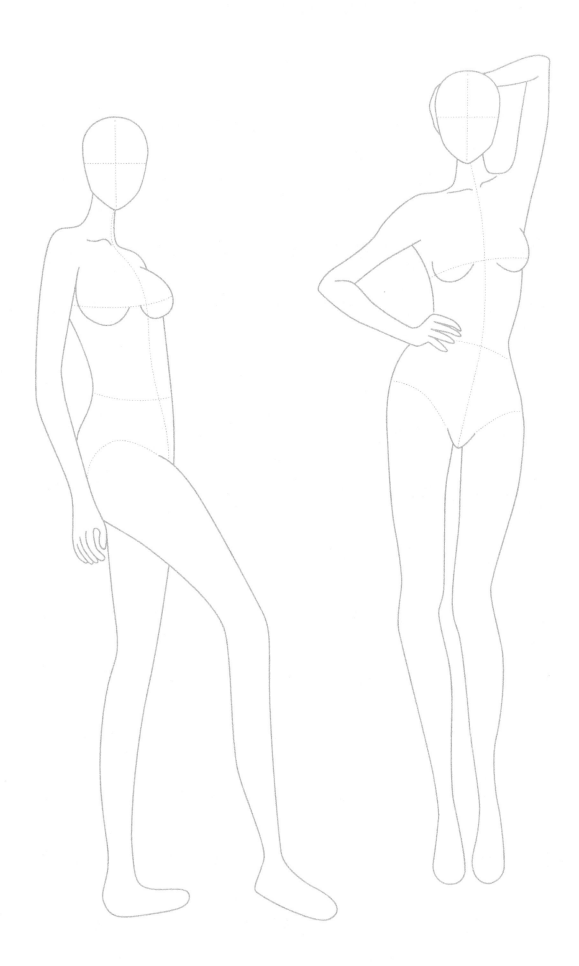

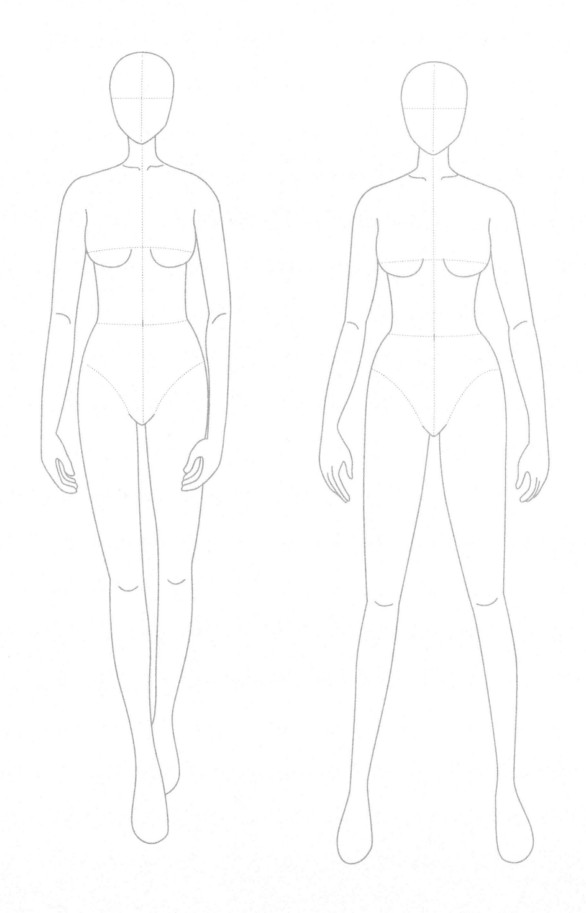

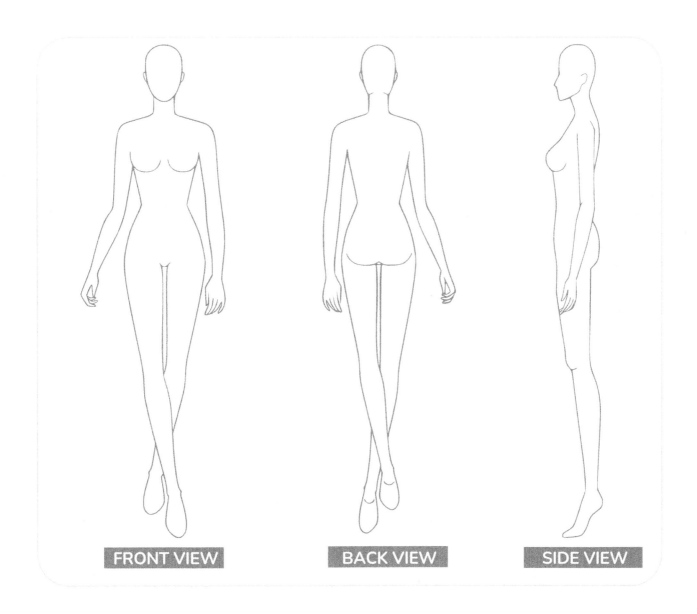

FRONT VIEW BACK VIEW SIDE VIEW

COLORS ◯ ◯ ◯ ◯ ◯ ◯ ◯ ◯ ◯ ◯ ◯ ◯ ◯ ◯ ◯

MATERIALS PATTERNS

ACCESSORIES

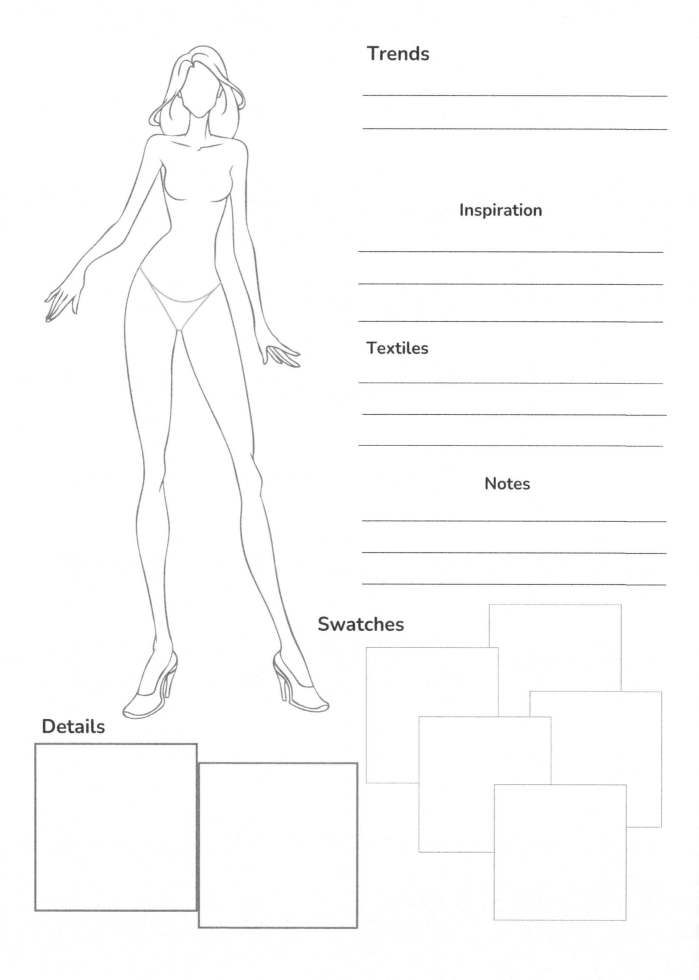

Trends

Inspiration

Textiles

Notes

Swatches

Details

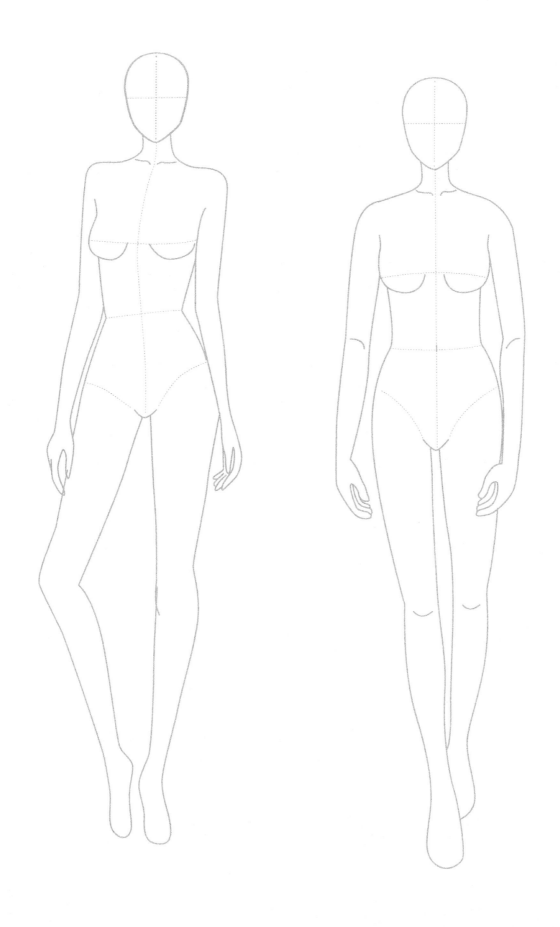

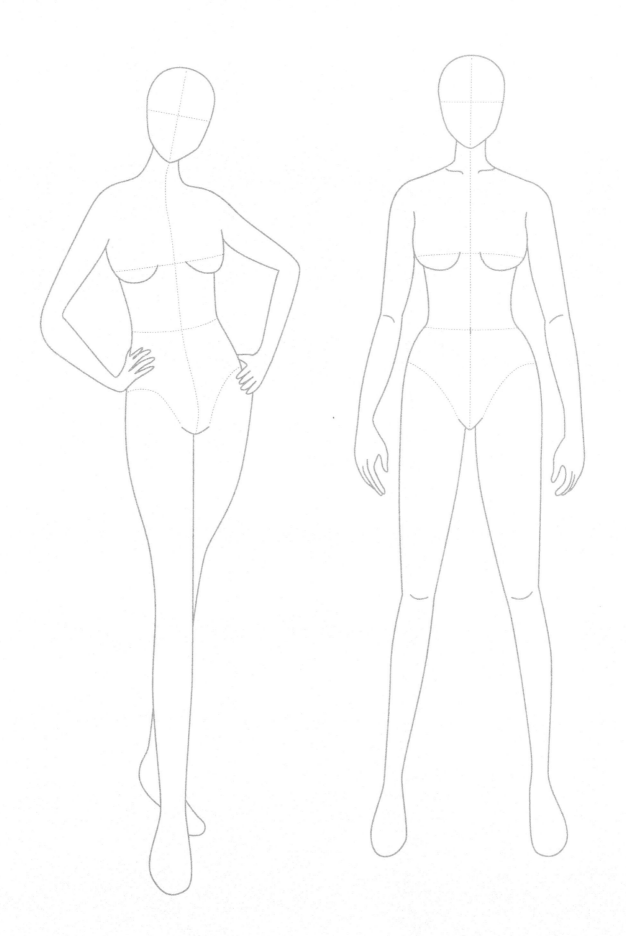

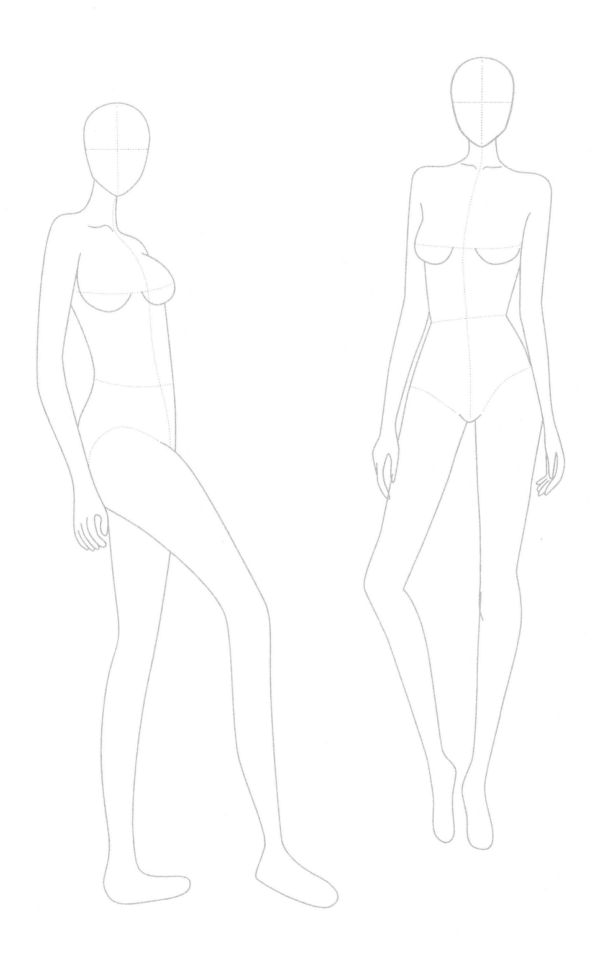

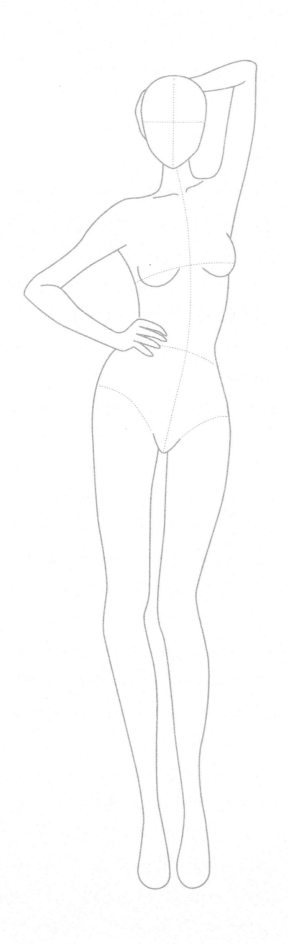

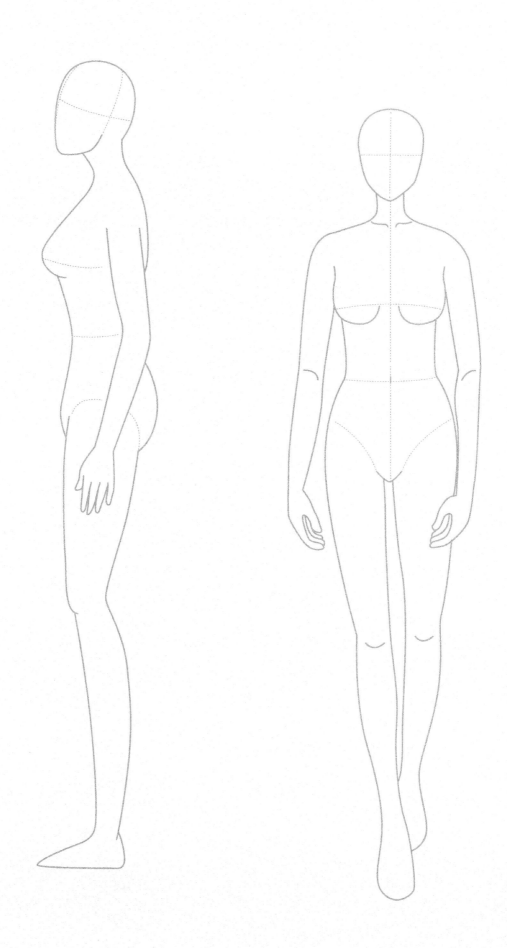

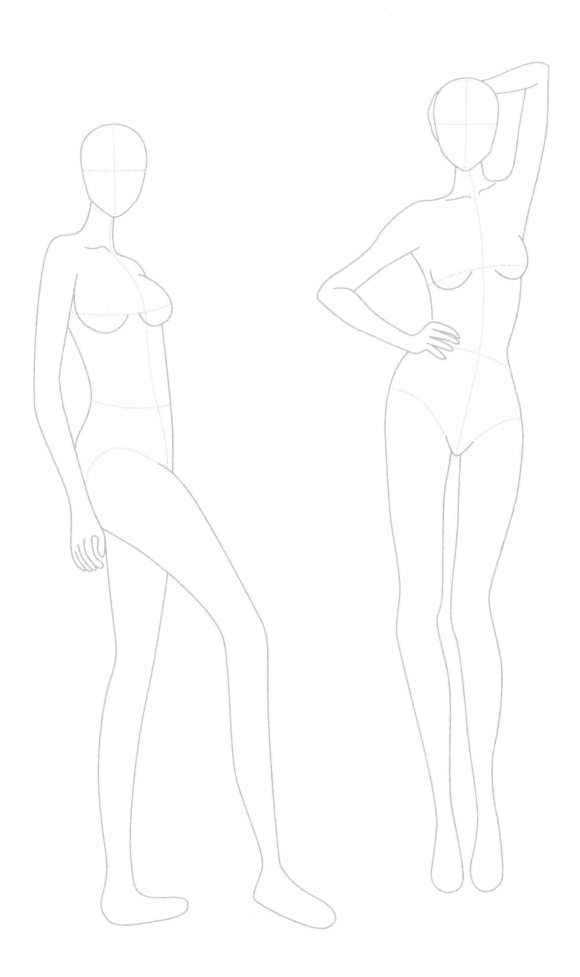

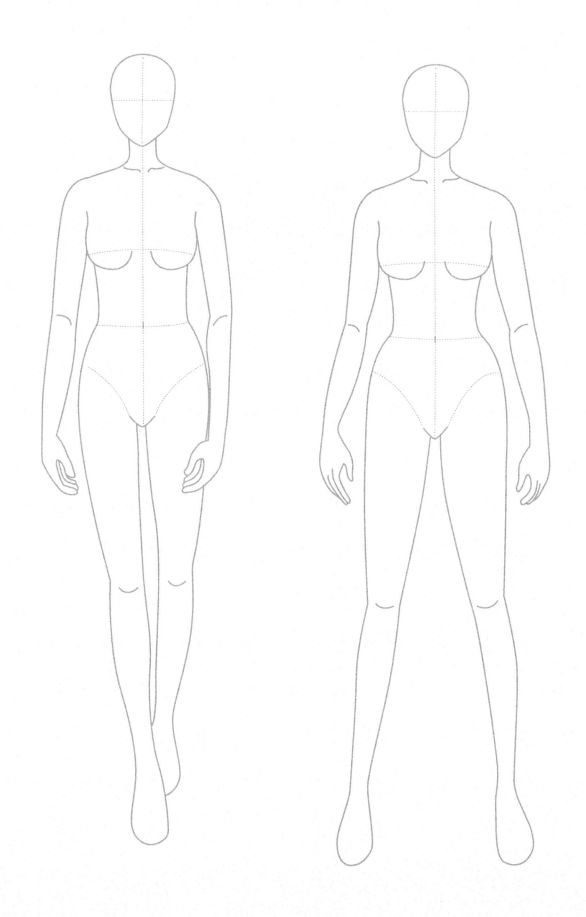

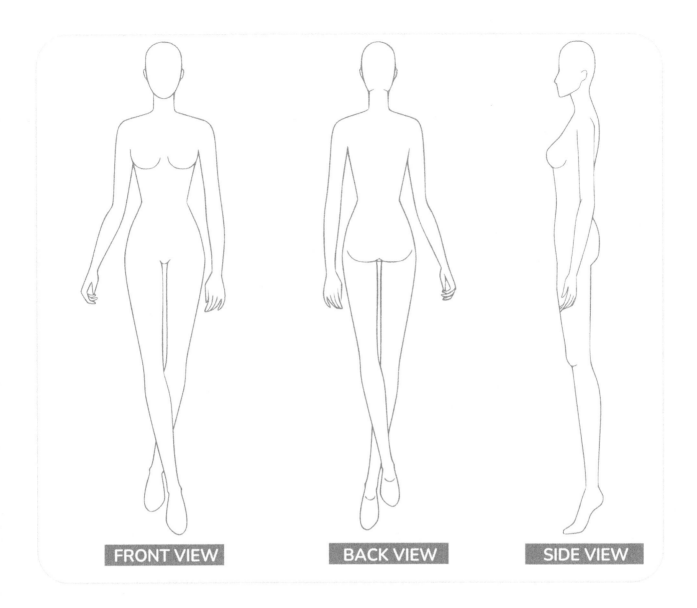

FRONT VIEW BACK VIEW SIDE VIEW

COLORS ◯◯◯◯◯◯◯◯◯◯◯◯◯◯◯

MATERIALS PATTERNS

ACCESSORIES

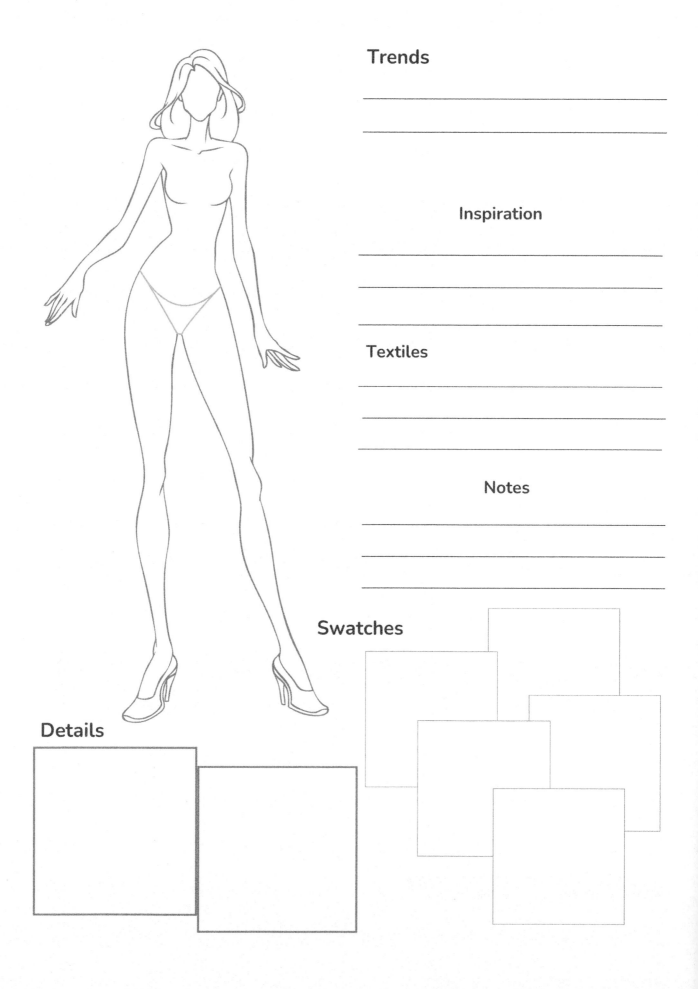

Trends

_____

_____

Inspiration

_____

_____

_____

Textiles

_____

_____

_____

Notes

_____

_____

_____

_____

Swatches

Details

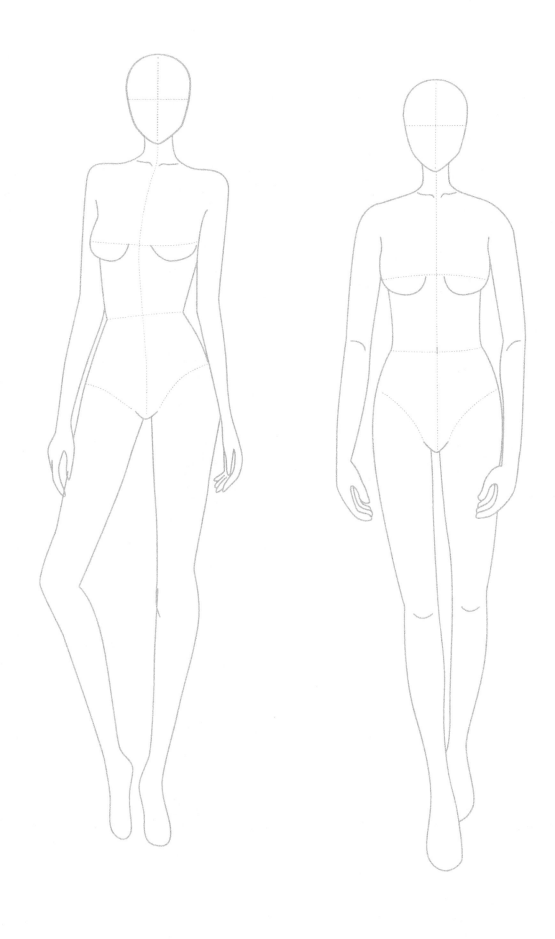

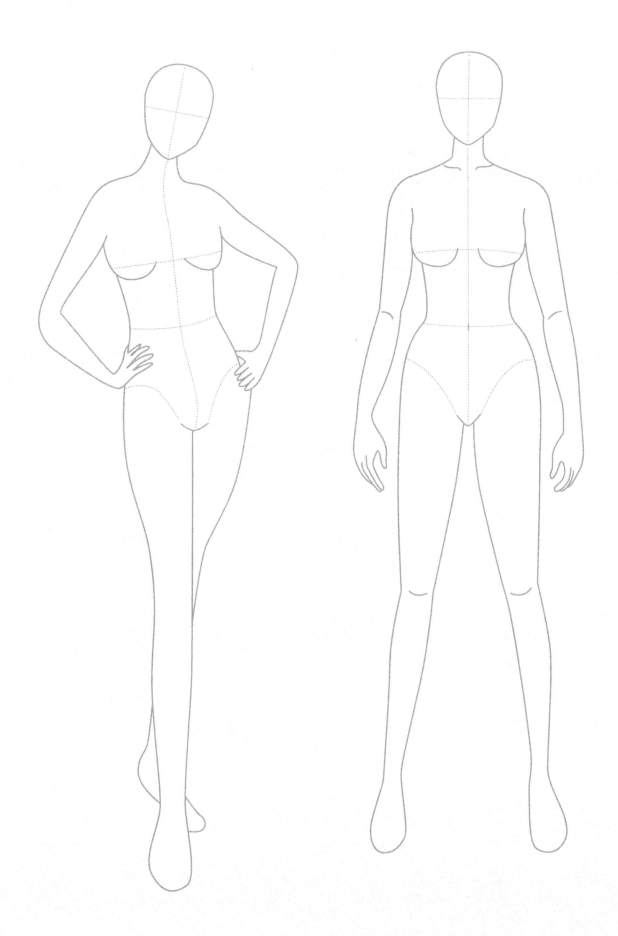

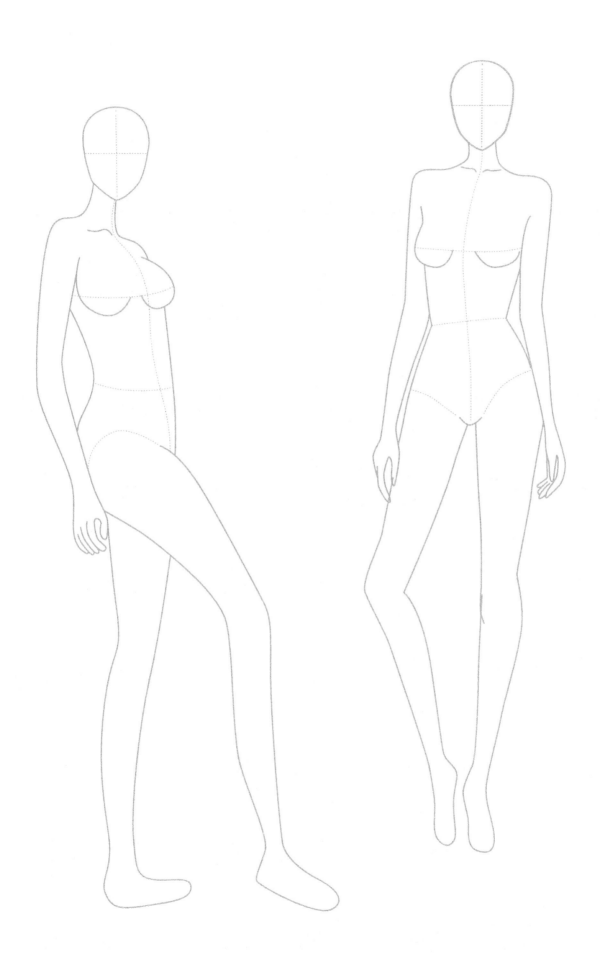

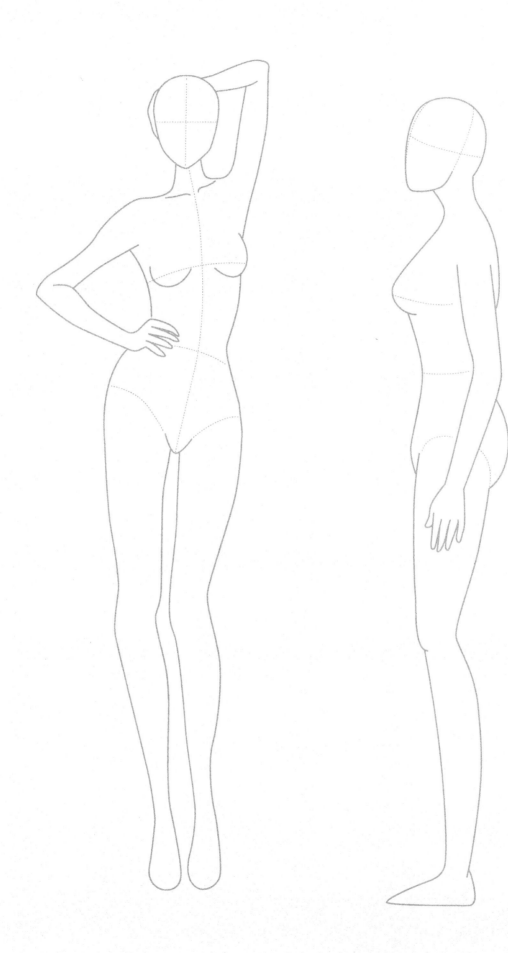

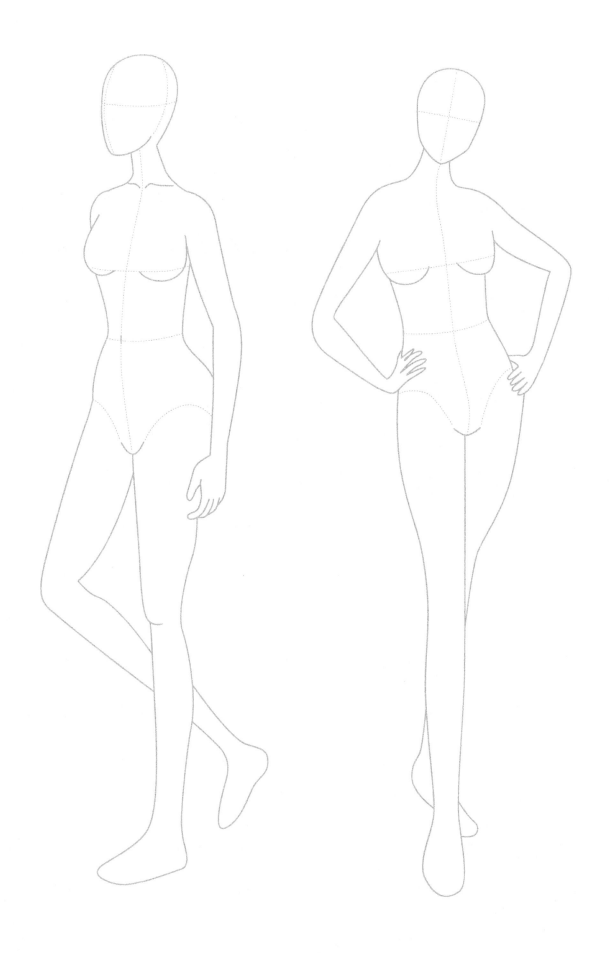

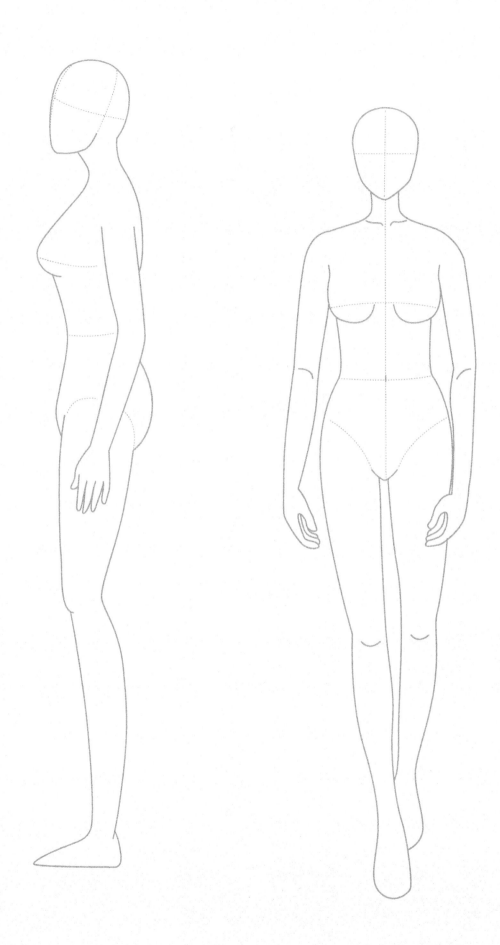

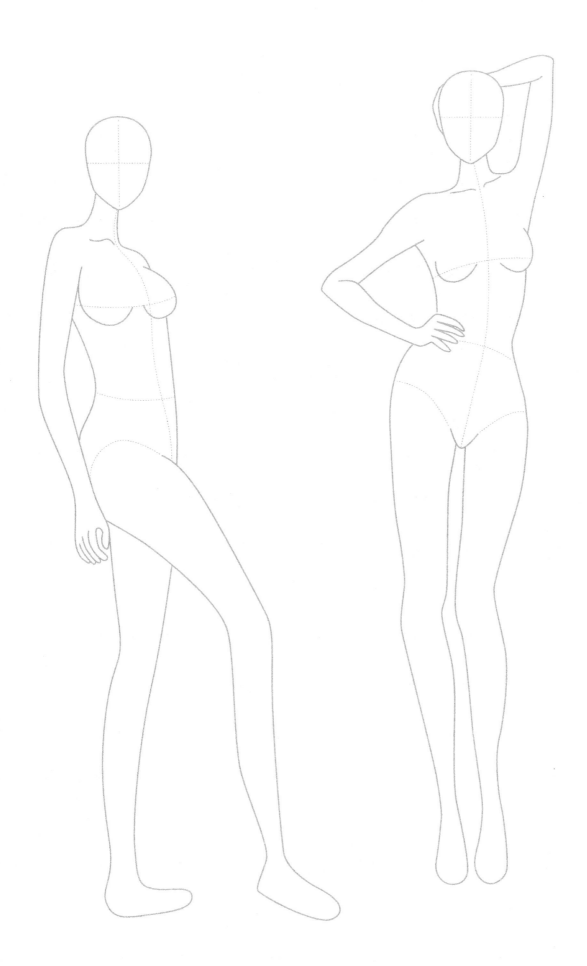

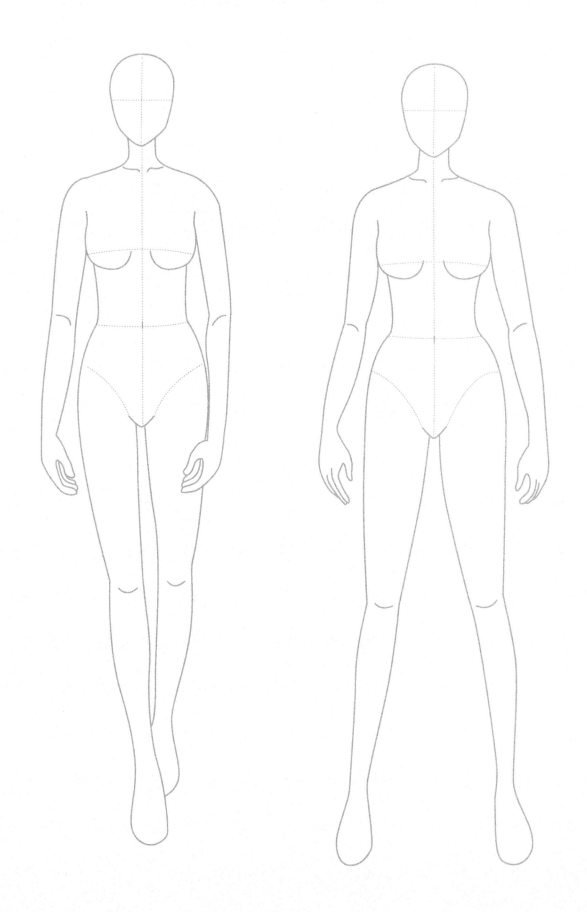

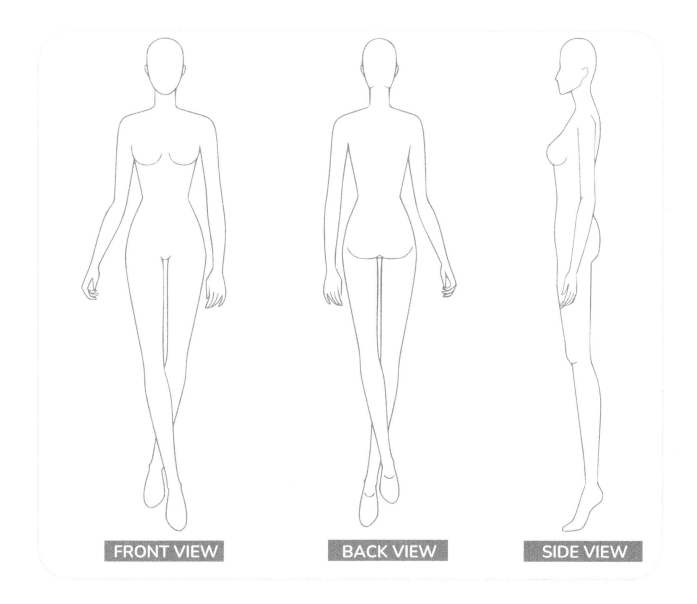

FRONT VIEW   BACK VIEW   SIDE VIEW

COLORS ◯ ◯ ◯ ◯ ◯ ◯ ◯ ◯ ◯ ◯ ◯ ◯ ◯ ◯ ◯

MATERIALS	PATTERNS

ACCESSORIES

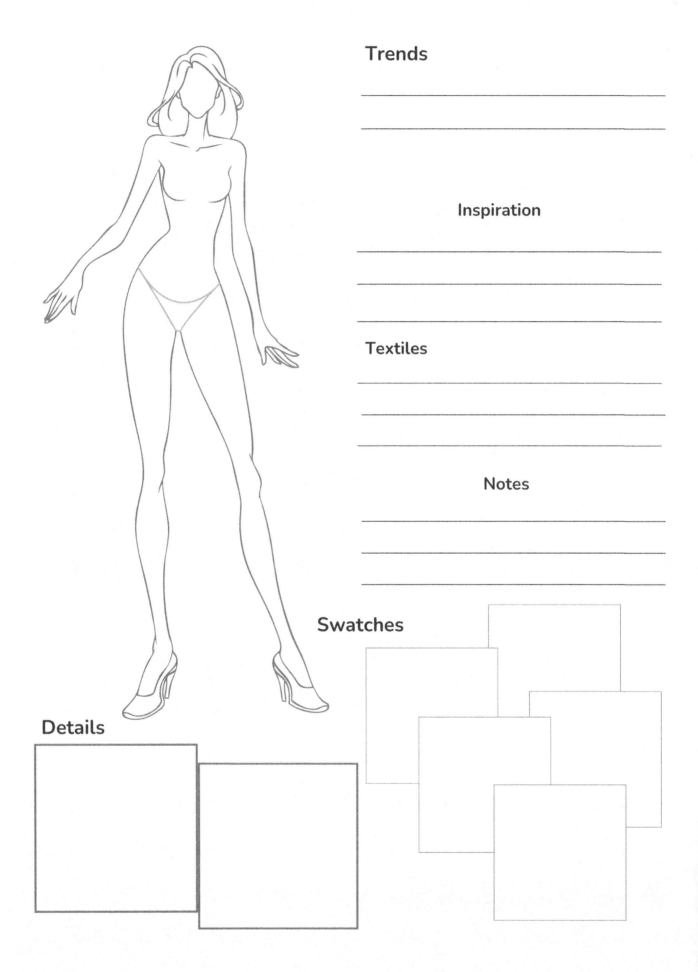

Trends

Inspiration

Textiles

Notes

Swatches

Details

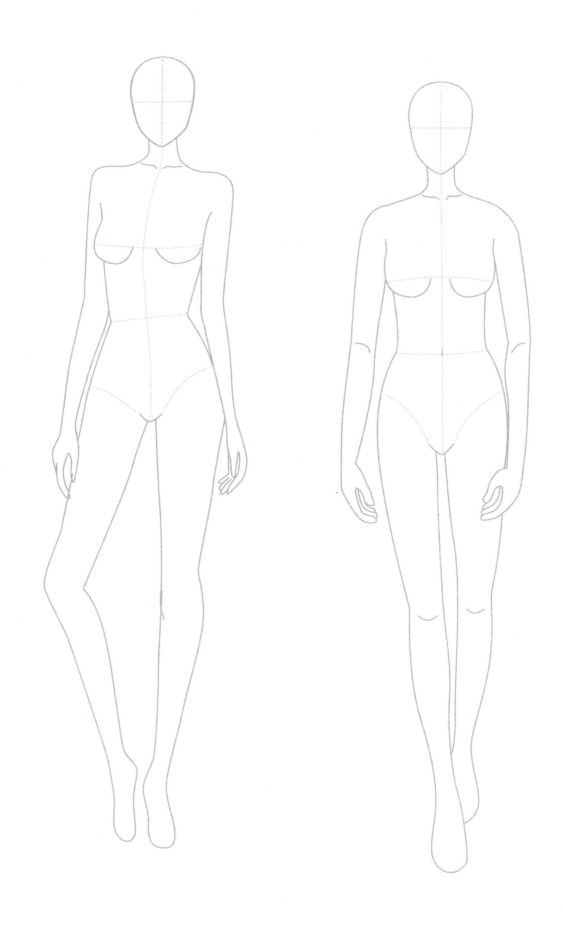

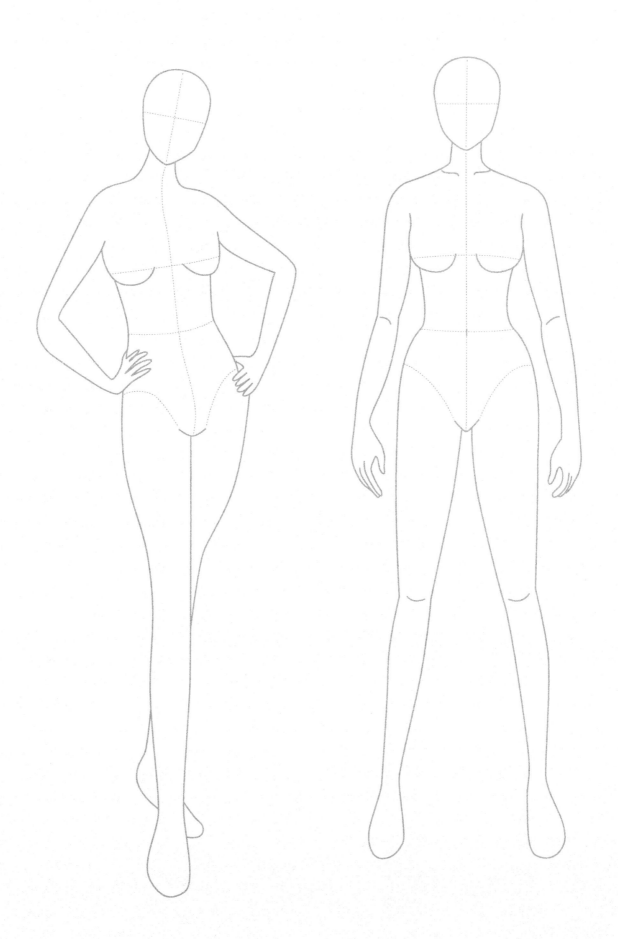

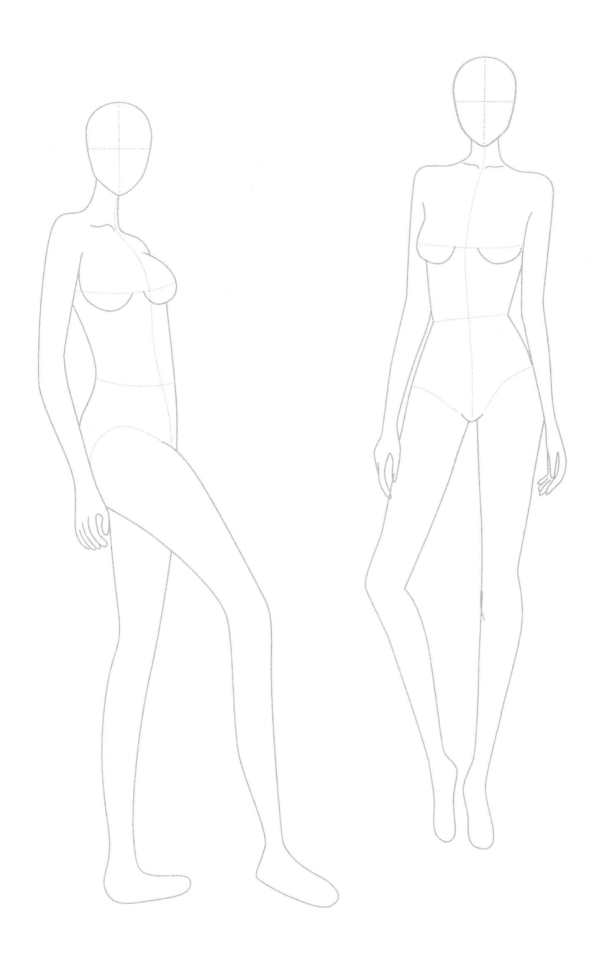

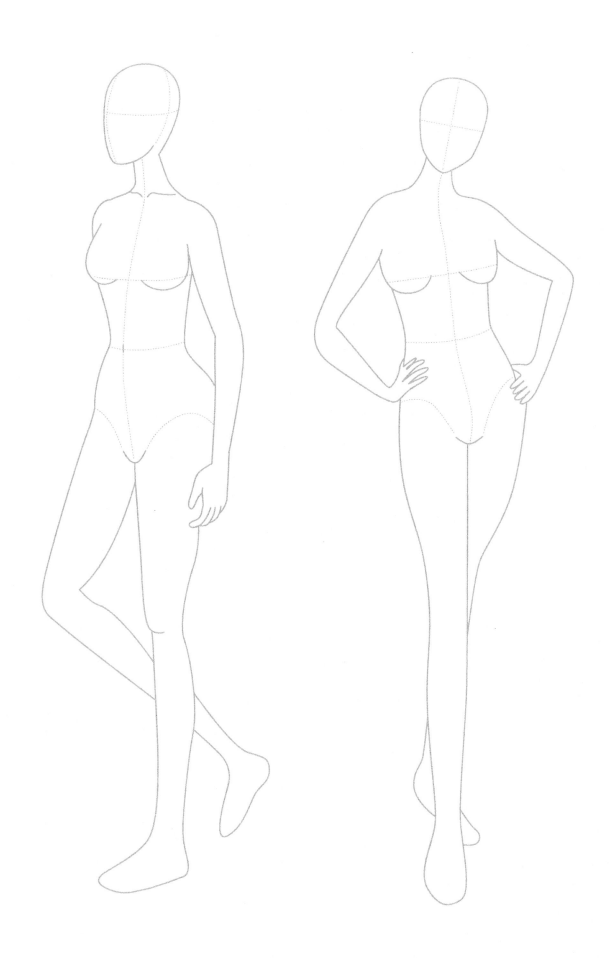

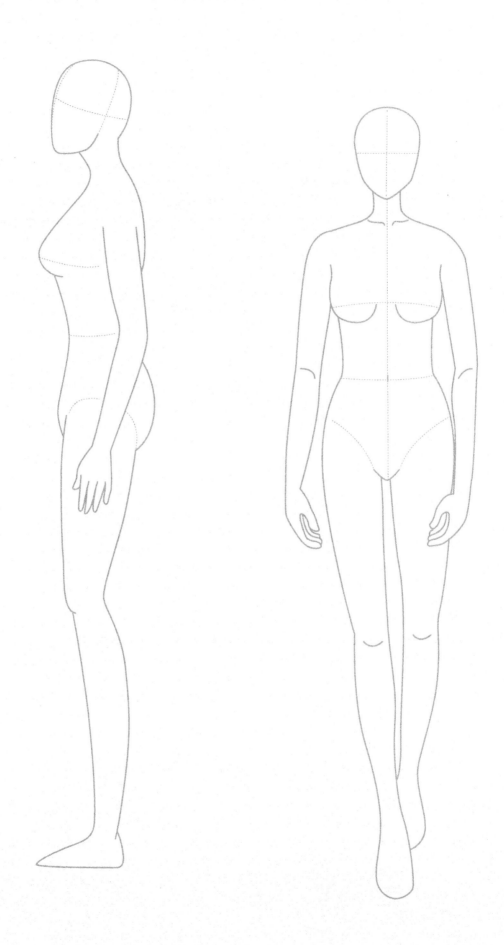

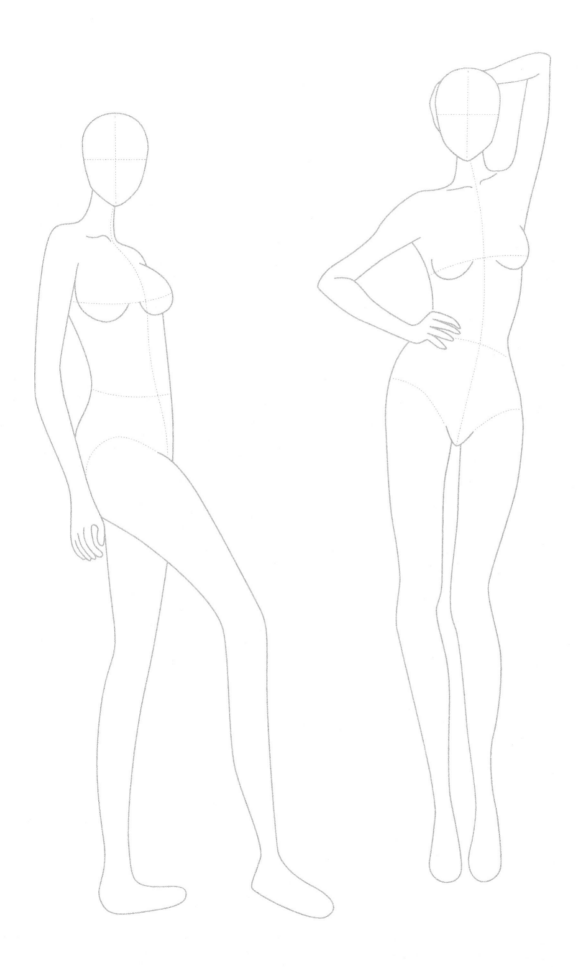

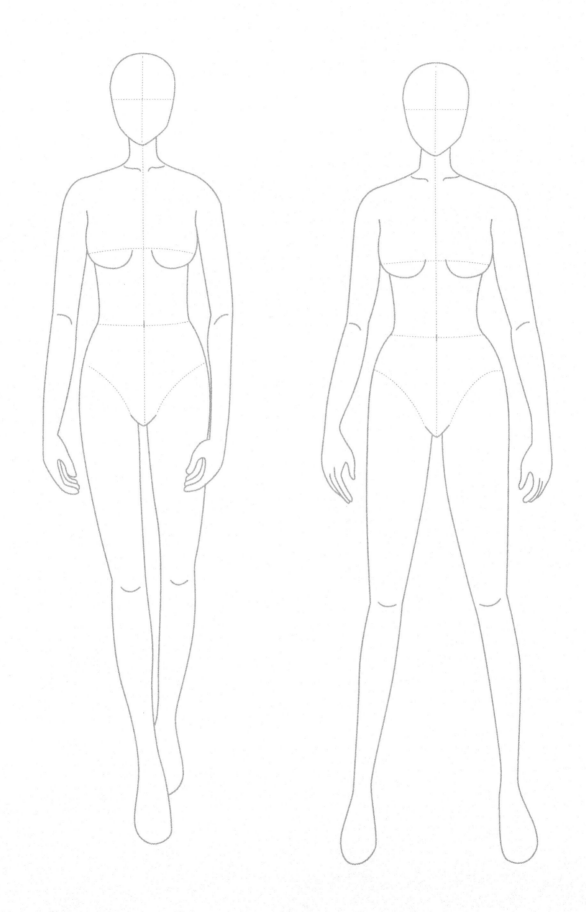

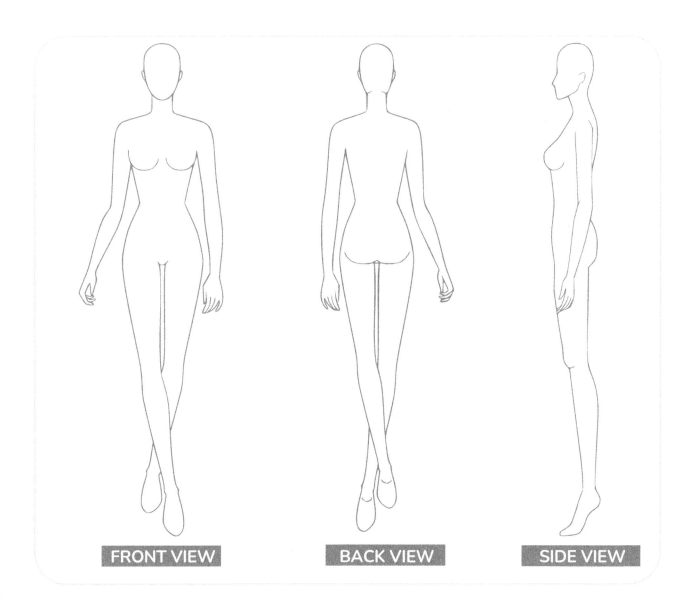

FRONT VIEW BACK VIEW SIDE VIEW

COLORS ◯ ◯ ◯ ◯ ◯ ◯ ◯ ◯ ◯ ◯ ◯ ◯ ◯ ◯ ◯

MATERIALS	PATTERNS

ACCESSORIES

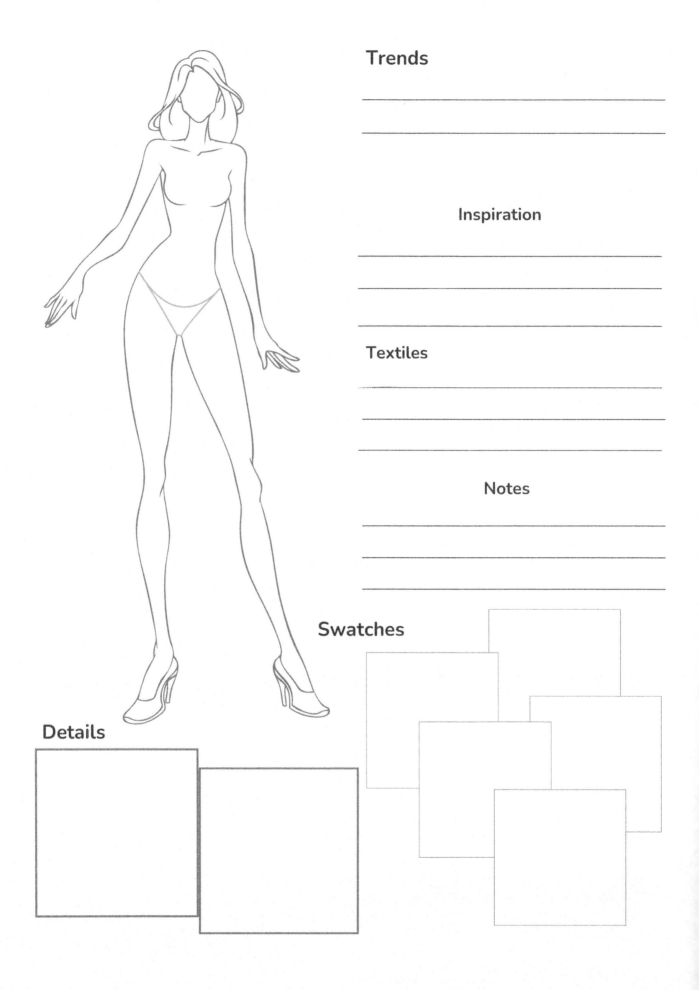

Trends

_____

_____

Inspiration

_____

_____

_____

Textiles

_____

_____

_____

Notes

_____

_____

_____

Swatches

Details

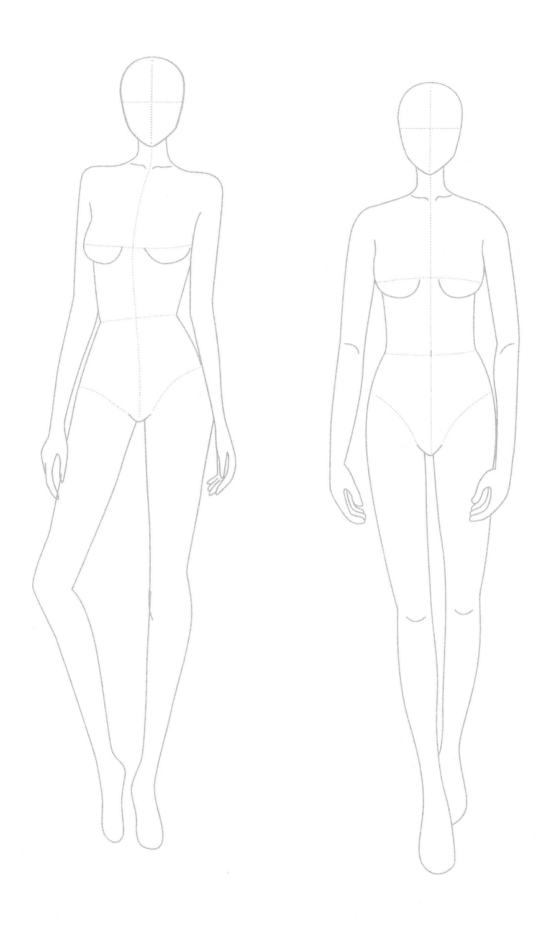

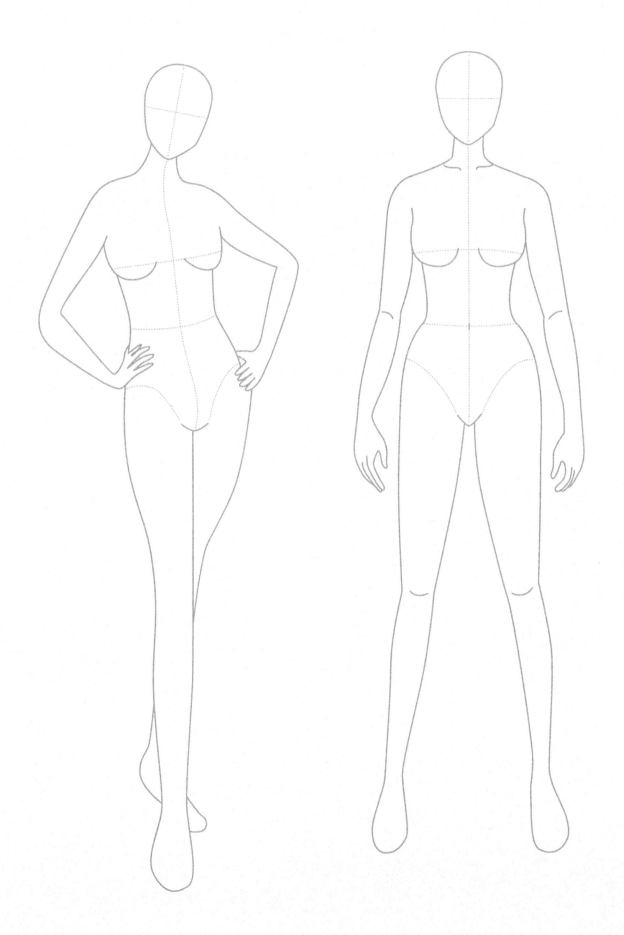

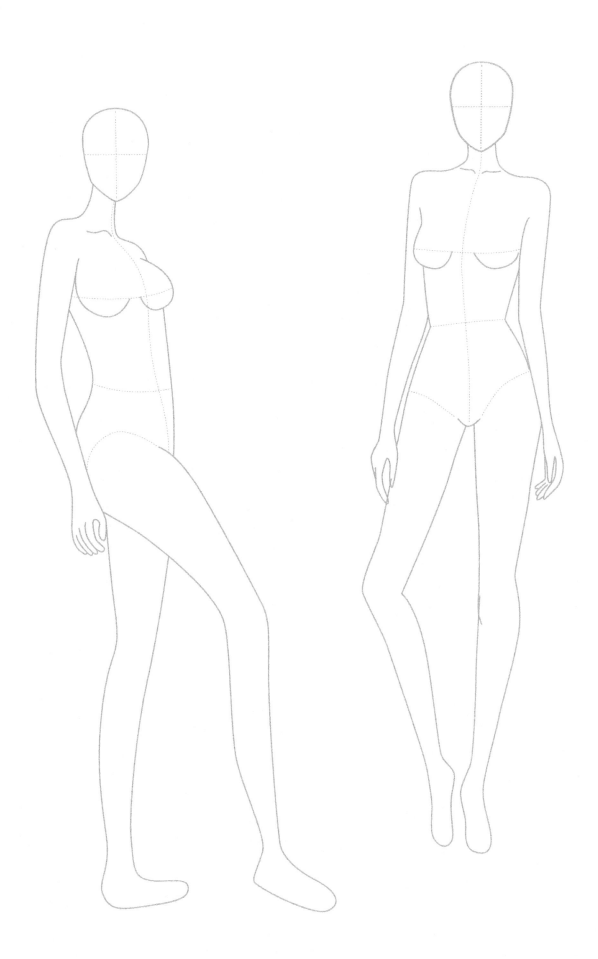

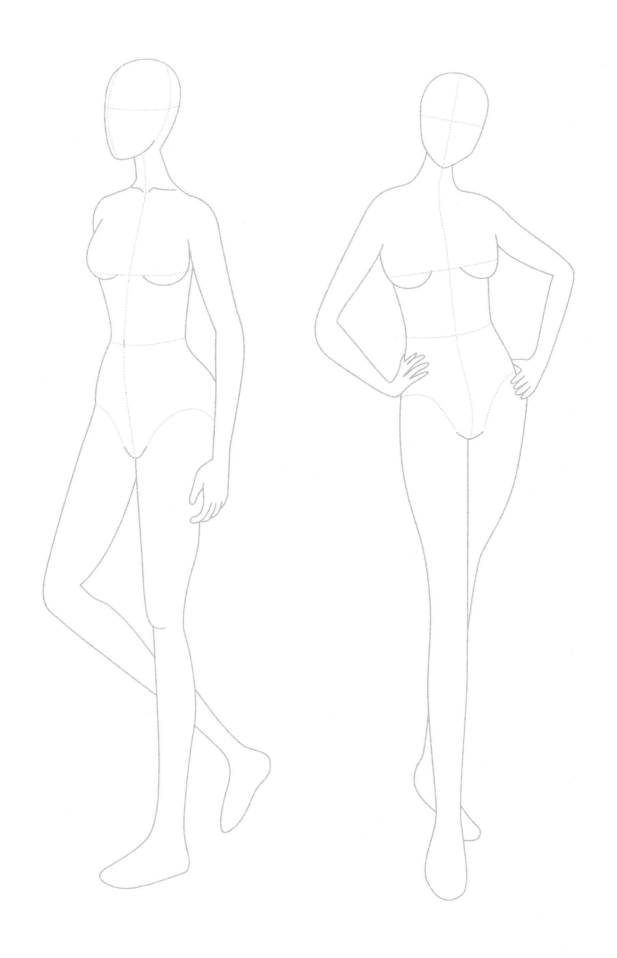

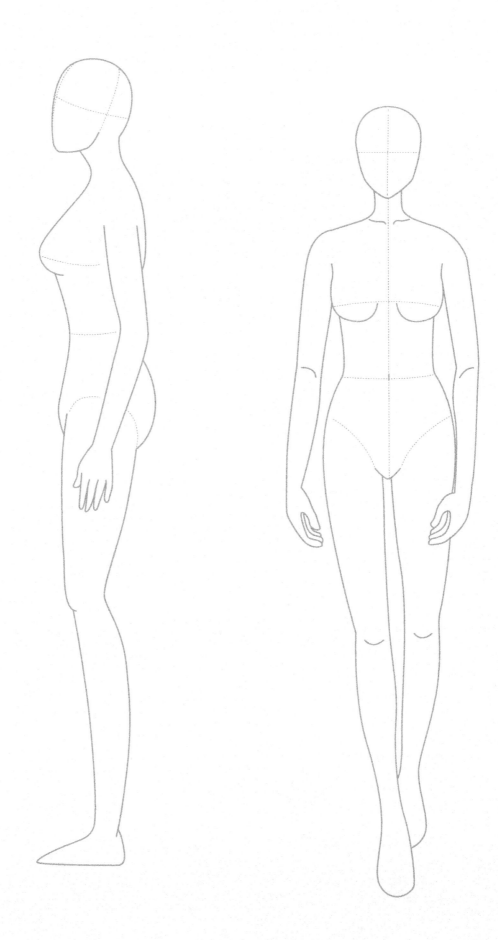

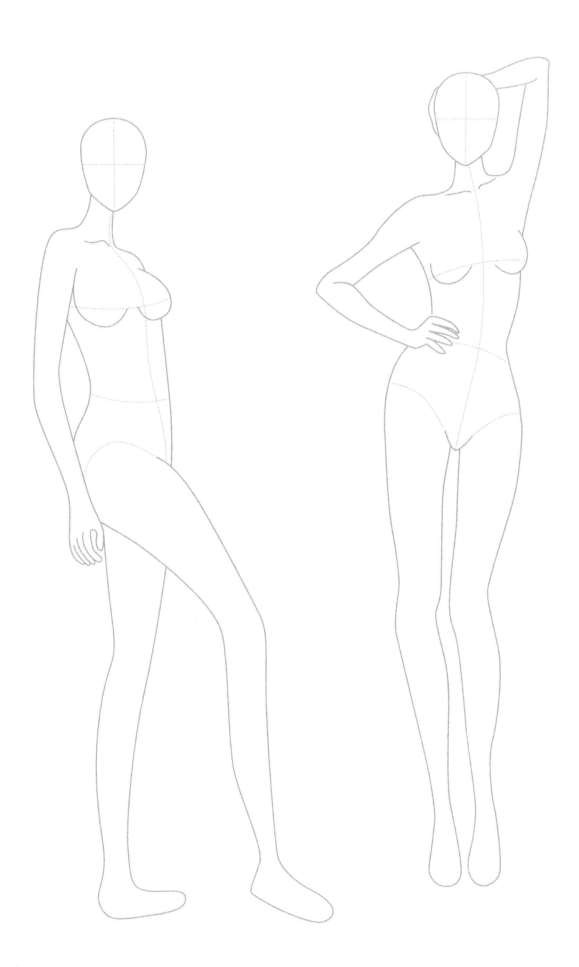

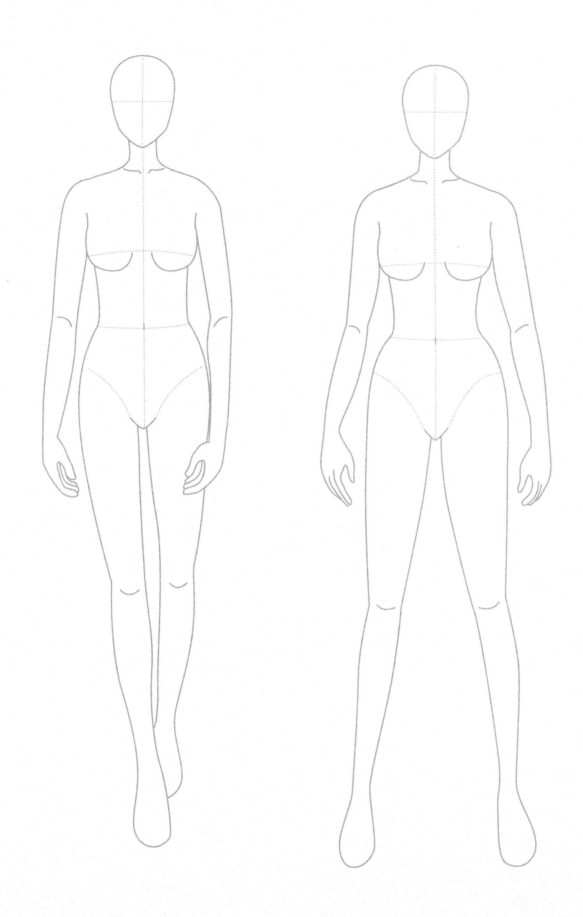

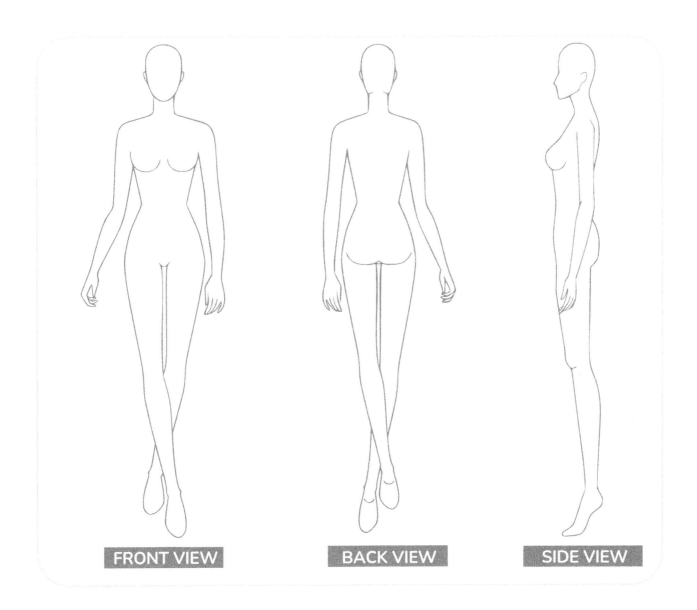

FRONT VIEW   BACK VIEW   SIDE VIEW

COLORS ◯ ◯ ◯ ◯ ◯ ◯ ◯ ◯ ◯ ◯ ◯ ◯ ◯ ◯ ◯ ◯

MATERIALS

PATTERNS

ACCESSORIES

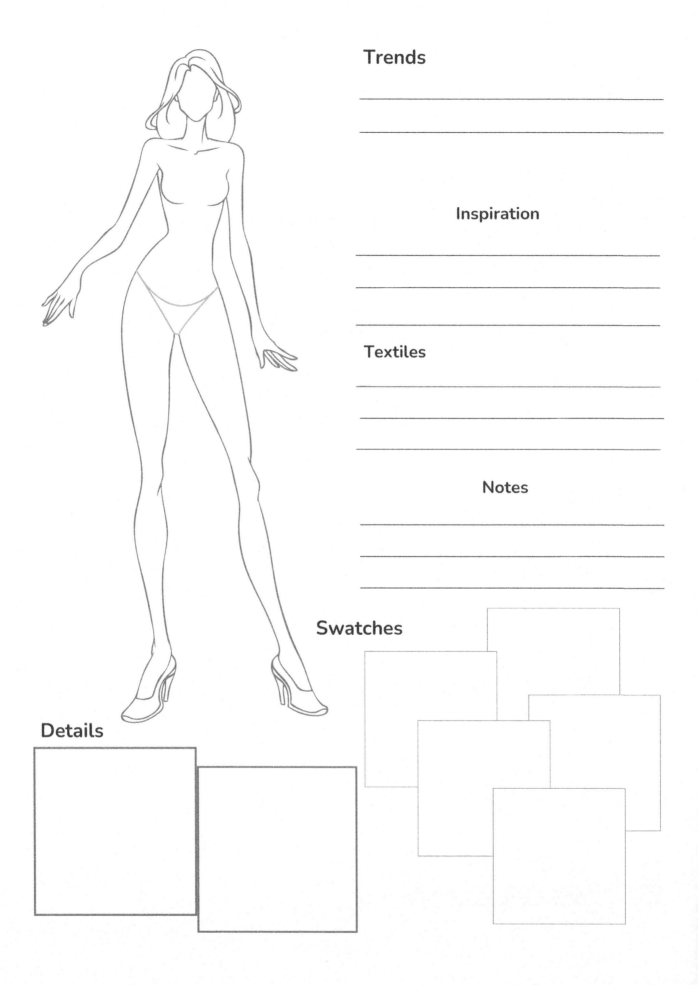

Trends

Inspiration

Textiles

Notes

Swatches

Details

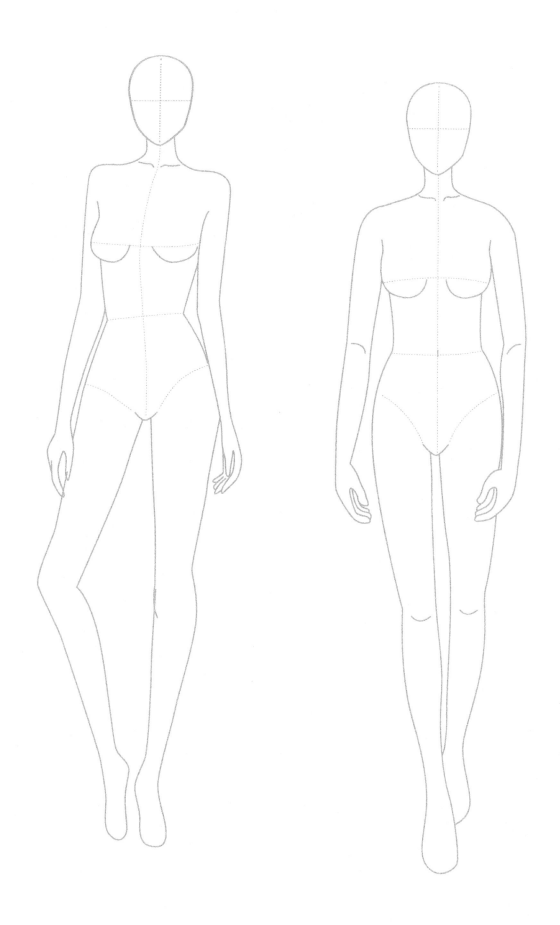

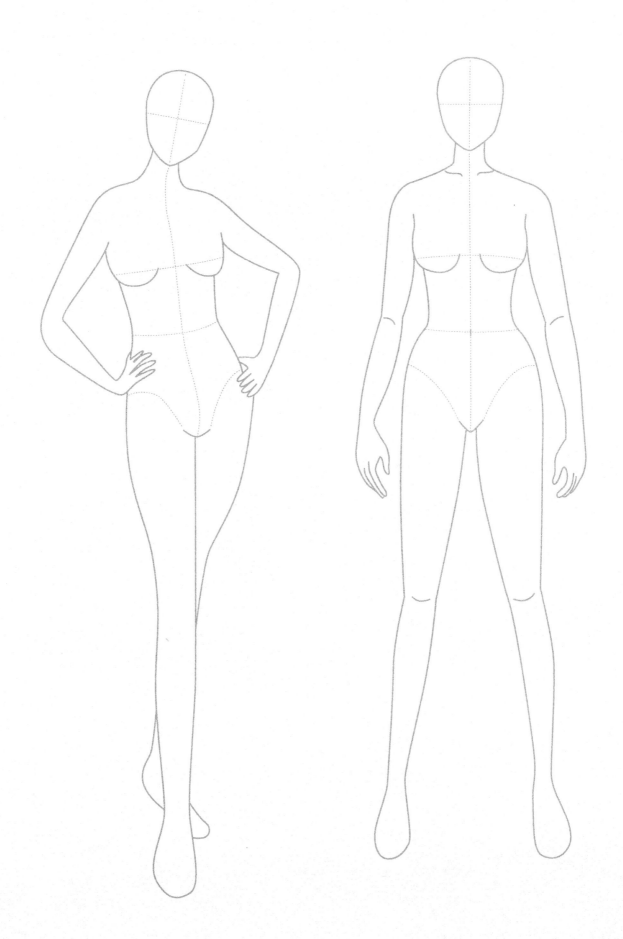

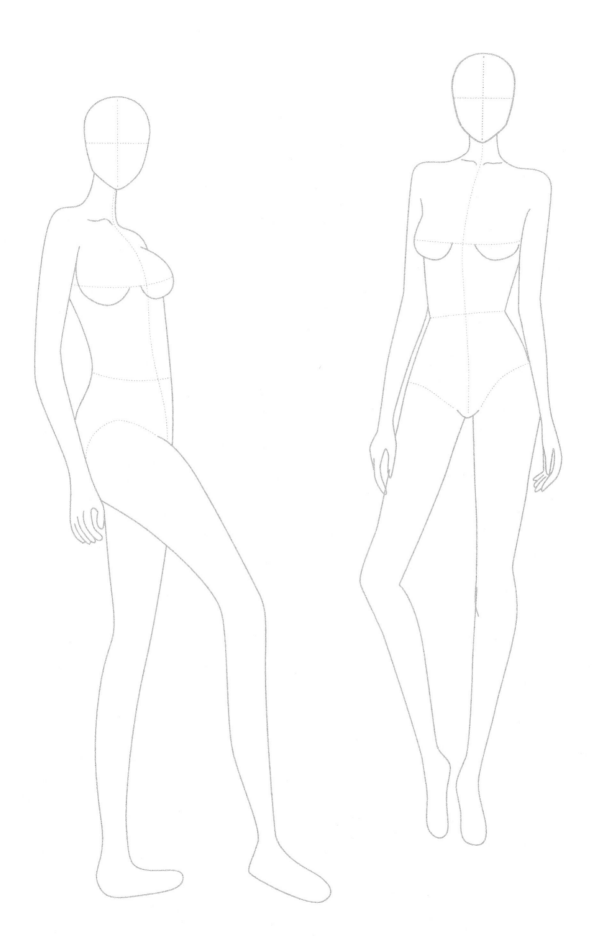

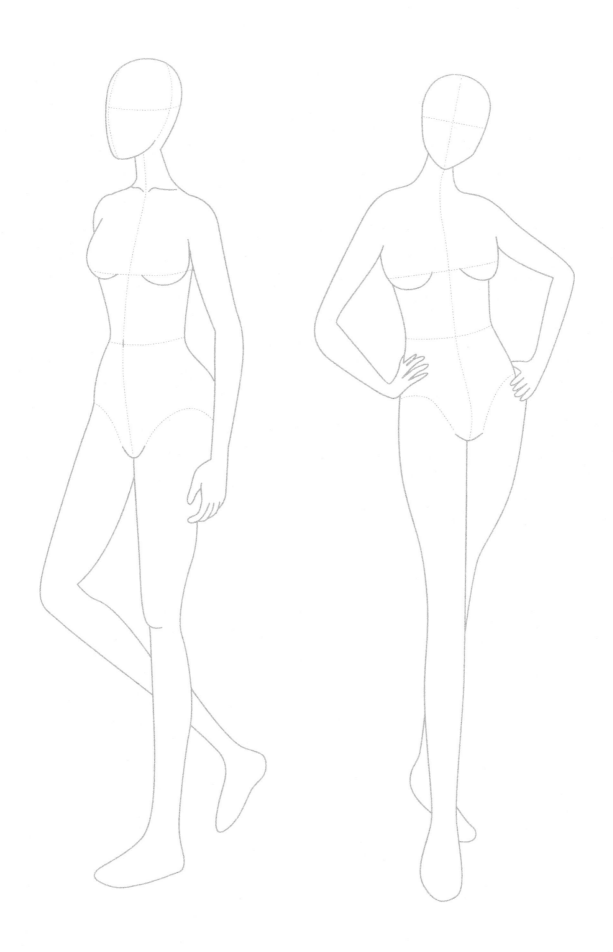

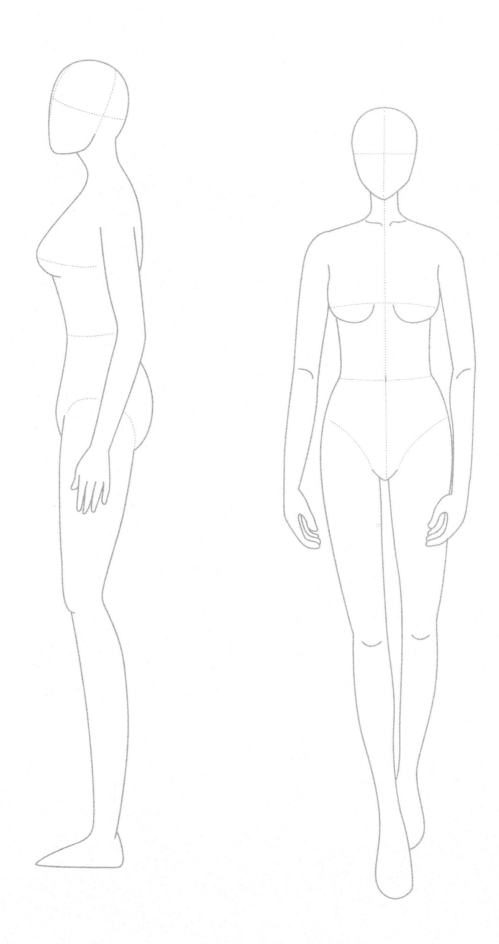

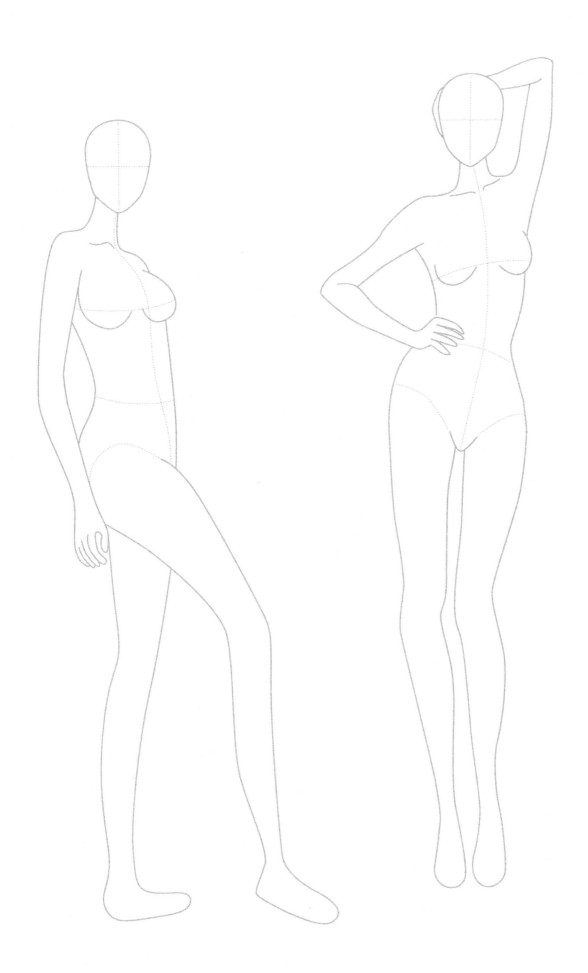

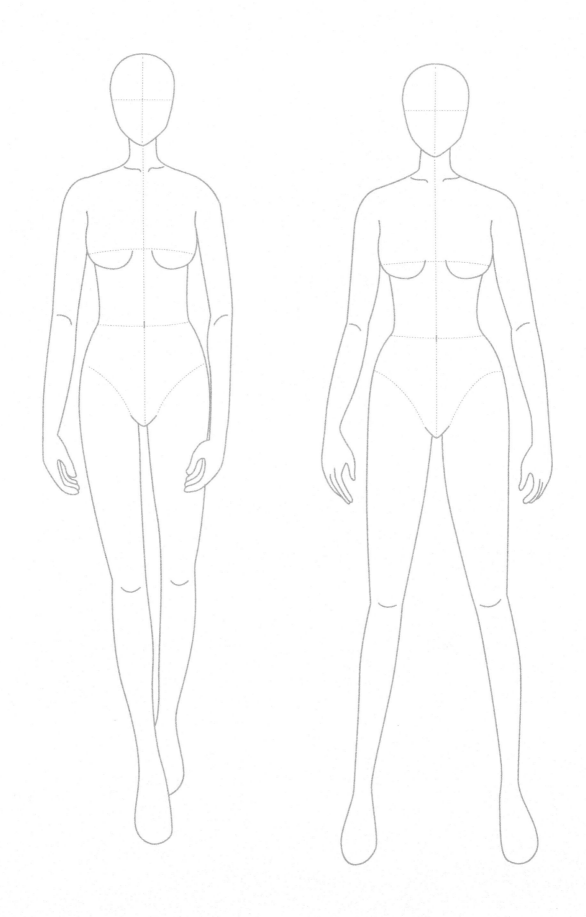

Made in the USA
Monee, IL
19 March 2022

93177945R00136